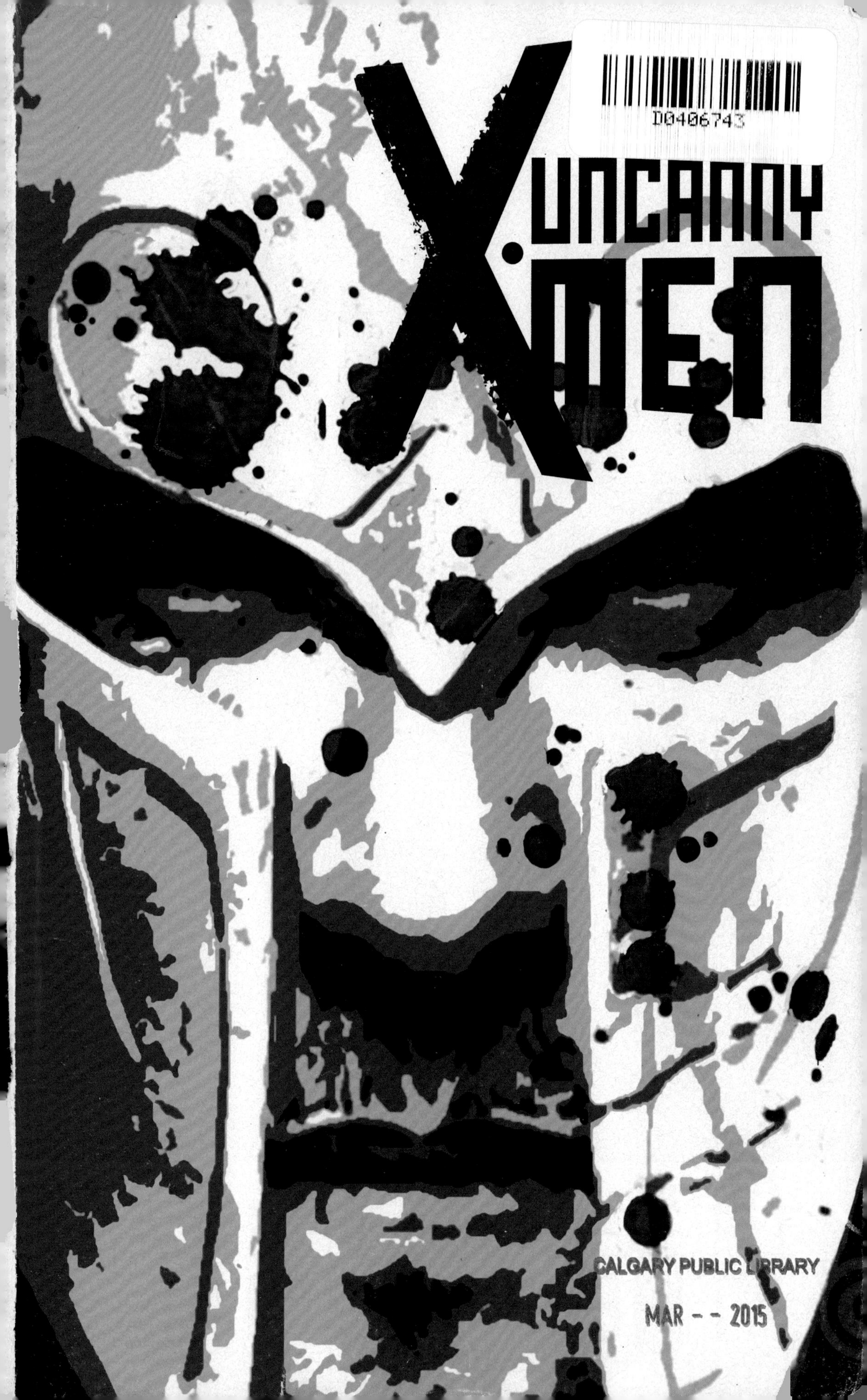
UNCANNY
X
MEN

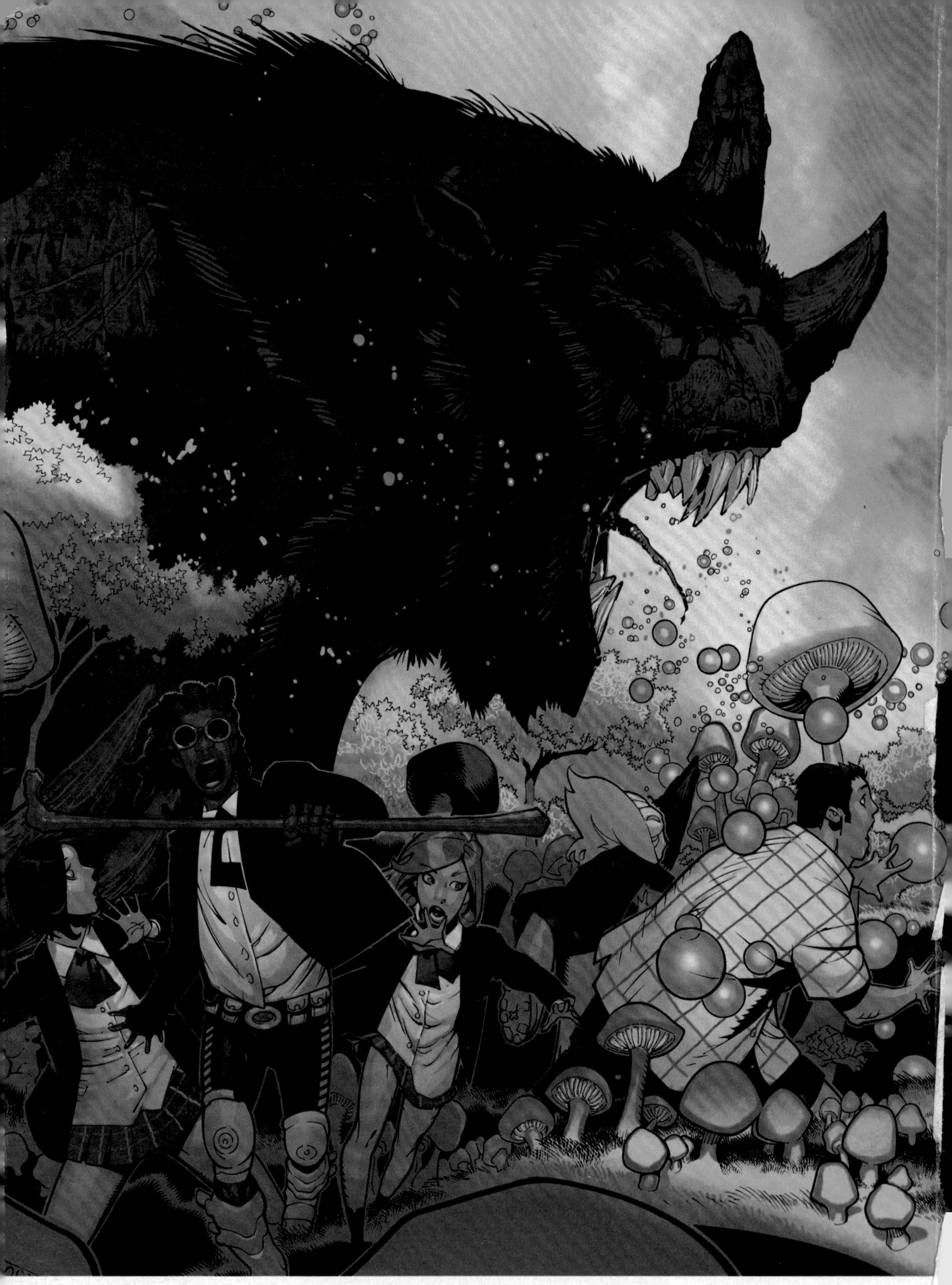

THE GOOD, THE BAD, THE INHUMAN

CYCLOPS
SCOTT SUMMERS

EMMA FROST

MAGNETO
ERIK LEHNSHERR

MAGIK
ILLYANA RASPUTIN

TRIAGE
CHRISTOPHER MUSE

TEMPUS
EVA BELL

FABIO MEDIA

BENJAMIN DEEDS

BRIAN MICHAEL
BENDIS
WRITER

CHRIS
BACHALO
PENCILER/COLORIST,
#14 & #16-17

TIM
TOWNSEND
WITH JAMIE MENDOZA, AL VEY,
MARK IRWIN & VICTOR OLAZABA
INKER, #14 & #16-17

KRIS
ANKA
ARTIST, #15

RAIN
BEREDO
COLOR ARTIST, #15

MARCO
RUDY
ARTIST, #18

VAL
STAPLES
COLOR ARTIST, #18

COVER ART: **CHRIS BACHALO & TIM TOWNSEND (#14 & #17),**
KRIS ANKA (#15-16) AND ALEXANDER LOZANO (#18)

VC'S JOE
CARAMAGNA
LETTERER
WITH **CHRIS ELIOPOULOS (#15)**

XANDER
JAROWEY
ASSISTANT EDITOR

JORDAN D.
WHITE
ASSOCIATE EDITOR

NICK
LOWE
EDITOR

X-MEN CREATED BY STAN LEE & JACK KIRBY

COLLECTION EDITOR: **JENNIFER GRÜNWALD**
ASSISTANT EDITOR: **SARAH BRUNSTAD**
ASSOCIATE MANAGING EDITOR: **ALEX STARBUCK**
EDITOR, SPECIAL PROJECTS: **MARK D. BEAZLEY**
SENIOR EDITOR, SPECIAL PROJECTS: **JEFF YOUNGQUIST**
SVP PRINT, SALES & MARKETING: **DAVID GABRIEL**

EDITOR IN CHIEF: **AXEL ALONSO**
CHIEF CREATIVE OFFICER: **JOE QUESADA**
PUBLISHER: **DAN BUCKLEY**
EXECUTIVE PRODUCER: **ALAN FINE**

UNCANNY X-MEN VOL. 3: THE GOOD, THE BAD, THE INHUMAN. Contains material originally published in magazine form as UNCANNY X-MEN #14-18. First printing 2015. ISBN# 978-0-7851-8937-4. Published by MARVEL WORLDWIDE, INC., a subsidiary of MARVEL ENTERTAINMENT, LLC. OFFICE OF PUBLICATION: 135 West 50th Street, New York, NY 10020. Copyright © 2015 Marvel Characters, Inc. All rights reserved. All characters featured in this issue and the distinctive names and likenesses thereof, and all related indicia are trademarks of Marvel Characters, Inc. No similarity between any of the names, characters, persons, and/or institutions in this magazine with those of any living or dead person or institution is intended, and any such similarity which may exist is purely coincidental. **Printed in Canada.** ALAN FINE, EVP - Office of the President, Marvel Worldwide, Inc. and EVP & CMO Marvel Characters B.V.; DAN BUCKLEY, Publisher & President - Print, Animation & Digital Divisions; JOE QUESADA, Chief Creative Officer; TOM BREVOORT, SVP of Publishing; DAVID BOGART, SVP of Operations & Procurement, Publishing; C.B. CEBULSKI, SVP of Creator & Content Development; DAVID GABRIEL, SVP Print, Sales & Marketing; JIM O'KEEFE, VP of Operations & Logistics; DAN CARR, Executive Director of Publishing Technology; SUSAN CRESPI, Editorial Operations Manager; ALEX MORALES, Publishing Operations Manager; STAN LEE, Chairman Emeritus. For information regarding advertising in Marvel Comics or on Marvel.com, please contact Niza Disla, Director of Marvel Partnerships, at ndisla@marvel.com. For Marvel subscription inquiries, please call 800-217-9158. **Manufactured between 11/21/2014 and 12/29/2014 by SOLISCO PRINTERS, SCOTT, QC, CANADA.**

10 9 8 7 6 5 4 3 2 1

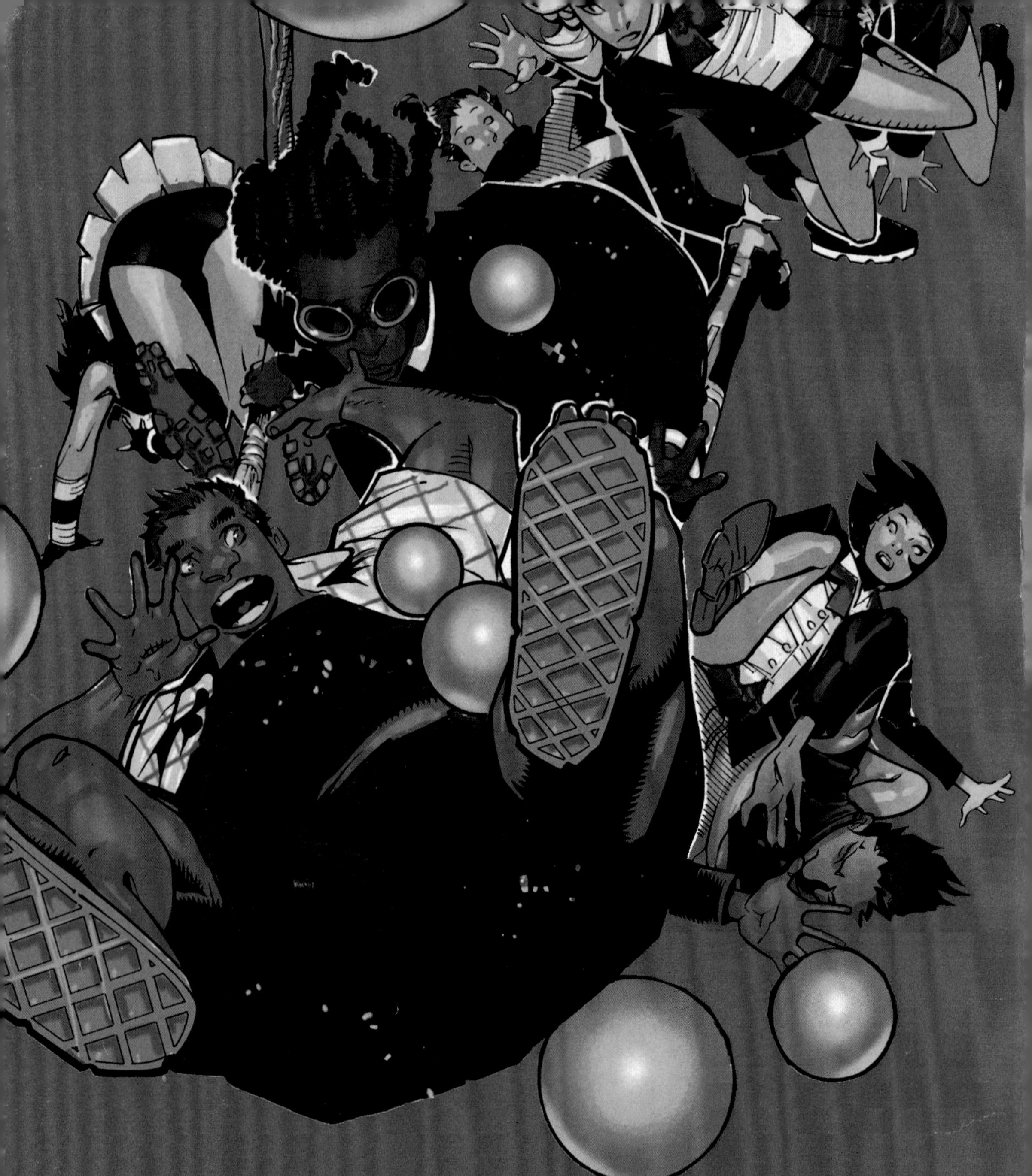

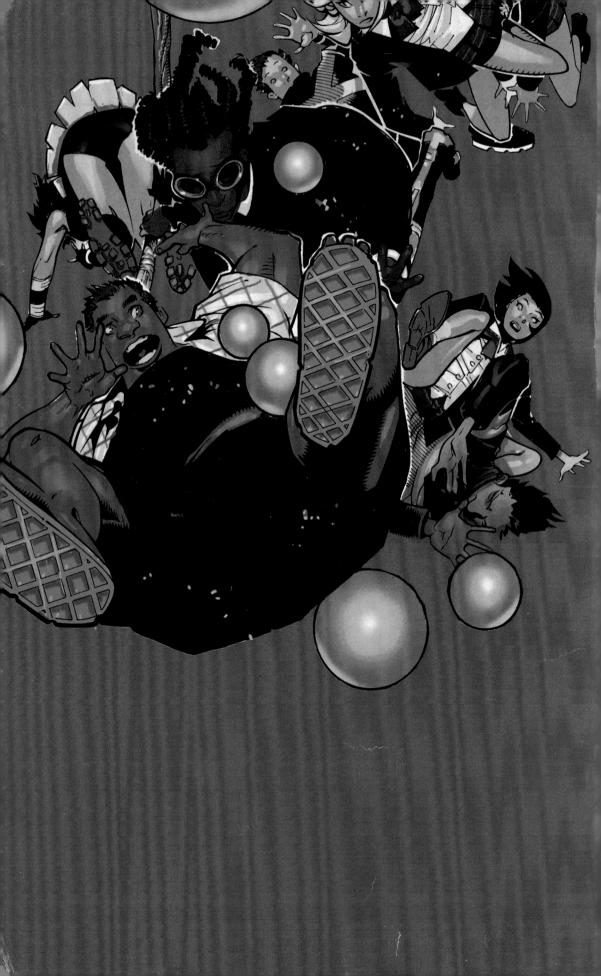

Born with genetic mutations that gave them abilities beyond those of normal humans, mutants are the next stage in evolution. As such, they are feared and hated by humanity. A group of mutants known as the X-Men fight for peaceful coexistence between mutants and humankind. But not all mutants see peaceful coextistence as a reality.

Scott Summers, A.K.A. Cyclops, is the face of the mutant revolution. he and his team of X-Men opened the new Charles Xavier School for the Gifted in order to train the next generation of mutants to defend themselves. The school has grown recently, as Kitty Pryde and the All-New X-Men have joined Cyclops after a falling out with the Jean Grey school.

Many of Cyclops' students have risen to the occassion of being X-Men and aided the team in combat situations. Benjamin Deeds is not one of those students. With little control over abilities that have limited utility in combat, Benjamin has been uncertain about his place with the Uncanny X-Men.

Meanwhile, as a consequence of Thanos' invasion of Earth, the Inhuman city of Attilan was destroyed, triggering a bomb spreading Terrigen — the chemical that activates the super powers in Inhumans — into the atmosphere.

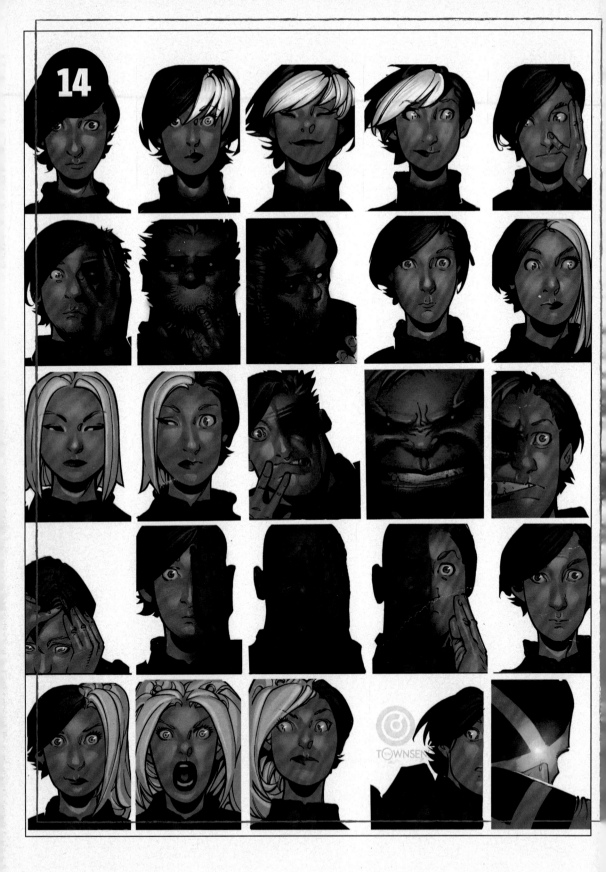

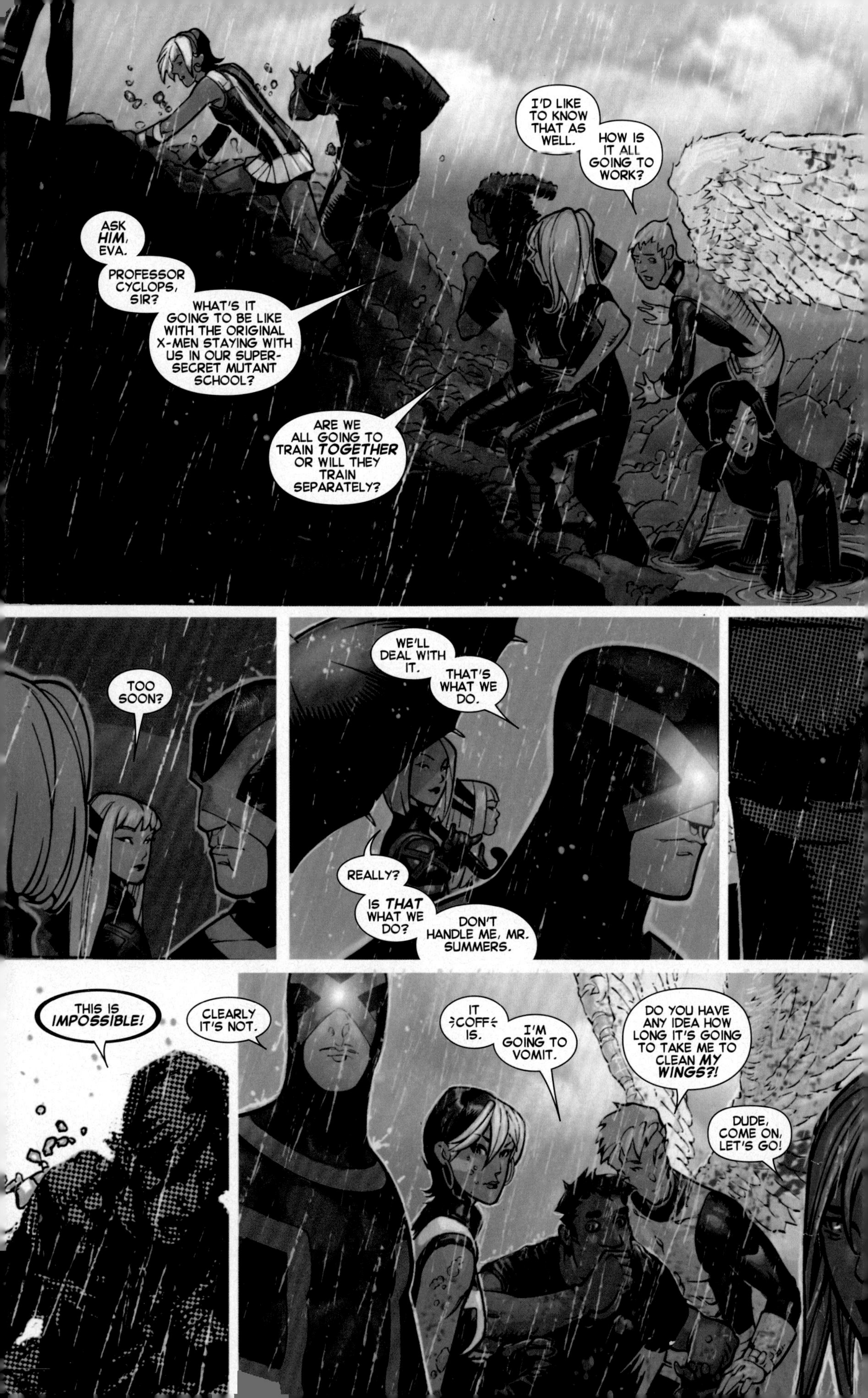
ASK HIM, EVA.
PROFESSOR CYCLOPS, SIR?
WHAT'S IT GOING TO BE LIKE WITH THE ORIGINAL X-MEN STAYING WITH US IN OUR SUPER-SECRET MUTANT SCHOOL?
ARE WE ALL GOING TO TRAIN TOGETHER OR WILL THEY TRAIN SEPARATELY?
I'D LIKE TO KNOW THAT AS WELL.
HOW IS IT ALL GOING TO WORK?
TOO SOON?
WE'LL DEAL WITH IT.
THAT'S WHAT WE DO.
REALLY?
IS THAT WHAT WE DO?
DON'T HANDLE ME, MR. SUMMERS.
THIS IS IMPOSSIBLE!
CLEARLY IT'S NOT.
IT *COFF* IS.
I'M GOING TO VOMIT.
DO YOU HAVE ANY IDEA HOW LONG IT'S GOING TO TAKE ME TO CLEAN MY WINGS?!
DUDE, COME ON, LET'S GO!

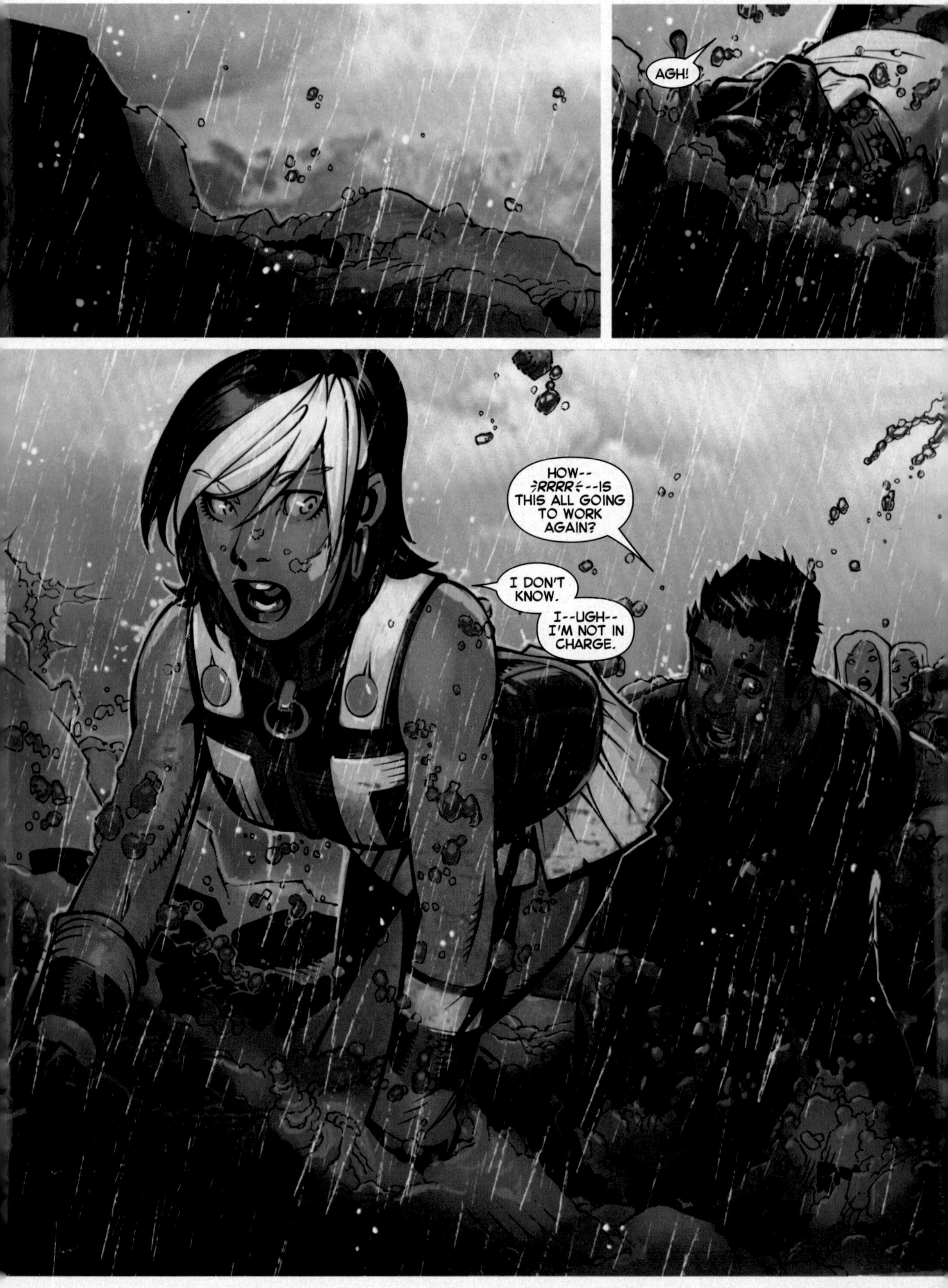
AGH!
HOW-- ≠RRRR≠--IS THIS ALL GOING TO WORK AGAIN?
I DON'T KNOW.
I--UGH-- I'M NOT IN CHARGE.

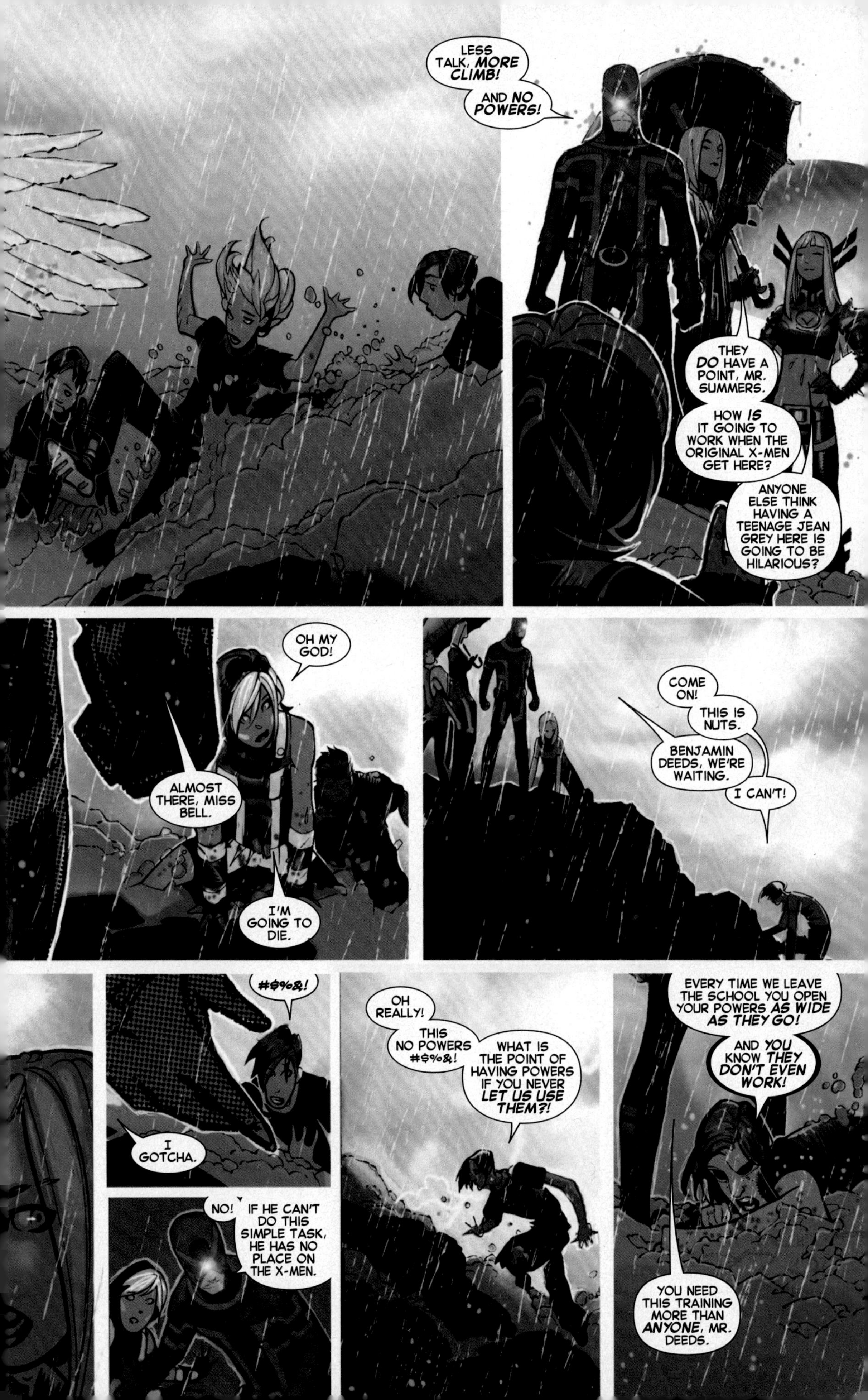
LESS TALK, MORE CLIMB!
AND NO POWERS!
THEY DO HAVE A POINT, MR. SUMMERS.
HOW IS IT GOING TO WORK WHEN THE ORIGINAL X-MEN GET HERE?
ANYONE ELSE THINK HAVING A TEENAGE JEAN GREY HERE IS GOING TO BE HILARIOUS?
OH MY GOD!
ALMOST THERE, MISS BELL.
I'M GOING TO DIE.
COME ON!
THIS IS NUTS.
BENJAMIN DEEDS, WE'RE WAITING.
I CAN'T!
#$%&!
I GOTCHA.
NO!
IF HE CAN'T DO THIS SIMPLE TASK, HE HAS NO PLACE ON THE X-MEN.
OH REALLY!
THIS NO POWERS #$%&!
WHAT IS THE POINT OF HAVING POWERS IF YOU NEVER LET US USE THEM?!
EVERY TIME WE LEAVE THE SCHOOL YOU OPEN YOUR POWERS AS WIDE AS THEY GO!
AND YOU KNOW THEY DON'T EVEN WORK!
YOU NEED THIS TRAINING MORE THAN ANYONE, MR. DEEDS.

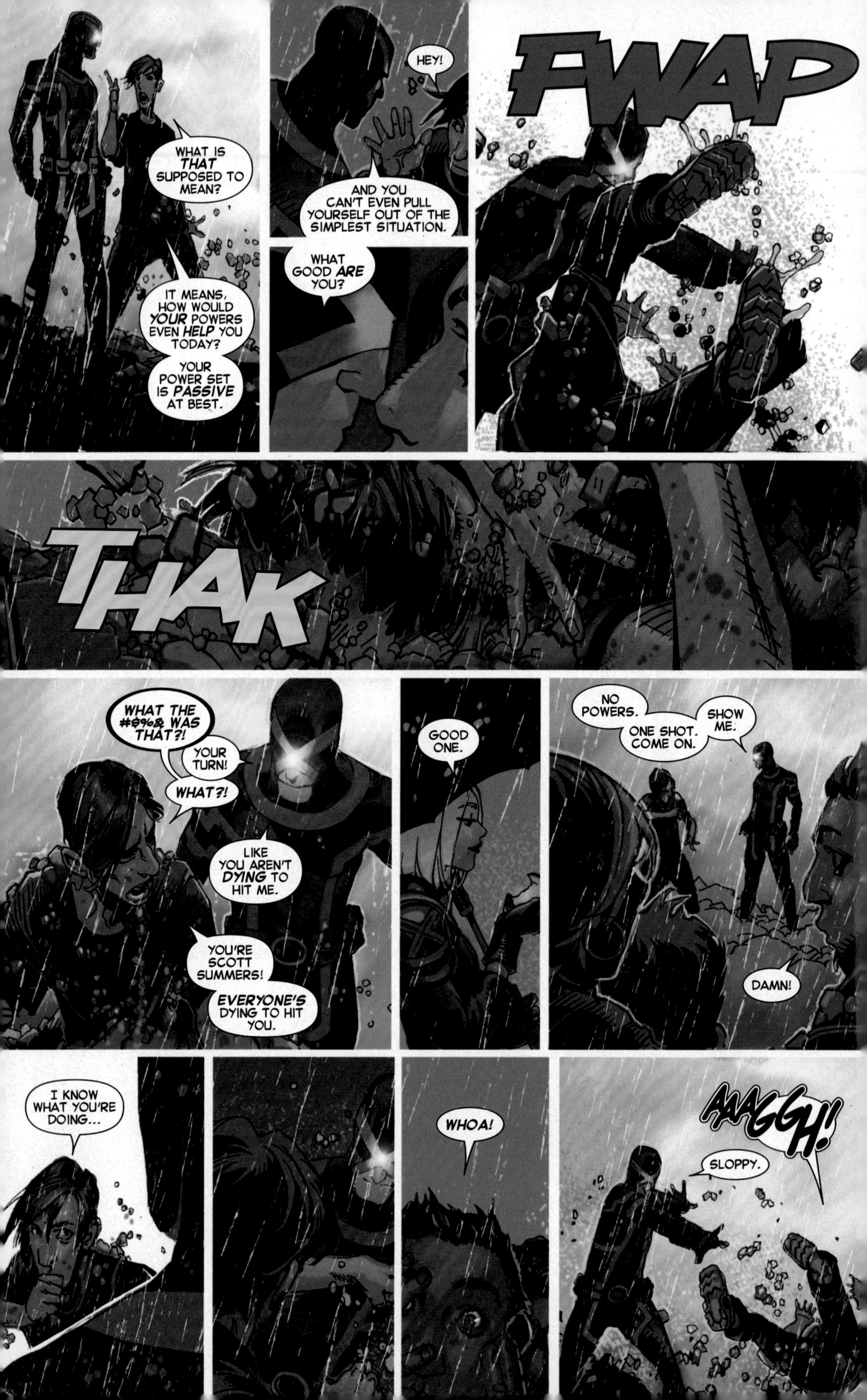

WHAT IS THAT SUPPOSED TO MEAN?
IT MEANS, HOW WOULD YOUR POWERS EVEN HELP YOU TODAY?
YOUR POWER SET IS PASSIVE AT BEST.
HEY!
AND YOU CAN'T EVEN PULL YOURSELF OUT OF THE SIMPLEST SITUATION.
WHAT GOOD ARE YOU?
FWAP
THAK
WHAT THE #$%& WAS THAT?!
YOUR TURN!
WHAT?!
LIKE YOU AREN'T DYING TO HIT ME.
YOU'RE SCOTT SUMMERS!
EVERYONE'S DYING TO HIT YOU.
GOOD ONE.
NO POWERS.
ONE SHOT. COME ON.
SHOW ME.
DAMN!
I KNOW WHAT YOU'RE DOING...
WHOA!
AAAGGH!
SLOPPY.

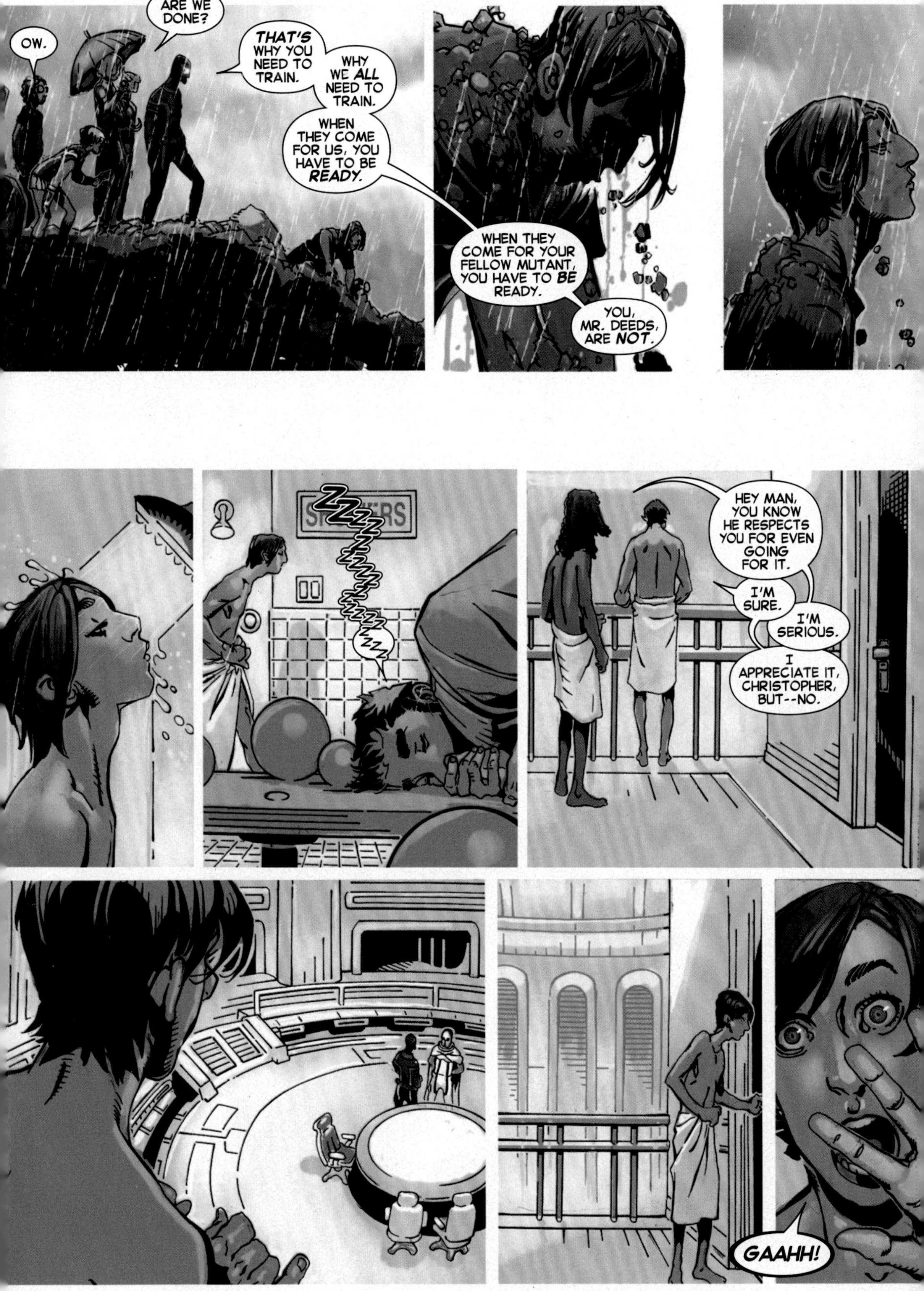

OW.
ARE WE DONE?
THAT'S WHY YOU NEED TO TRAIN.
WHY WE ALL NEED TO TRAIN.
WHEN THEY COME FOR US, YOU HAVE TO BE READY.
WHEN THEY COME FOR YOUR FELLOW MUTANT, YOU HAVE TO BE READY.
YOU, MR. DEEDS, ARE NOT.
SHOWERS
ZZZZZZZZZZZZ
HEY MAN, YOU KNOW HE RESPECTS YOU FOR EVEN GOING FOR IT.
I'M SURE.
I'M SERIOUS.
I APPRECIATE IT, CHRISTOPHER, BUT--NO.
GAAHH!

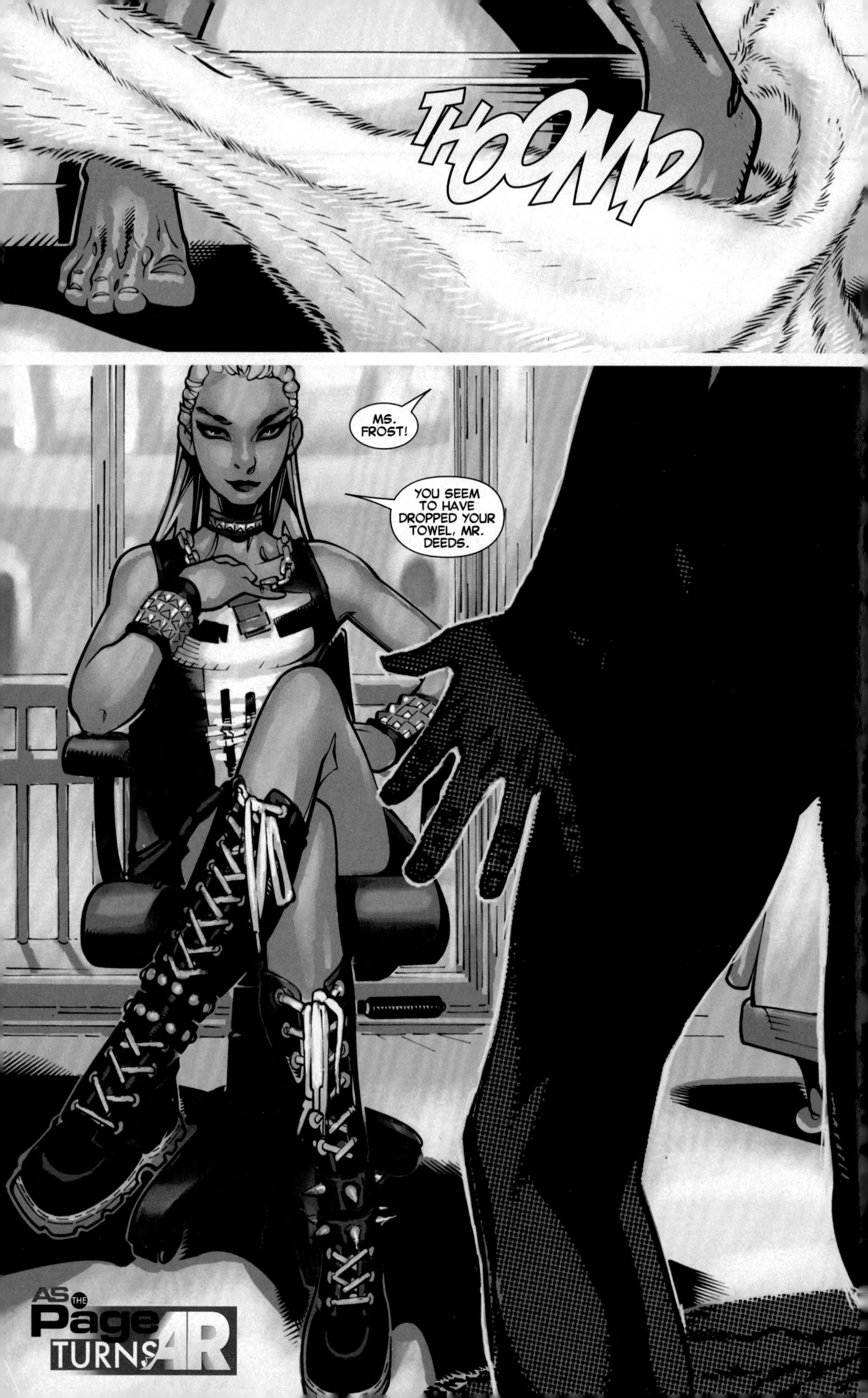
THOOMP
MS. FROST!
YOU SEEM TO HAVE DROPPED YOUR TOWEL, MR. DEEDS.
AS THE Page TURNS AR

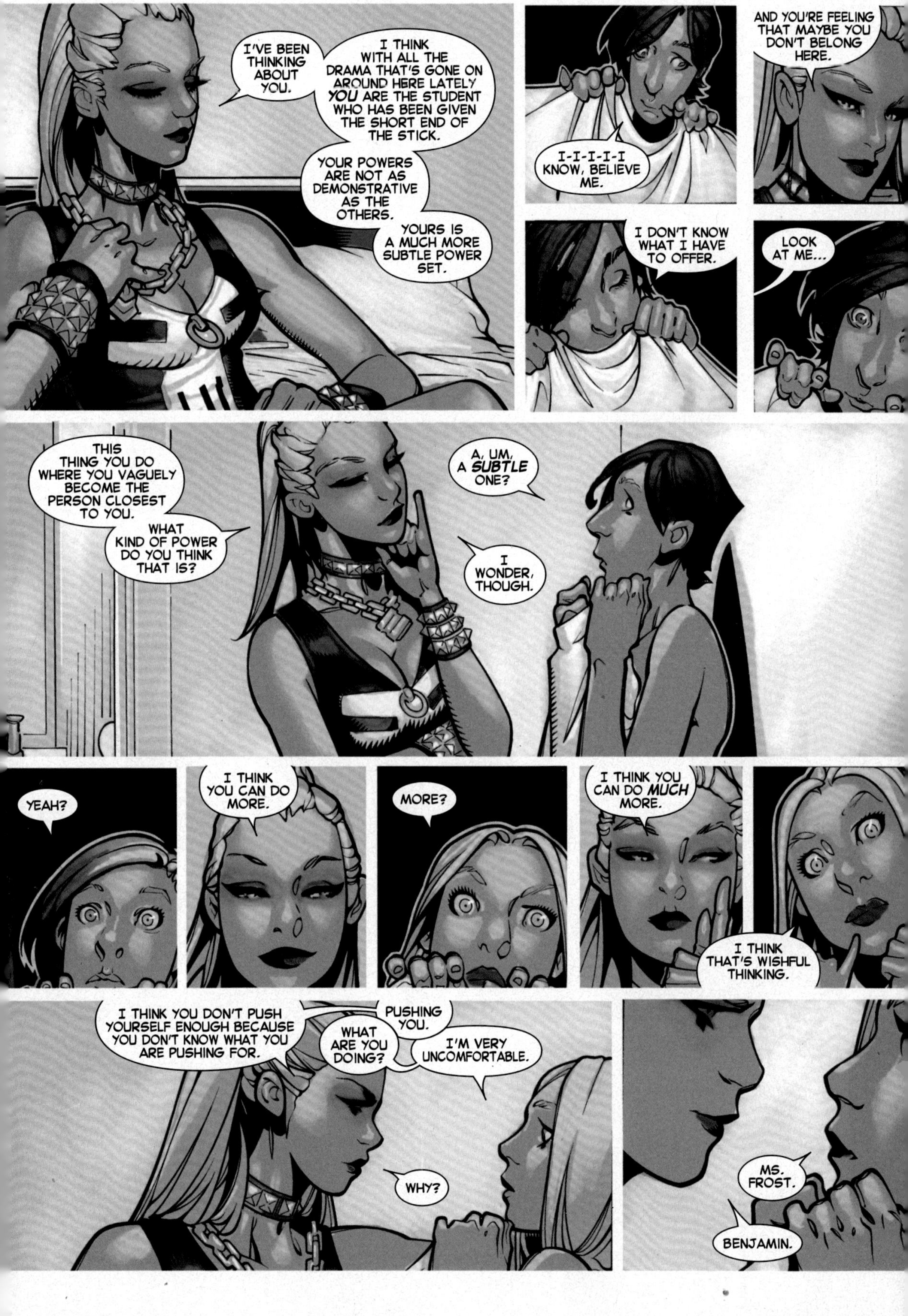
I'VE BEEN THINKING ABOUT YOU.
I THINK WITH ALL THE DRAMA THAT'S GONE ON AROUND HERE LATELY *YOU* ARE THE STUDENT WHO HAS BEEN GIVEN THE SHORT END OF THE STICK.
YOUR POWERS ARE NOT AS DEMONSTRATIVE AS THE OTHERS.
YOURS IS A MUCH MORE SUBTLE POWER SET.
I-I-I-I-I KNOW, BELIEVE ME.
AND YOU'RE FEELING THAT MAYBE YOU DON'T BELONG HERE.
I DON'T KNOW WHAT I HAVE TO OFFER.
LOOK AT ME...
THIS THING YOU DO WHERE YOU VAGUELY BECOME THE PERSON CLOSEST TO YOU.
WHAT KIND OF POWER DO YOU THINK THAT IS?
A, UM, A *SUBTLE* ONE?
I WONDER, THOUGH.
YEAH?
I THINK YOU CAN DO MORE.
MORE?
I THINK YOU CAN DO *MUCH* MORE.
I THINK THAT'S WISHFUL THINKING.
I THINK YOU DON'T PUSH YOURSELF ENOUGH BECAUSE YOU DON'T KNOW WHAT YOU ARE PUSHING FOR.
PUSHING YOU.
WHAT ARE YOU DOING?
I'M VERY UNCOMFORTABLE.
WHY?
MS. FROST.
BENJAMIN.

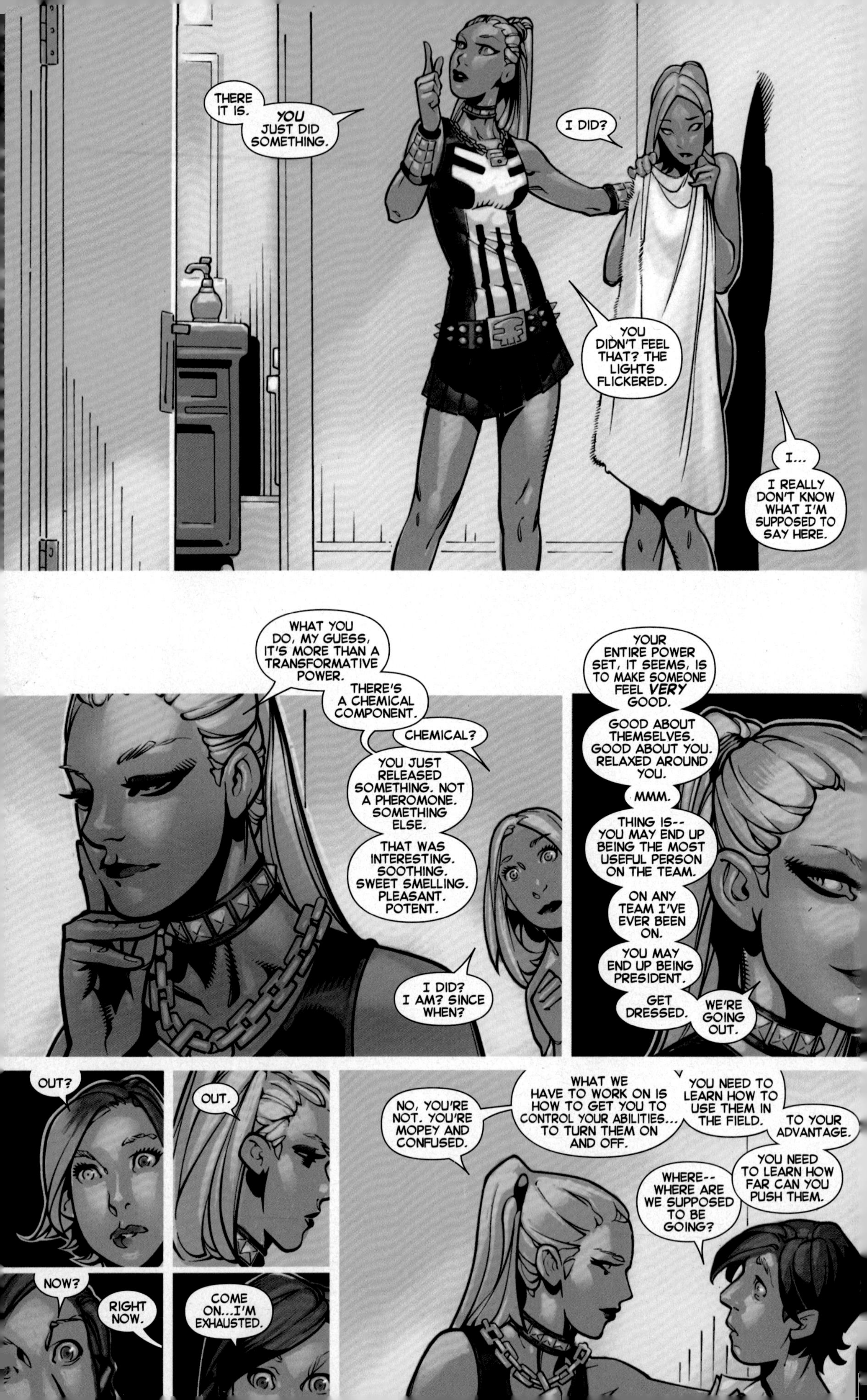
THERE IT IS. *YOU* JUST DID SOMETHING.
I DID?
YOU DIDN'T FEEL THAT? THE LIGHTS FLICKERED.
I...
I REALLY DON'T KNOW WHAT I'M SUPPOSED TO SAY HERE.
WHAT YOU DO, MY GUESS, IT'S MORE THAN A TRANSFORMATIVE POWER.
THERE'S A CHEMICAL COMPONENT.
CHEMICAL?
YOU JUST RELEASED SOMETHING. NOT A PHEROMONE. SOMETHING ELSE.
THAT WAS INTERESTING. SOOTHING. SWEET SMELLING. PLEASANT. POTENT.
I DID? I AM? SINCE WHEN?
YOUR ENTIRE POWER SET, IT SEEMS, IS TO MAKE SOMEONE FEEL *VERY* GOOD.
GOOD ABOUT THEMSELVES. GOOD ABOUT YOU. RELAXED AROUND YOU.
MMM.
THING IS-- YOU MAY END UP BEING THE MOST USEFUL PERSON ON THE TEAM.
ON ANY TEAM I'VE EVER BEEN ON.
YOU MAY END UP BEING PRESIDENT.
GET DRESSED.
WE'RE GOING OUT.
OUT?
OUT.
NOW?
RIGHT NOW.
COME ON...I'M EXHAUSTED.
NO, YOU'RE NOT. YOU'RE MOPEY AND CONFUSED.
WHAT WE HAVE TO WORK ON IS HOW TO GET YOU TO CONTROL YOUR ABILITIES... TO TURN THEM ON AND OFF.
YOU NEED TO LEARN HOW TO USE THEM IN THE FIELD.
TO YOUR ADVANTAGE.
YOU NEED TO LEARN HOW FAR CAN YOU PUSH THEM.
WHERE-- WHERE ARE WE SUPPOSED TO BE GOING?

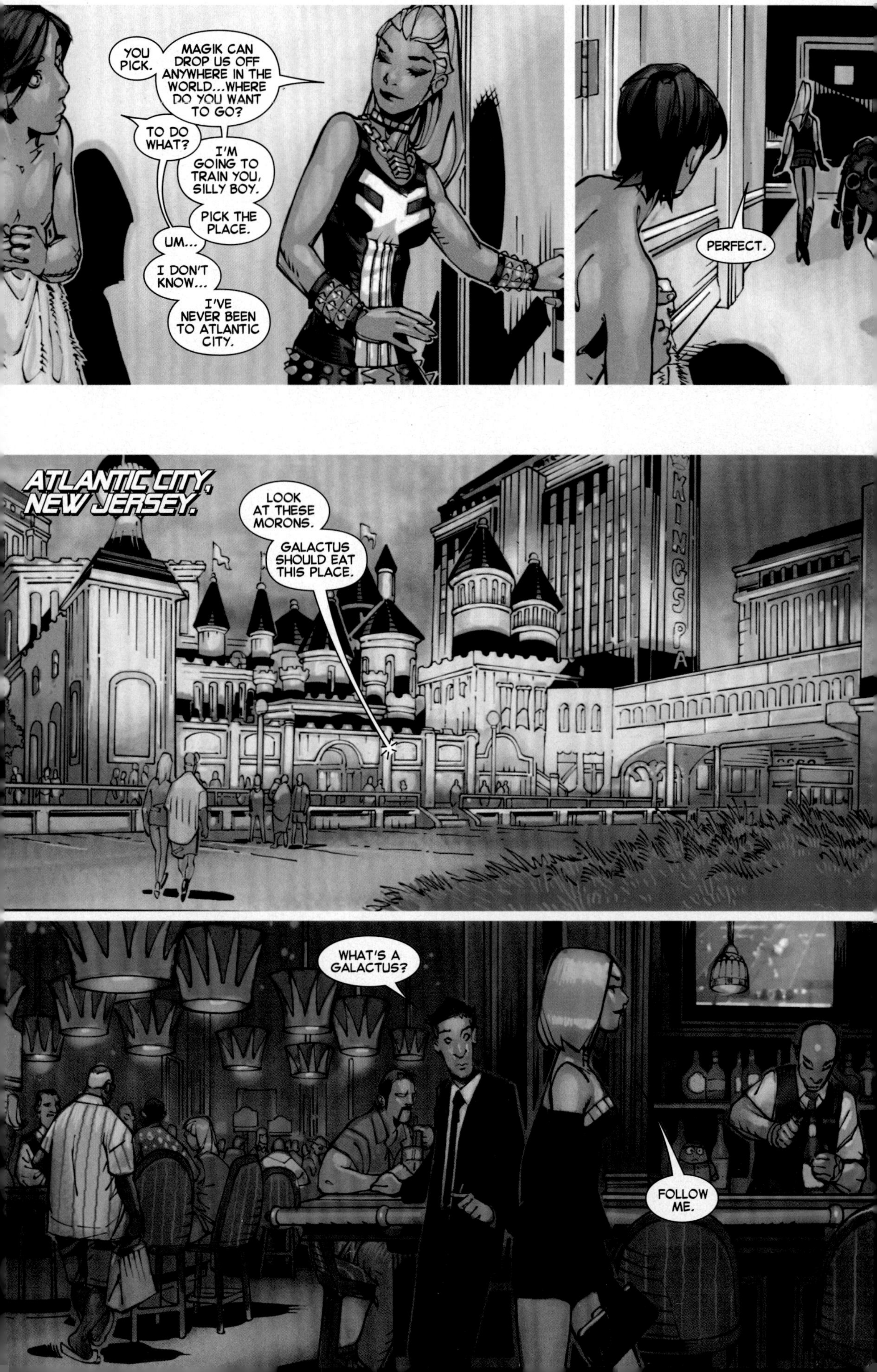
YOU PICK.
MAGIK CAN DROP US OFF ANYWHERE IN THE WORLD...WHERE DO YOU WANT TO GO?
TO DO WHAT?
I'M GOING TO TRAIN YOU, SILLY BOY.
PICK THE PLACE.
UM...
I DON'T KNOW...
I'VE NEVER BEEN TO ATLANTIC CITY.
PERFECT.
ATLANTIC CITY, NEW JERSEY.
LOOK AT THESE MORONS.
GALACTUS SHOULD EAT THIS PLACE.
WHAT'S A GALACTUS?
FOLLOW ME.

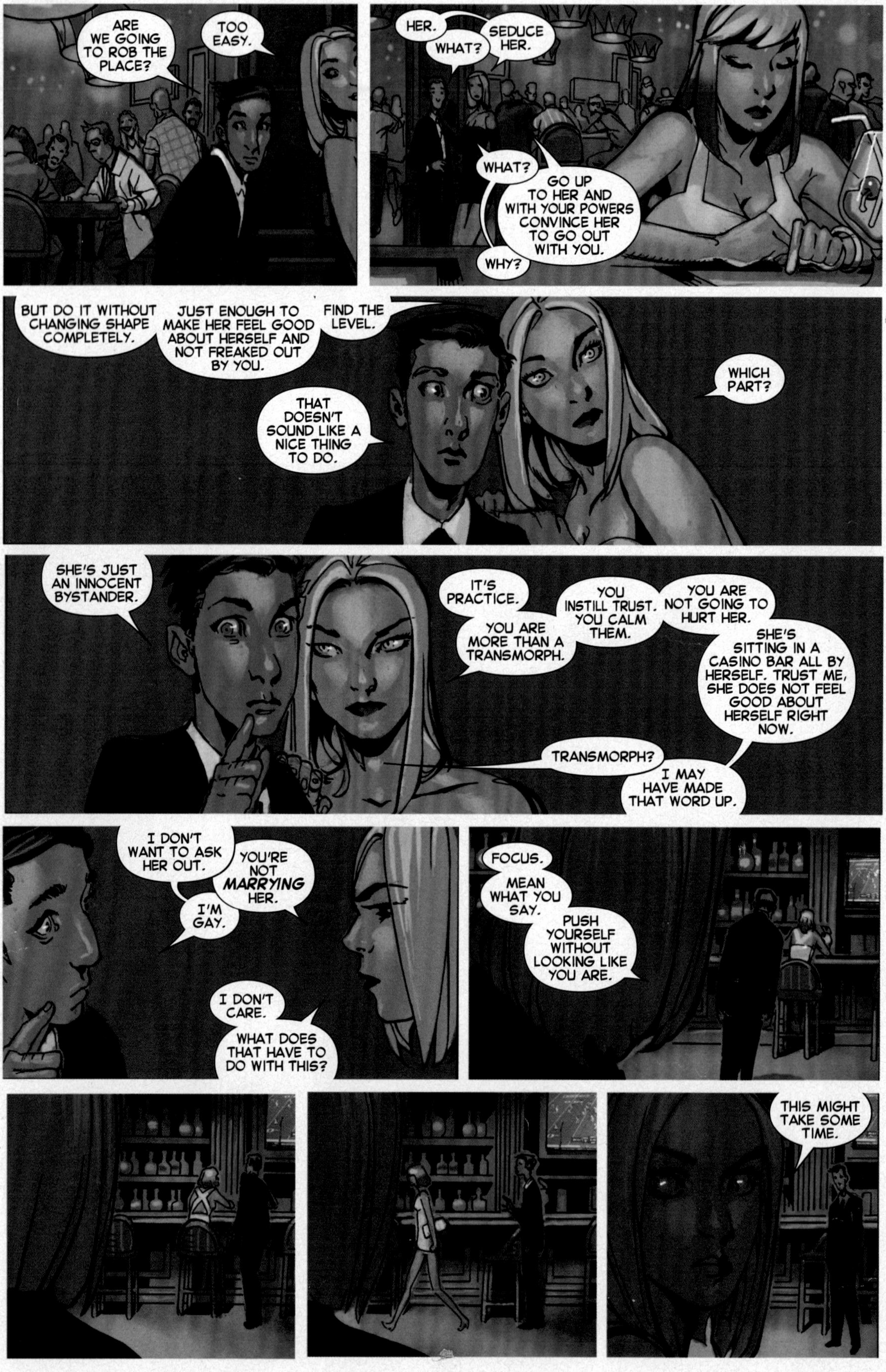
ARE WE GOING TO ROB THE PLACE?
TOO EASY.
HER.
WHAT?
SEDUCE HER.
WHAT?
GO UP TO HER AND WITH YOUR POWERS CONVINCE HER TO GO OUT WITH YOU.
WHY?
WHICH PART?
FIND THE LEVEL.
JUST ENOUGH TO MAKE HER FEEL GOOD ABOUT HERSELF AND NOT FREAKED OUT BY YOU.
BUT DO IT WITHOUT CHANGING SHAPE COMPLETELY.
THAT DOESN'T SOUND LIKE A NICE THING TO DO.
SHE'S JUST AN INNOCENT BYSTANDER.
IT'S PRACTICE.
YOU ARE MORE THAN A TRANSMORPH.
YOU INSTILL TRUST. YOU CALM THEM.
YOU ARE NOT GOING TO HURT HER.
SHE'S SITTING IN A CASINO BAR ALL BY HERSELF. TRUST ME, SHE DOES NOT FEEL GOOD ABOUT HERSELF RIGHT NOW.
TRANSMORPH?
I MAY HAVE MADE THAT WORD UP.
I DON'T WANT TO ASK HER OUT.
YOU'RE NOT *MARRYING* HER.
I'M GAY.
I DON'T CARE.
WHAT DOES THAT HAVE TO DO WITH THIS?
FOCUS.
MEAN WHAT YOU SAY.
PUSH YOURSELF WITHOUT LOOKING LIKE YOU ARE.
THIS MIGHT TAKE SOME TIME.

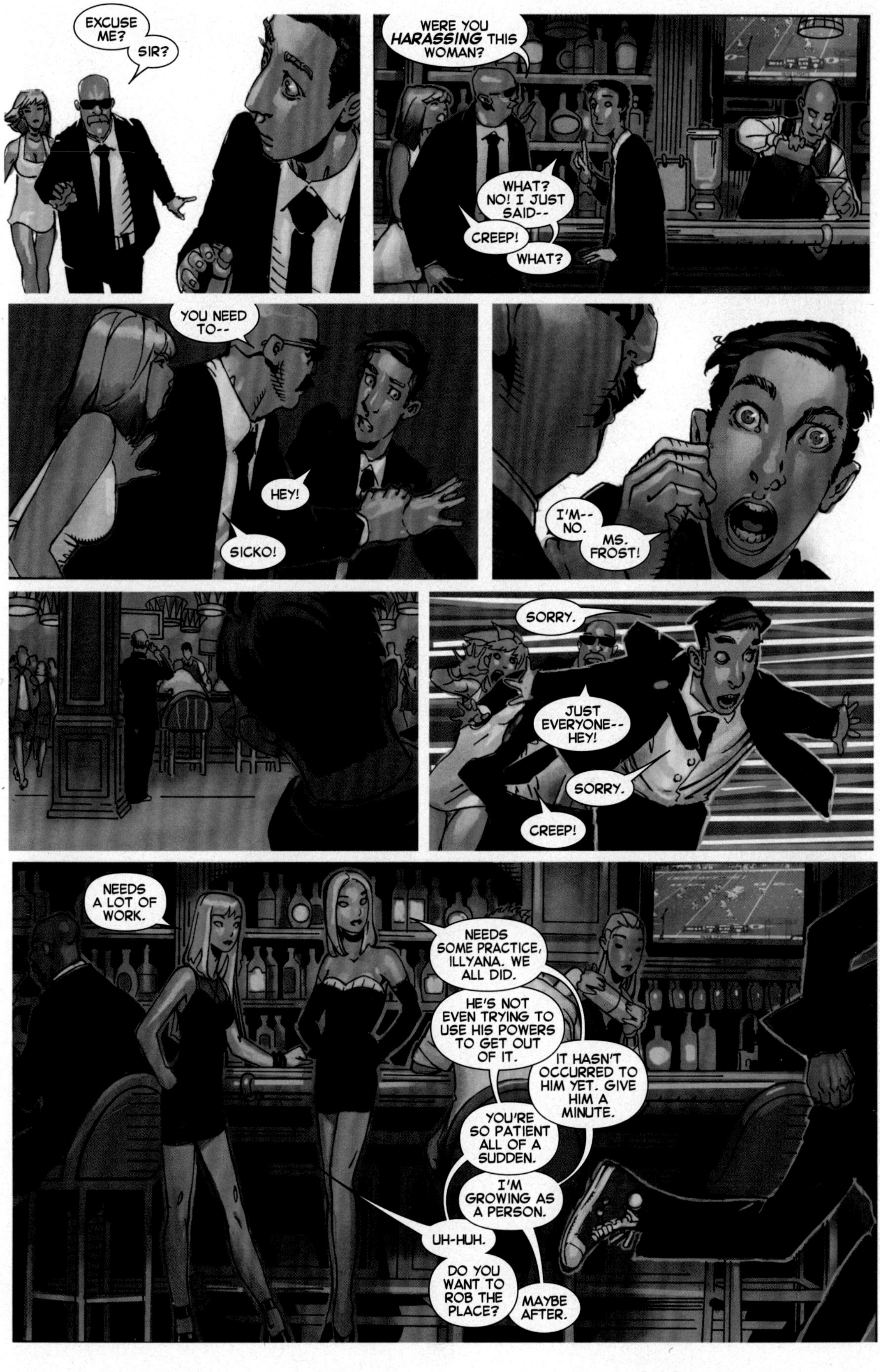
EXCUSE ME?
SIR?
WERE YOU HARASSING THIS WOMAN?
WHAT? NO! I JUST SAID--
CREEP!
WHAT?
YOU NEED TO--
HEY!
SICKO!
I'M-- NO.
MS. FROST!
SORRY.
JUST EVERYONE-- HEY!
SORRY.
CREEP!
NEEDS A LOT OF WORK.
NEEDS SOME PRACTICE, ILLYANA. WE ALL DID.
HE'S NOT EVEN TRYING TO USE HIS POWERS TO GET OUT OF IT.
IT HASN'T OCCURRED TO HIM YET. GIVE HIM A MINUTE.
YOU'RE SO PATIENT ALL OF A SUDDEN.
I'M GROWING AS A PERSON.
UH-HUH.
DO YOU WANT TO ROB THE PLACE?
MAYBE AFTER.

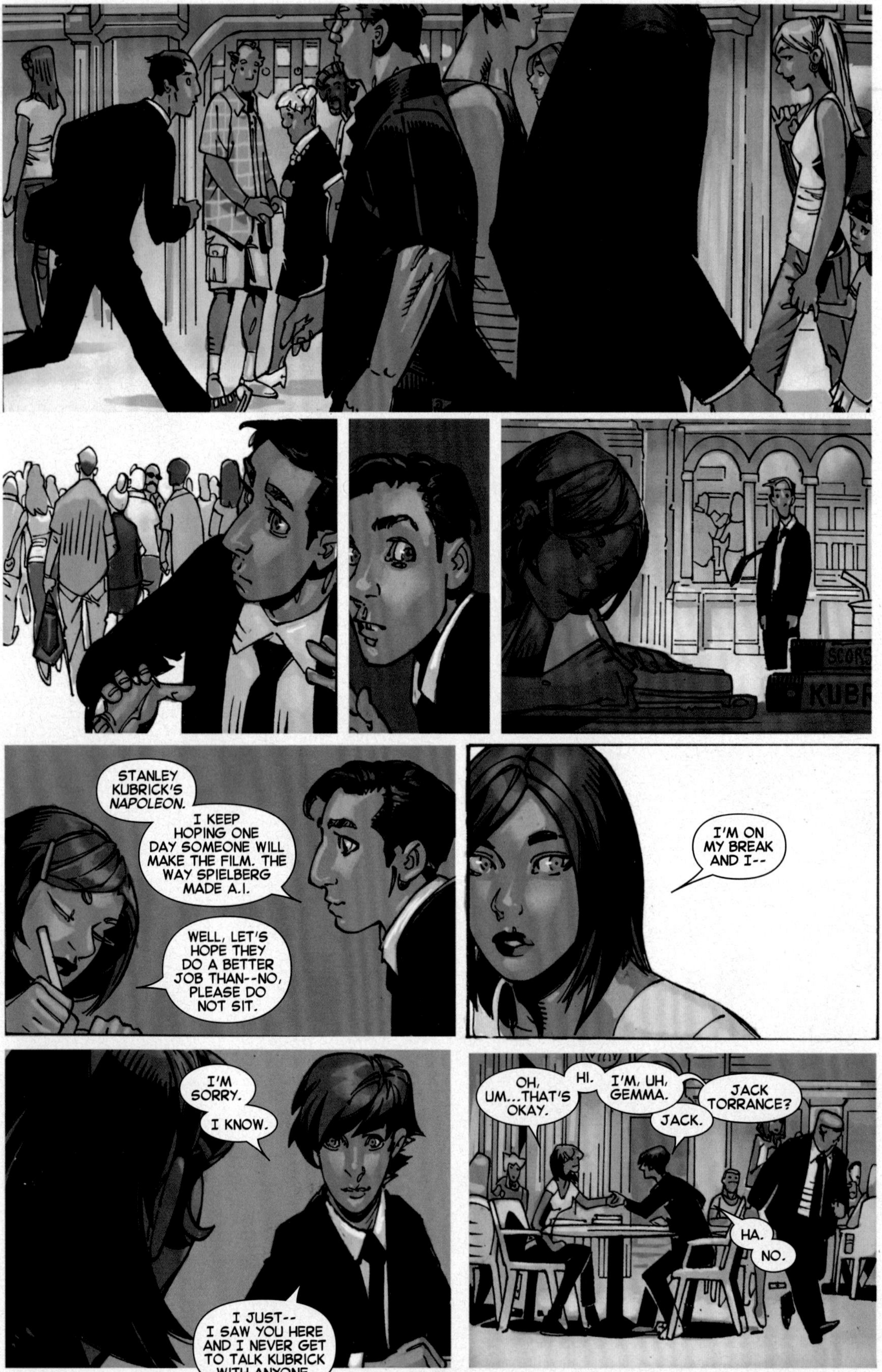
SCORS
KUBR
STANLEY KUBRICK'S NAPOLEON.
I KEEP HOPING ONE DAY SOMEONE WILL MAKE THE FILM. THE WAY SPIELBERG MADE A.I.
WELL, LET'S HOPE THEY DO A BETTER JOB THAN--NO, PLEASE DO NOT SIT.
I'M ON MY BREAK AND I--
I'M SORRY.
I KNOW.
I JUST-- I SAW YOU HERE AND I NEVER GET TO TALK KUBRICK WITH ANYONE.
OH, UM...THAT'S OKAY.
HI.
I'M, UH, GEMMA.
JACK.
JACK TORRANCE?
HA.
NO.

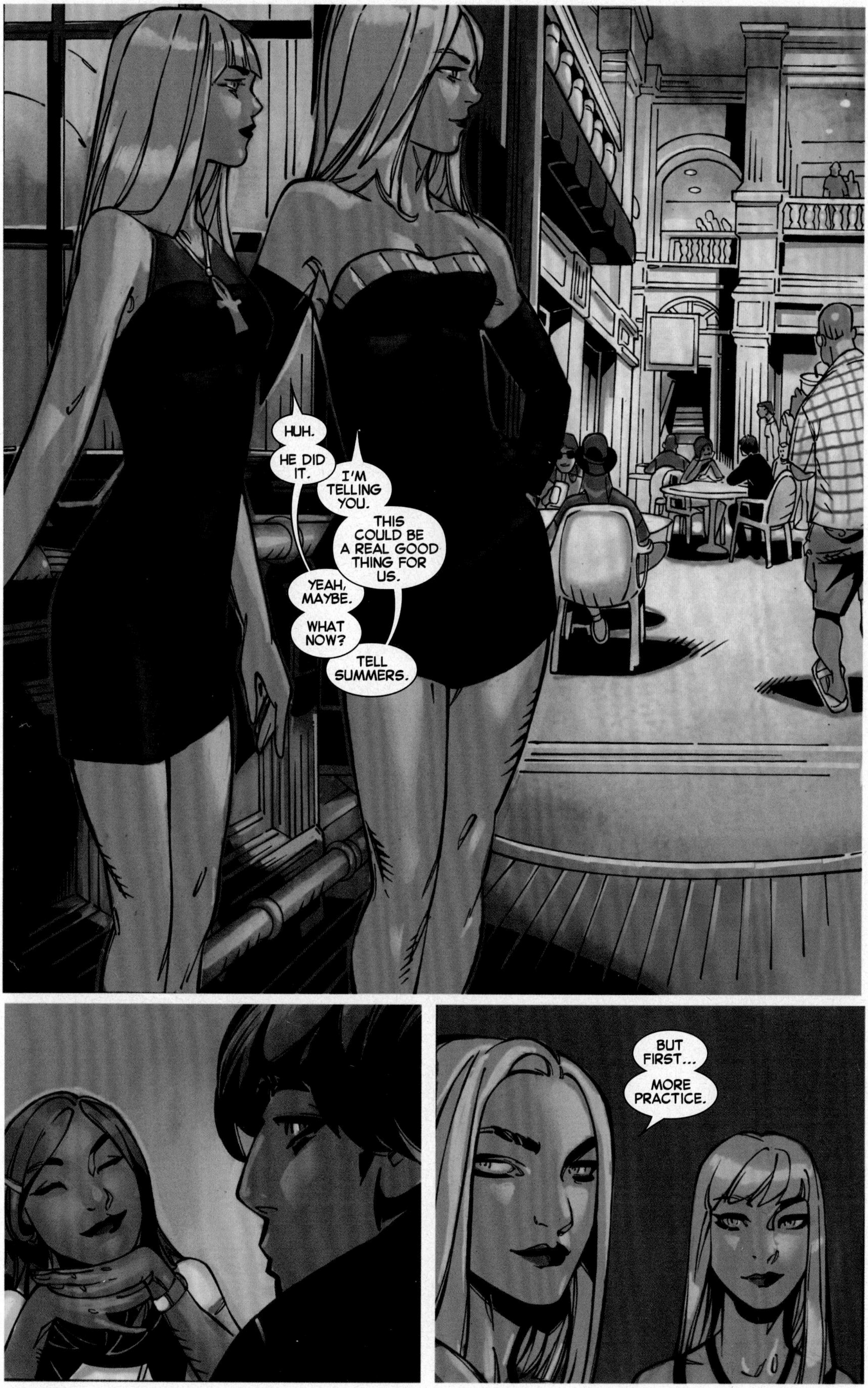
HUH.
HE DID IT.
I'M TELLING YOU.
THIS COULD BE A REAL GOOD THING FOR US.
YEAH, MAYBE.
WHAT NOW?
TELL SUMMERS.
BUT FIRST...
MORE PRACTICE.

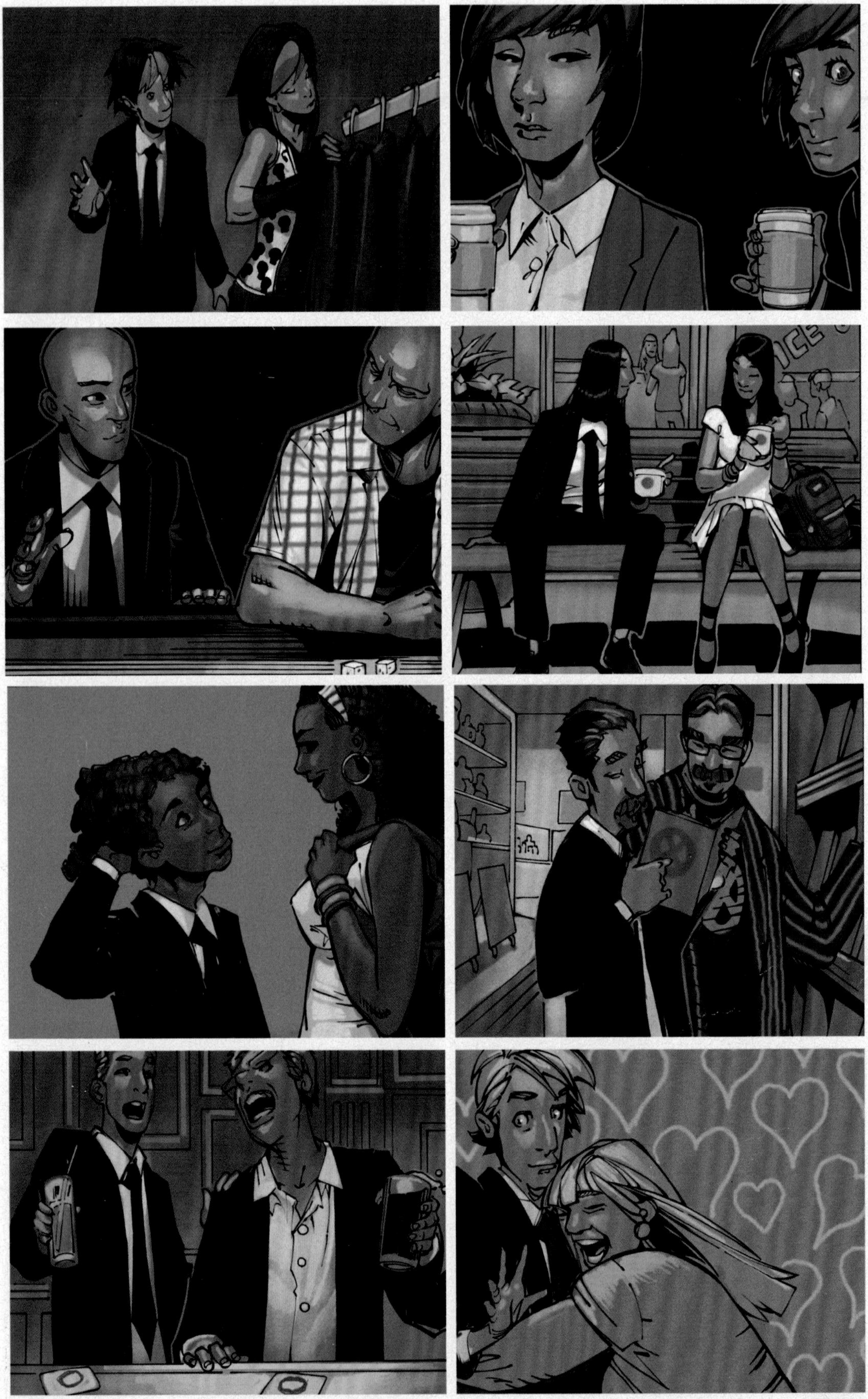

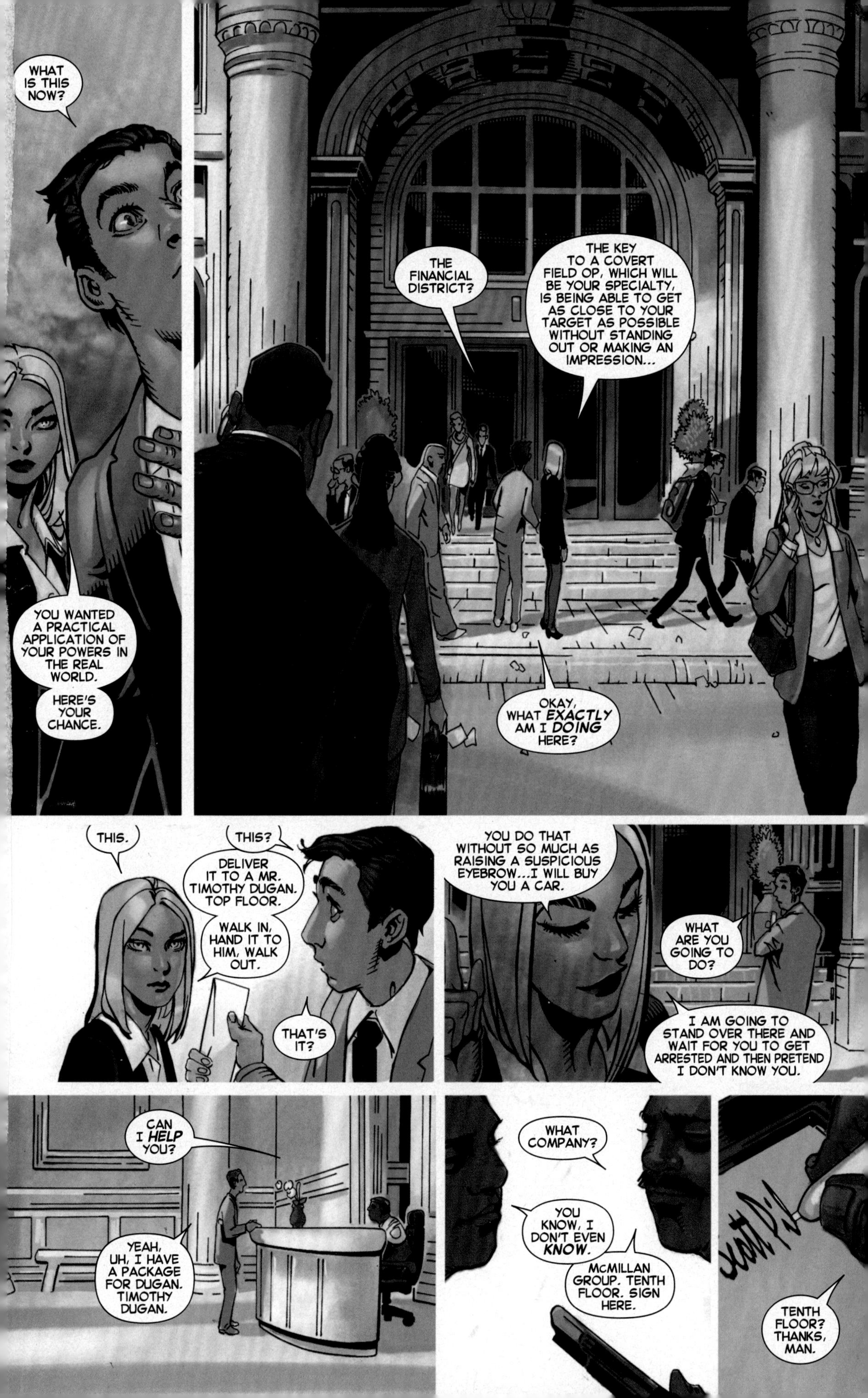
WHAT IS THIS NOW?
THE FINANCIAL DISTRICT?
THE KEY TO A COVERT FIELD OP, WHICH WILL BE YOUR SPECIALTY, IS BEING ABLE TO GET AS CLOSE TO YOUR TARGET AS POSSIBLE WITHOUT STANDING OUT OR MAKING AN IMPRESSION...
YOU WANTED A PRACTICAL APPLICATION OF YOUR POWERS IN THE REAL WORLD.
HERE'S YOUR CHANCE.
OKAY, WHAT *EXACTLY* AM I *DOING* HERE?
THIS.
THIS?
DELIVER IT TO A MR. TIMOTHY DUGAN. TOP FLOOR.
WALK IN, HAND IT TO HIM, WALK OUT.
THAT'S IT?
YOU DO THAT WITHOUT SO MUCH AS RAISING A SUSPICIOUS EYEBROW...I WILL BUY YOU A CAR.
WHAT ARE YOU GOING TO DO?
I AM GOING TO STAND OVER THERE AND WAIT FOR YOU TO GET ARRESTED AND THEN PRETEND I DON'T KNOW YOU.
CAN I *HELP* YOU?
YEAH, UH, I HAVE A PACKAGE FOR DUGAN. TIMOTHY DUGAN.
WHAT COMPANY?
YOU KNOW, I DON'T EVEN *KNOW*.
McMILLAN GROUP. TENTH FLOOR. SIGN HERE.
TENTH FLOOR? THANKS, MAN.

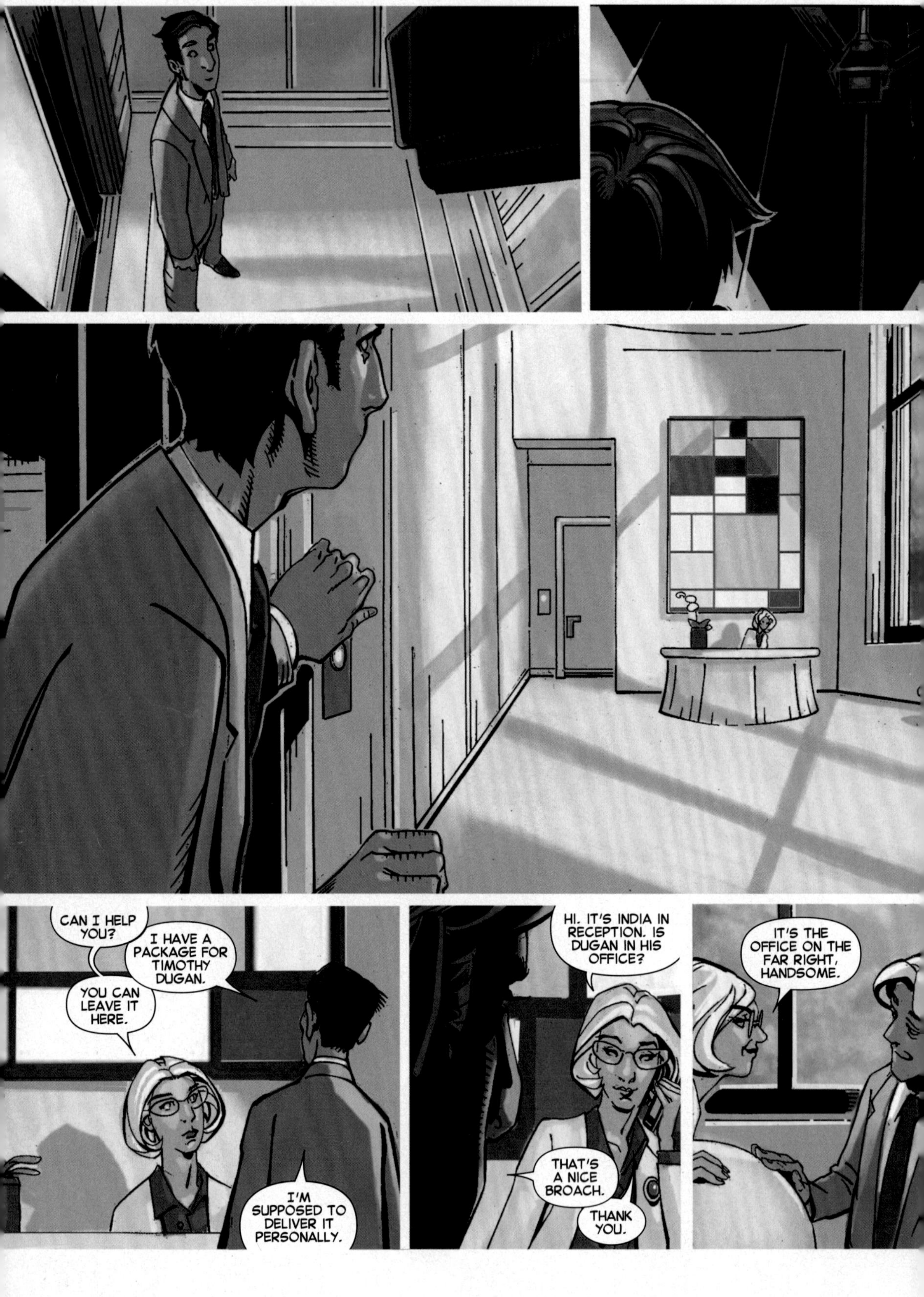
CAN I HELP YOU?
I HAVE A PACKAGE FOR TIMOTHY DUGAN.
YOU CAN LEAVE IT HERE.
I'M SUPPOSED TO DELIVER IT PERSONALLY.
HI. IT'S INDIA IN RECEPTION. IS DUGAN IN HIS OFFICE?
THAT'S A NICE BROACH.
THANK YOU.
IT'S THE OFFICE ON THE FAR RIGHT, HANDSOME.

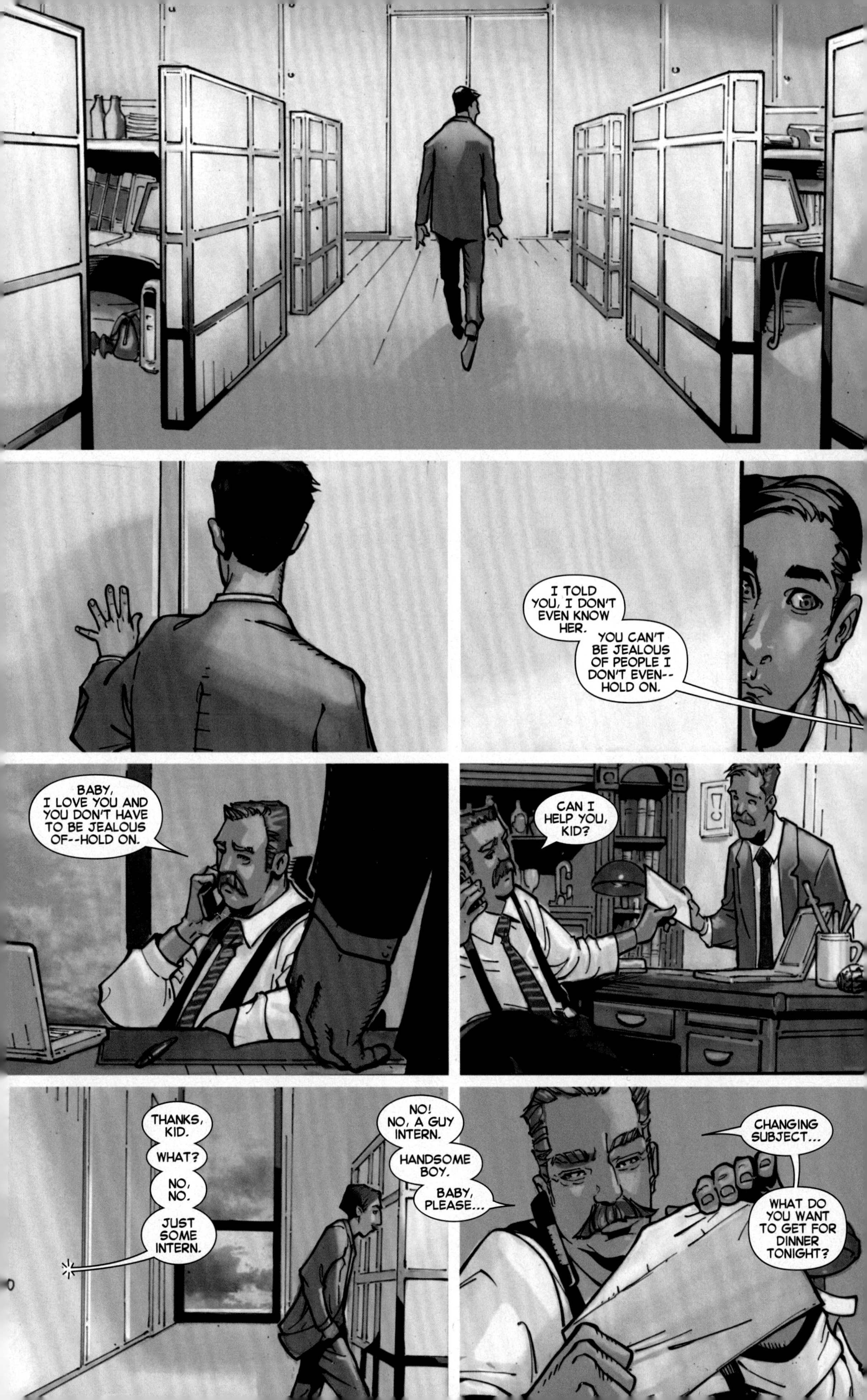
I TOLD YOU, I DON'T EVEN KNOW HER.
YOU CAN'T BE JEALOUS OF PEOPLE I DON'T EVEN--HOLD ON.
BABY, I LOVE YOU AND YOU DON'T HAVE TO BE JEALOUS OF--HOLD ON.
CAN I HELP YOU, KID?
THANKS, KID.
WHAT?
NO, NO.
JUST SOME INTERN.
NO! NO, A GUY INTERN.
HANDSOME BOY.
BABY, PLEASE...
CHANGING SUBJECT...
WHAT DO YOU WANT TO GET FOR DINNER TONIGHT?

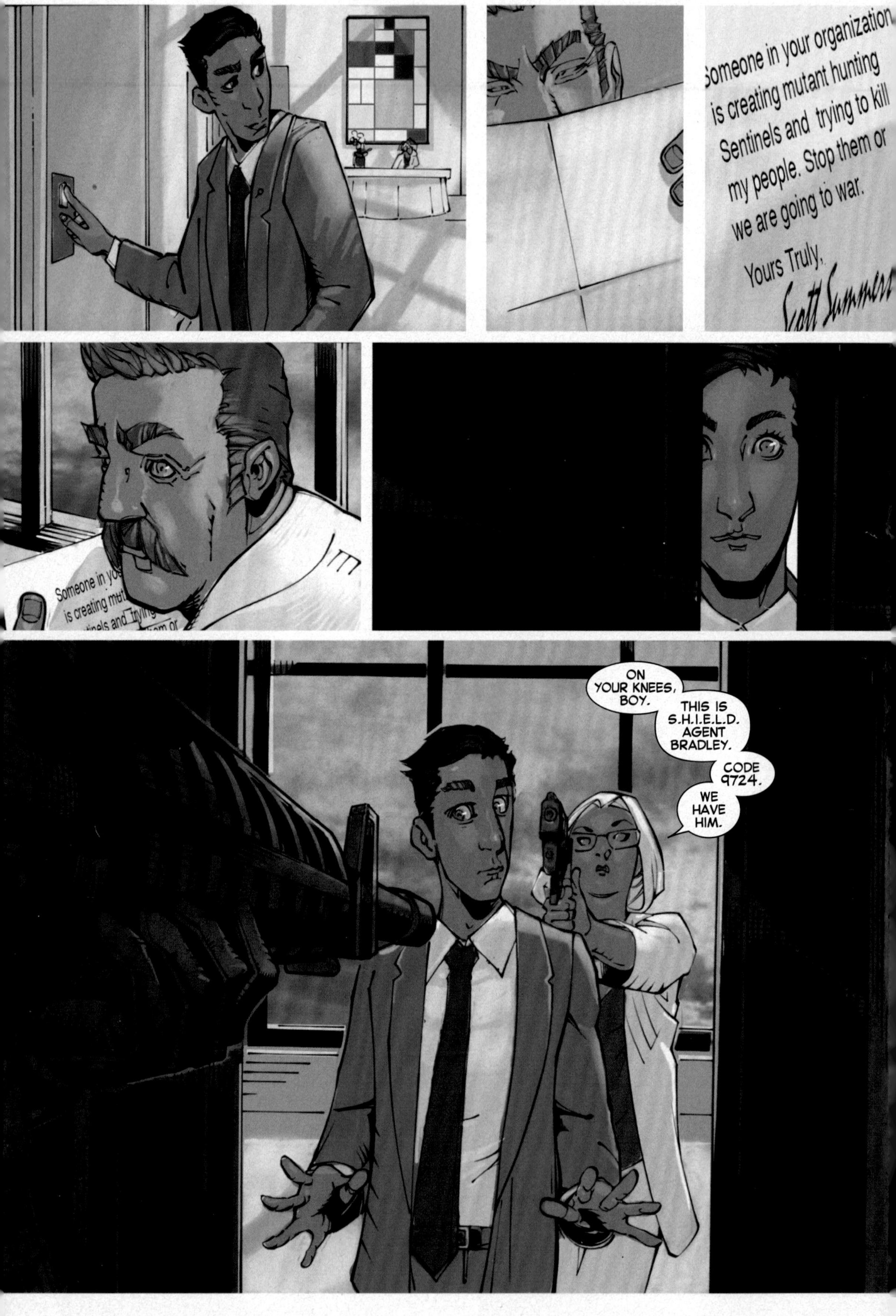
Someone in your organization is creating mutant hunting Sentinels and trying to kill my people. Stop them or we are going to war.
Yours Truly,
Scott Summers
ON YOUR KNEES, BOY.
THIS IS S.H.I.E.L.D. AGENT BRADLEY.
CODE 9724.
WE HAVE HIM.

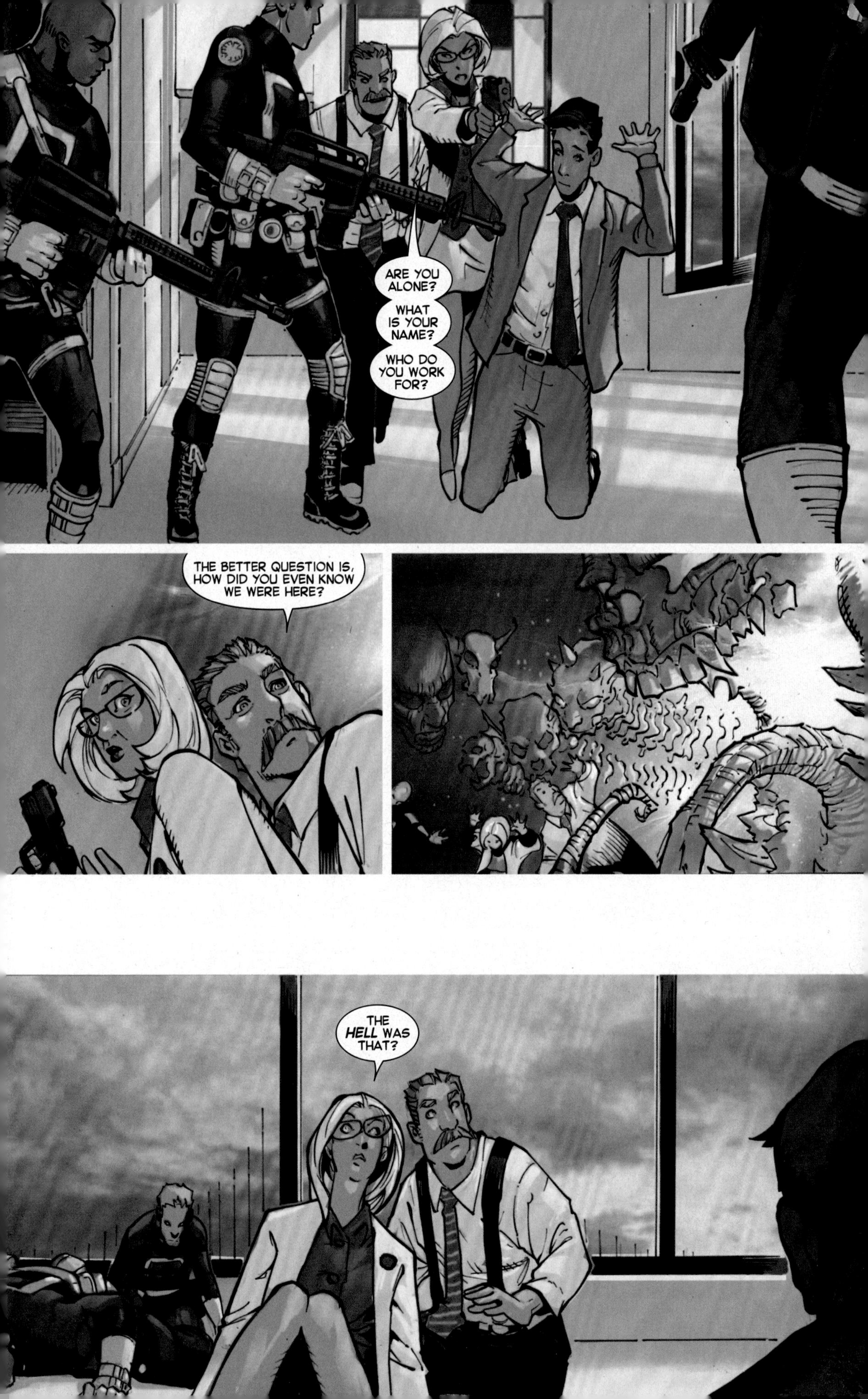
ARE YOU ALONE?
WHAT IS YOUR NAME?
WHO DO YOU WORK FOR?
THE BETTER QUESTION IS, HOW DID YOU EVEN KNOW WE WERE HERE?
THE *HELL* WAS THAT?

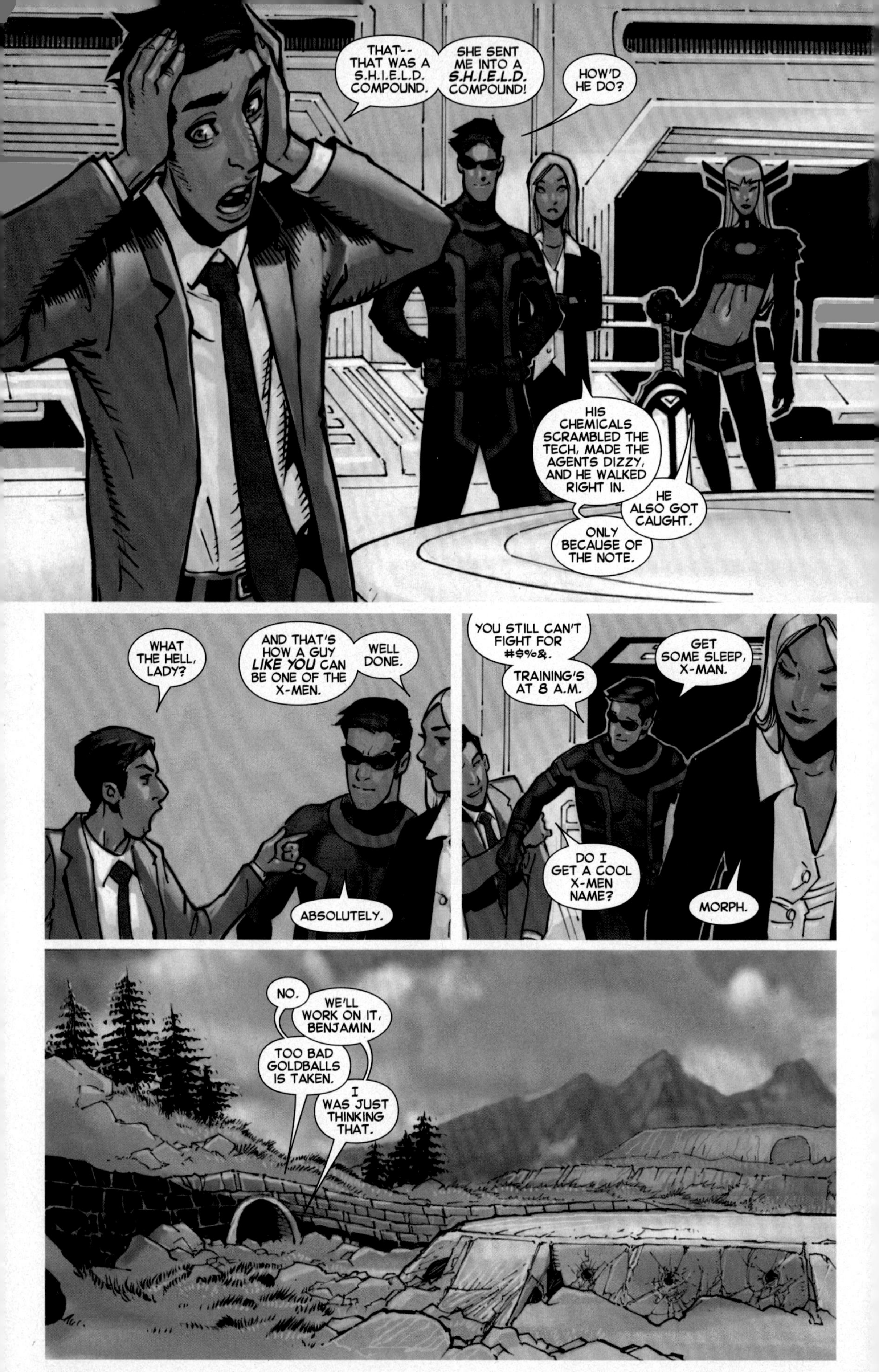
THAT-- THAT WAS A S.H.I.E.L.D. COMPOUND.
SHE SENT ME INTO A S.H.I.E.L.D. COMPOUND!
HOW'D HE DO?
HIS CHEMICALS SCRAMBLED THE TECH, MADE THE AGENTS DIZZY, AND HE WALKED RIGHT IN.
HE ALSO GOT CAUGHT.
ONLY BECAUSE OF THE NOTE.
WHAT THE HELL, LADY?
AND THAT'S HOW A GUY LIKE YOU CAN BE ONE OF THE X-MEN.
WELL DONE.
ABSOLUTELY.
YOU STILL CAN'T FIGHT FOR #$%&.
TRAINING'S AT 8 A.M.
GET SOME SLEEP, X-MAN.
DO I GET A COOL X-MEN NAME?
MORPH.
NO.
WE'LL WORK ON IT, BENJAMIN.
TOO BAD GOLDBALLS IS TAKEN.
I WAS JUST THINKING THAT.

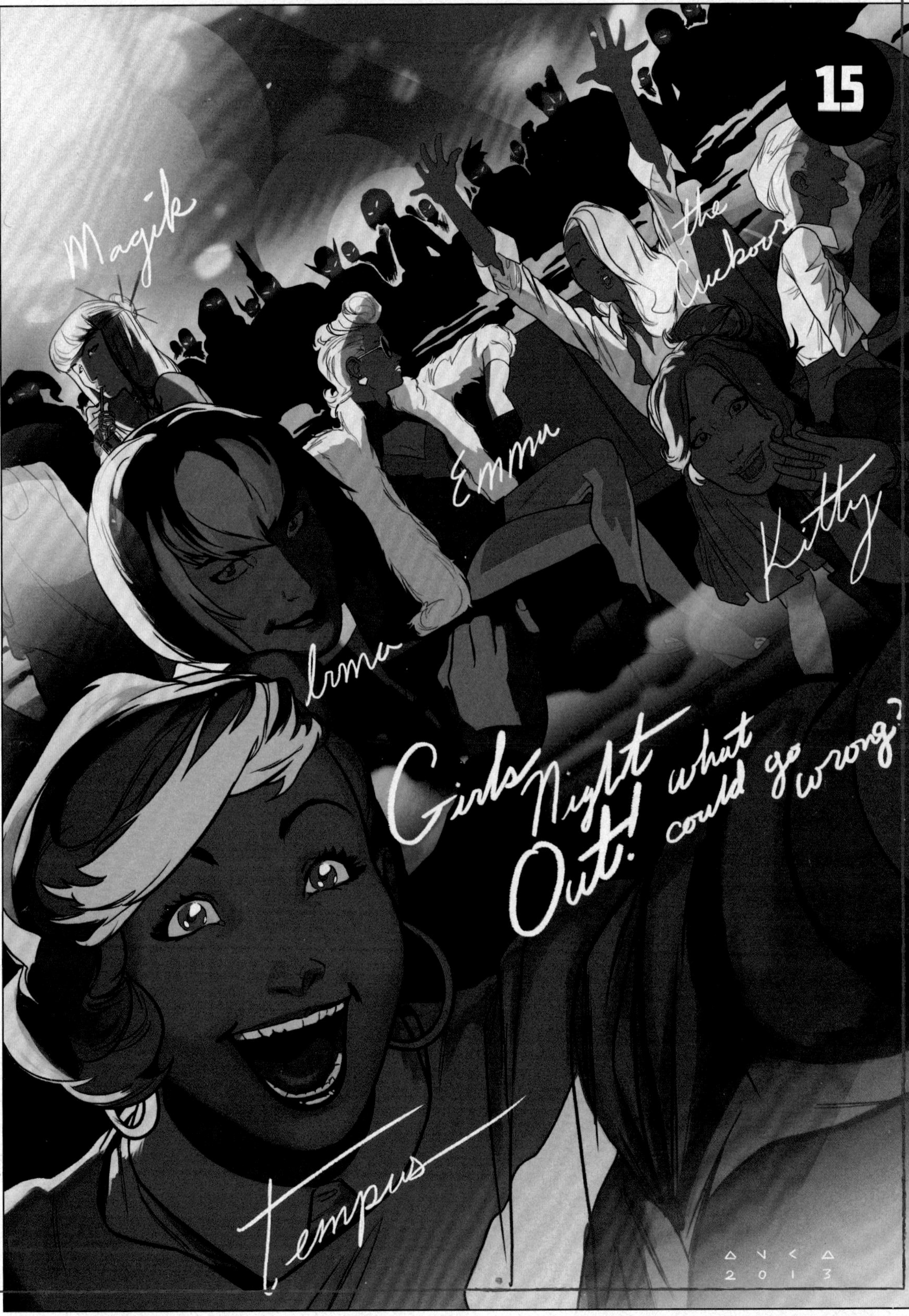
15
Magik
the Cuckoos
Emma
Kitty
Irma
Girls Night Out! what could go wrong?
Tempus
2013

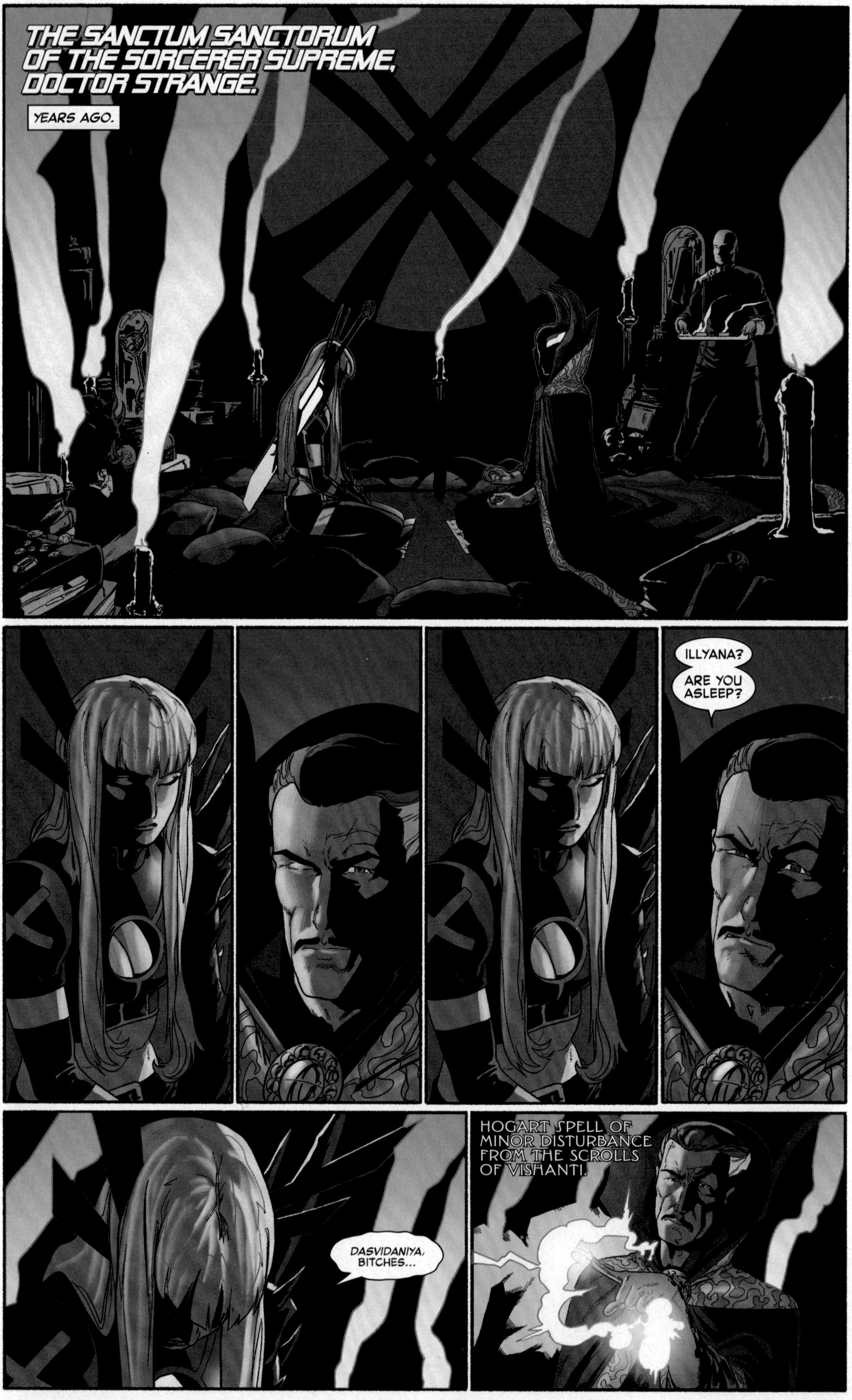
THE SANCTUM SANCTORUM OF THE SORCERER SUPREME, DOCTOR STRANGE.
YEARS AGO.
ILLYANA?
ARE YOU ASLEEP?
DASVIDANIYA, BITCHES...
HOGART SPELL OF MINOR DISTURBANCE FROM THE SCROLLS OF VISHANTI.

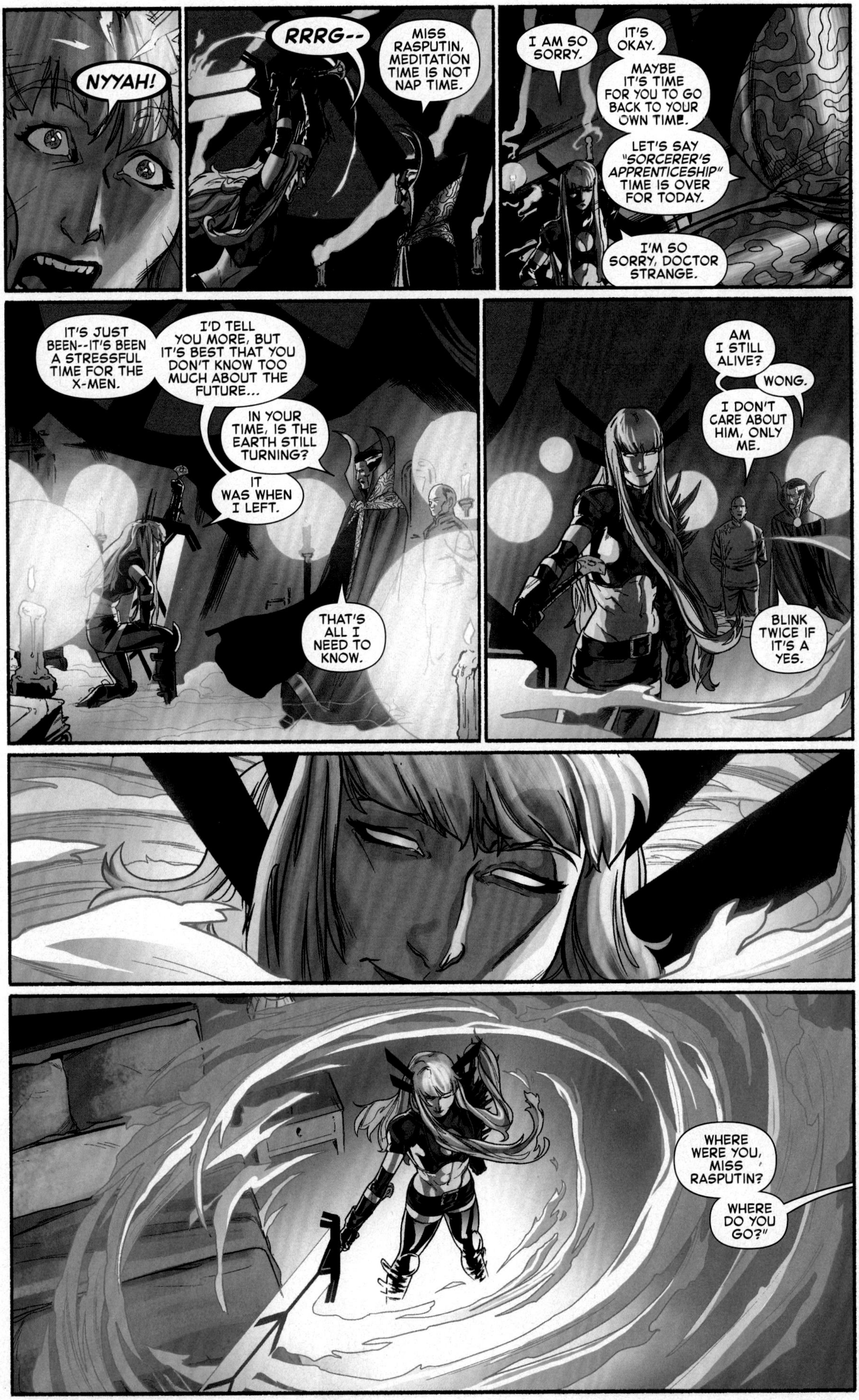
NYYAH!
RRRG--
MISS RASPUTIN, MEDITATION TIME IS NOT NAP TIME.
I AM SO SORRY.
IT'S OKAY.
MAYBE IT'S TIME FOR YOU TO GO BACK TO YOUR OWN TIME.
LET'S SAY "SORCERER'S APPRENTICESHIP" TIME IS OVER FOR TODAY.
I'M SO SORRY, DOCTOR STRANGE.
IT'S JUST BEEN--IT'S BEEN A STRESSFUL TIME FOR THE X-MEN.
I'D TELL YOU MORE, BUT IT'S BEST THAT YOU DON'T KNOW TOO MUCH ABOUT THE FUTURE...
IN YOUR TIME, IS THE EARTH STILL TURNING?
IT WAS WHEN I LEFT.
THAT'S ALL I NEED TO KNOW.
AM I STILL ALIVE?
WONG.
I DON'T CARE ABOUT HIM, ONLY ME.
BLINK TWICE IF IT'S A YES.
WHERE WERE YOU, MISS RASPUTIN?
WHERE DO YOU GO?"

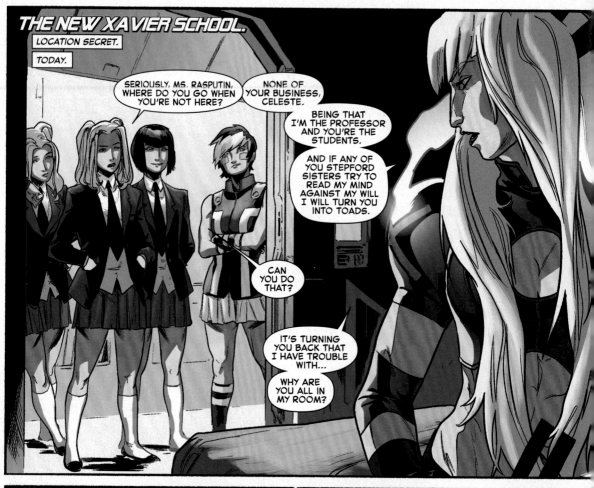

THE NEW XAVIER SCHOOL.

LOCATION SECRET.

TODAY.

SERIOUSLY, MS. RASPUTIN, WHERE DO YOU GO WHEN YOU'RE NOT HERE?

NONE OF YOUR BUSINESS, CELESTE.

BEING THAT I'M THE PROFESSOR AND YOU'RE THE STUDENTS.

AND IF ANY OF YOU STEPFORD SISTERS TRY TO READ MY MIND AGAINST MY WILL I WILL TURN YOU INTO TOADS.

CAN YOU DO THAT?

IT'S TURNING YOU BACK THAT I HAVE TROUBLE WITH...

WHY ARE YOU ALL IN MY ROOM?

OI! JEAN GREY!

WHAT'S GOING ON?

JEAN GREY, GET IN HERE.

WHAT?

WE DON'T WANT YOU TO JUDGE US.

JUDGE?

WE'RE ALL X-MEN.

POWERFUL WOMEN STANDING ON OUR OWN TWO FEET.

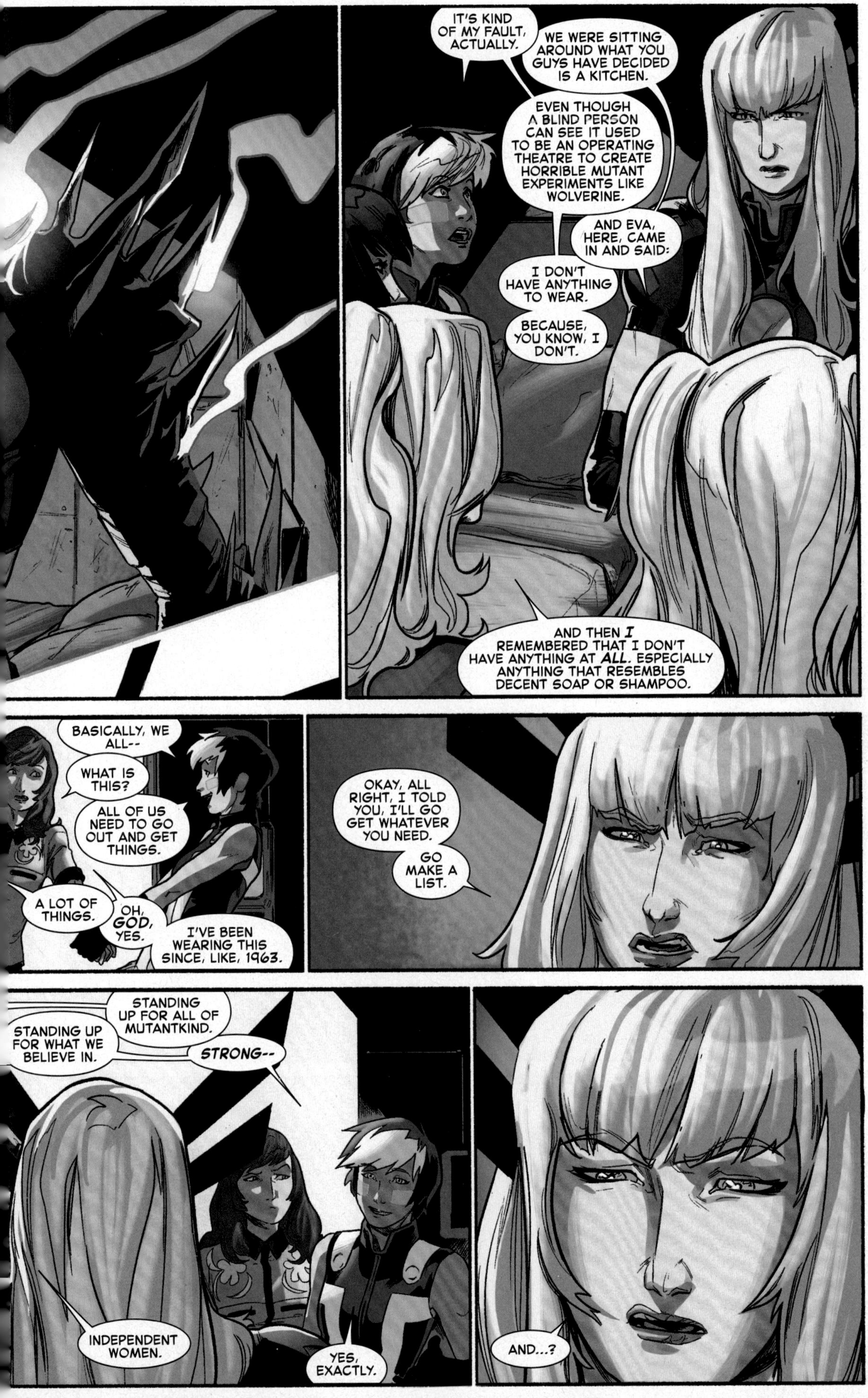
IT'S KIND OF MY FAULT, ACTUALLY.
WE WERE SITTING AROUND WHAT YOU GUYS HAVE DECIDED IS A KITCHEN.
EVEN THOUGH A BLIND PERSON CAN SEE IT USED TO BE AN OPERATING THEATRE TO CREATE HORRIBLE MUTANT EXPERIMENTS LIKE WOLVERINE.
AND EVA, HERE, CAME IN AND SAID:
I DON'T HAVE ANYTHING TO WEAR.
BECAUSE, YOU KNOW, I DON'T.
AND THEN I REMEMBERED THAT I DON'T HAVE ANYTHING AT ALL. ESPECIALLY ANYTHING THAT RESEMBLES DECENT SOAP OR SHAMPOO.
BASICALLY, WE ALL--
WHAT IS THIS?
ALL OF US NEED TO GO OUT AND GET THINGS.
A LOT OF THINGS.
OH, GOD, YES.
I'VE BEEN WEARING THIS SINCE, LIKE, 1963.
OKAY, ALL RIGHT, I TOLD YOU, I'LL GO GET WHATEVER YOU NEED.
GO MAKE A LIST.
STANDING UP FOR WHAT WE BELIEVE IN.
STANDING UP FOR ALL OF MUTANTKIND.
STRONG--
INDEPENDENT WOMEN.
YES, EXACTLY.
AND...?

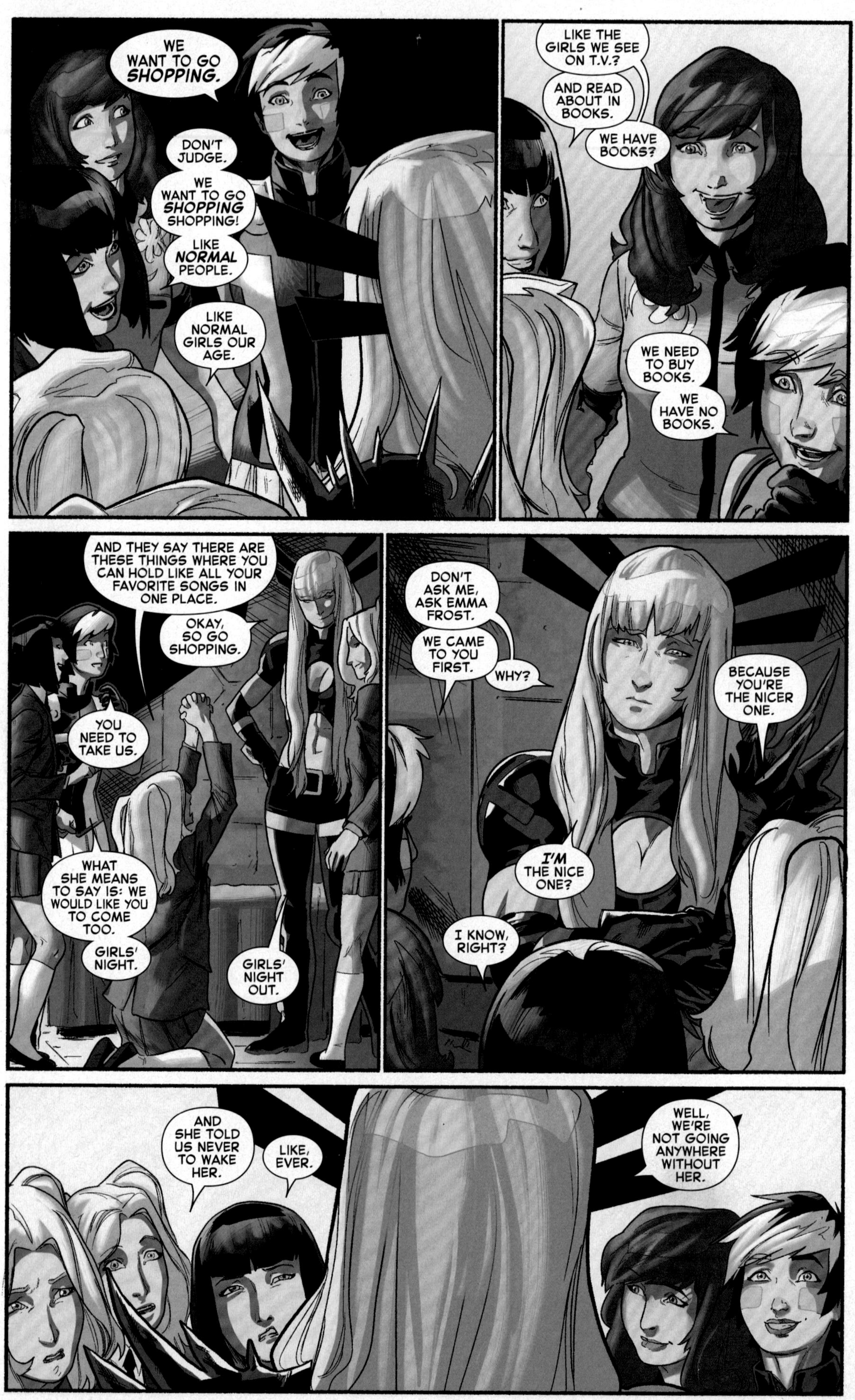
WE WANT TO GO SHOPPING.
DON'T JUDGE.
WE WANT TO GO SHOPPING SHOPPING!
LIKE NORMAL PEOPLE.
LIKE NORMAL GIRLS OUR AGE.
LIKE THE GIRLS WE SEE ON T.V.?
AND READ ABOUT IN BOOKS.
WE HAVE BOOKS?
WE NEED TO BUY BOOKS.
WE HAVE NO BOOKS.
AND THEY SAY THERE ARE THESE THINGS WHERE YOU CAN HOLD LIKE ALL YOUR FAVORITE SONGS IN ONE PLACE.
OKAY, SO GO SHOPPING.
YOU NEED TO TAKE US.
WHAT SHE MEANS TO SAY IS: WE WOULD LIKE YOU TO COME TOO.
GIRLS' NIGHT.
GIRLS' NIGHT OUT.
DON'T ASK ME, ASK EMMA FROST.
WE CAME TO YOU FIRST.
WHY?
BECAUSE YOU'RE THE NICER ONE.
I'M THE NICE ONE?
I KNOW, RIGHT?
AND SHE TOLD US NEVER TO WAKE HER.
LIKE, EVER.
WELL, WE'RE NOT GOING ANYWHERE WITHOUT HER.

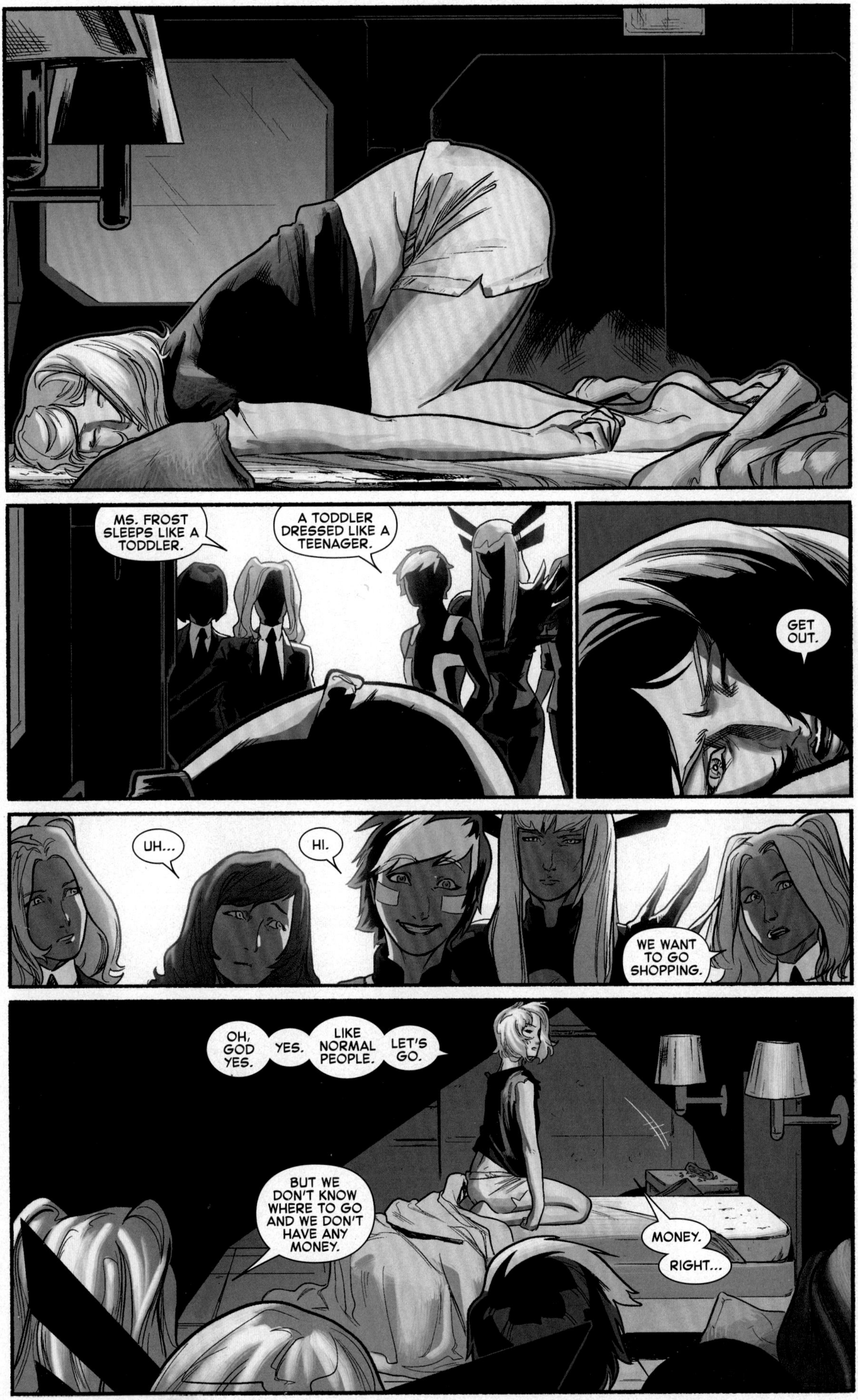
MS. FROST SLEEPS LIKE A TODDLER.
A TODDLER DRESSED LIKE A TEENAGER.
GET OUT.
UH...
HI.
WE WANT TO GO SHOPPING.
OH, GOD YES.
YES.
LIKE NORMAL PEOPLE.
LET'S GO.
BUT WE DON'T KNOW WHERE TO GO AND WE DON'T HAVE ANY MONEY.
MONEY.
RIGHT...

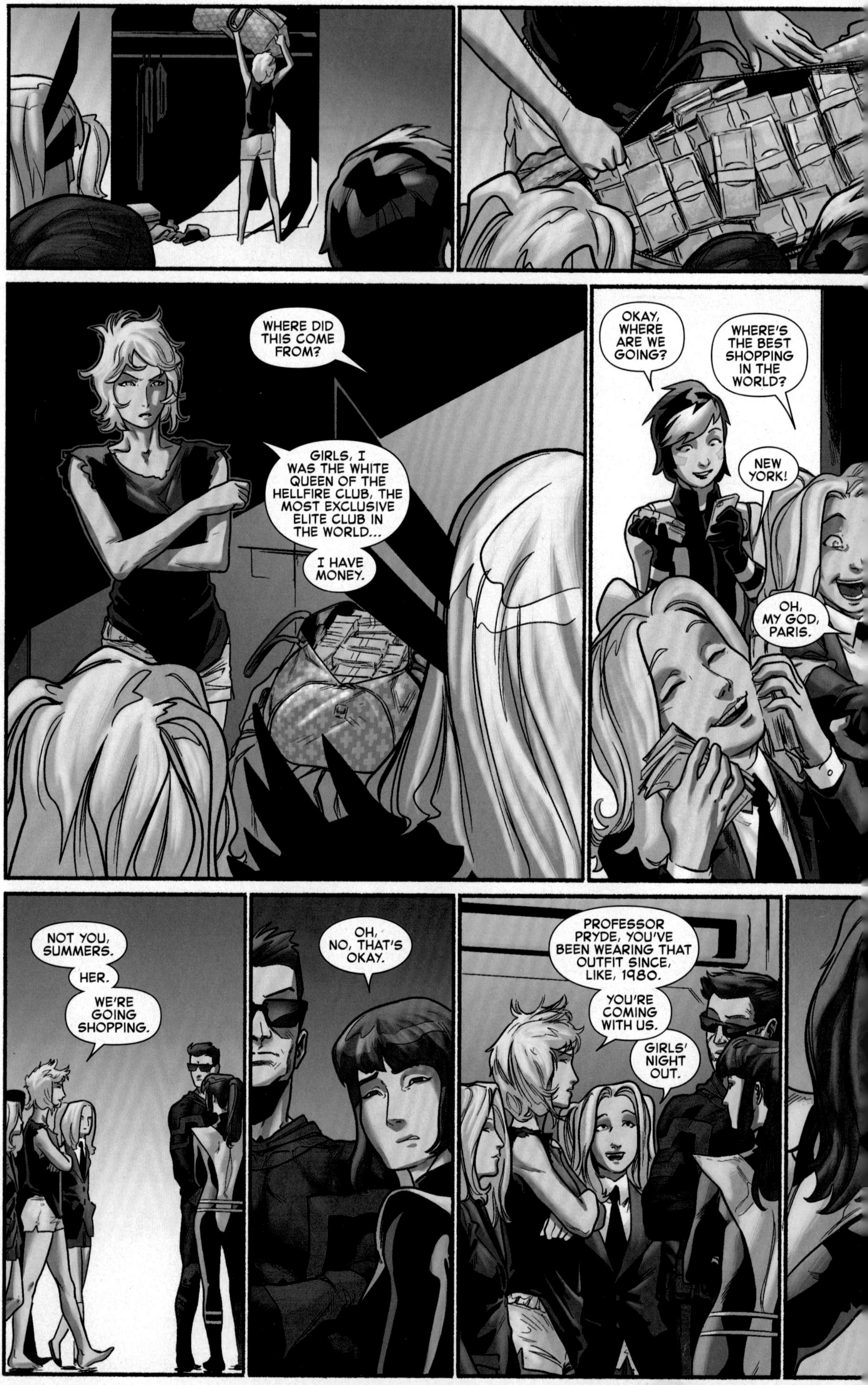
WHERE DID THIS COME FROM?
GIRLS, I WAS THE WHITE QUEEN OF THE HELLFIRE CLUB, THE MOST EXCLUSIVE ELITE CLUB IN THE WORLD...
I HAVE MONEY.
OKAY, WHERE ARE WE GOING?
WHERE'S THE BEST SHOPPING IN THE WORLD?
NEW YORK!
OH, MY GOD, PARIS.
NOT YOU, SUMMERS.
HER.
WE'RE GOING SHOPPING.
OH, NO, THAT'S OKAY.
PROFESSOR PRYDE, YOU'VE BEEN WEARING THAT OUTFIT SINCE, LIKE, 1980.
YOU'RE COMING WITH US.
GIRLS' NIGHT OUT.

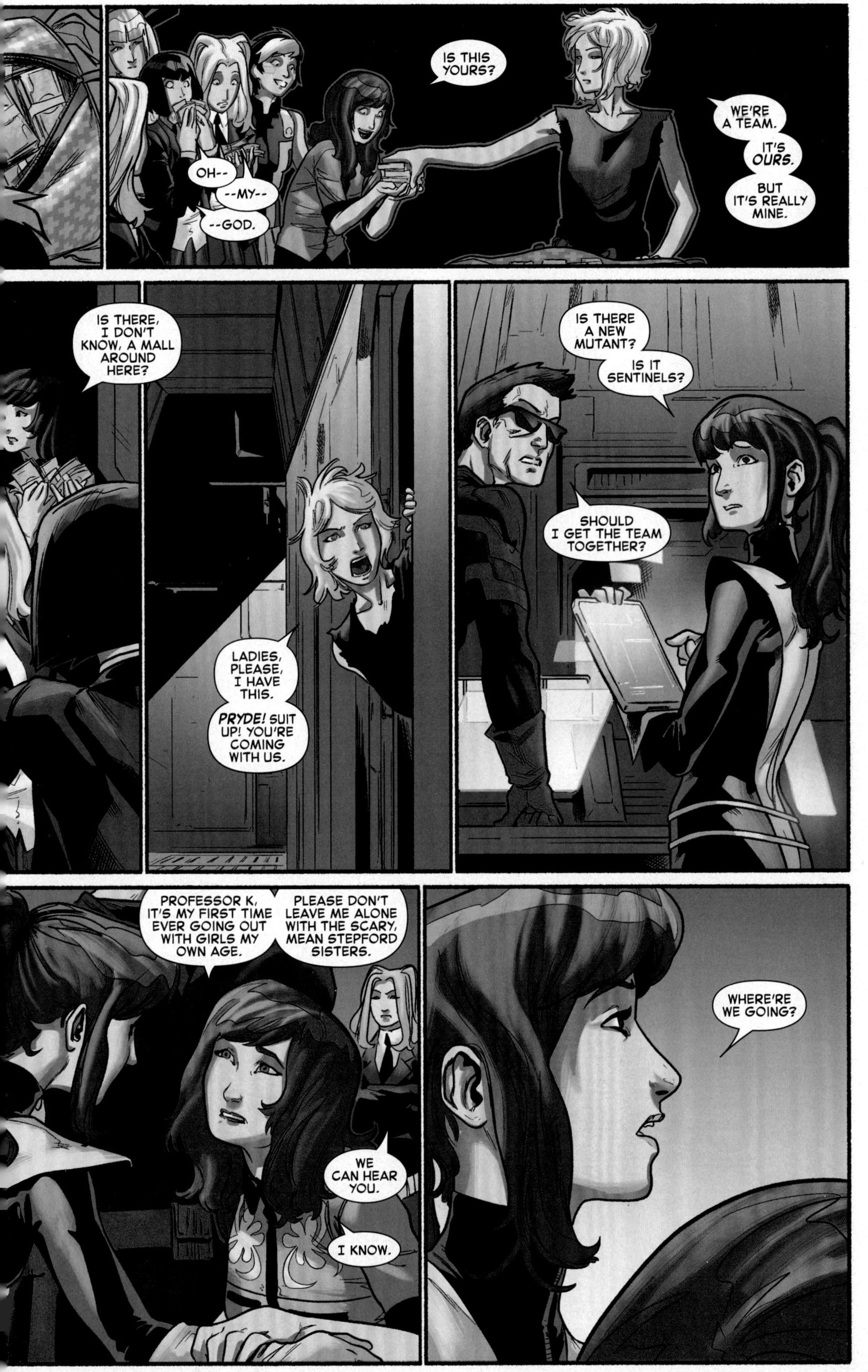
IS THIS YOURS?
OH--
--MY--
--GOD.
WE'RE A TEAM.
IT'S OURS.
BUT IT'S REALLY MINE.
IS THERE, I DON'T KNOW, A MALL AROUND HERE?
LADIES, PLEASE, I HAVE THIS.
PRYDE! SUIT UP! YOU'RE COMING WITH US.
IS THERE A NEW MUTANT?
IS IT SENTINELS?
SHOULD I GET THE TEAM TOGETHER?
PROFESSOR K, IT'S MY FIRST TIME EVER GOING OUT WITH GIRLS MY OWN AGE.
PLEASE DON'T LEAVE ME ALONE WITH THE SCARY, MEAN STEPFORD SISTERS.
WE CAN HEAR YOU.
I KNOW.
WHERE'RE WE GOING?

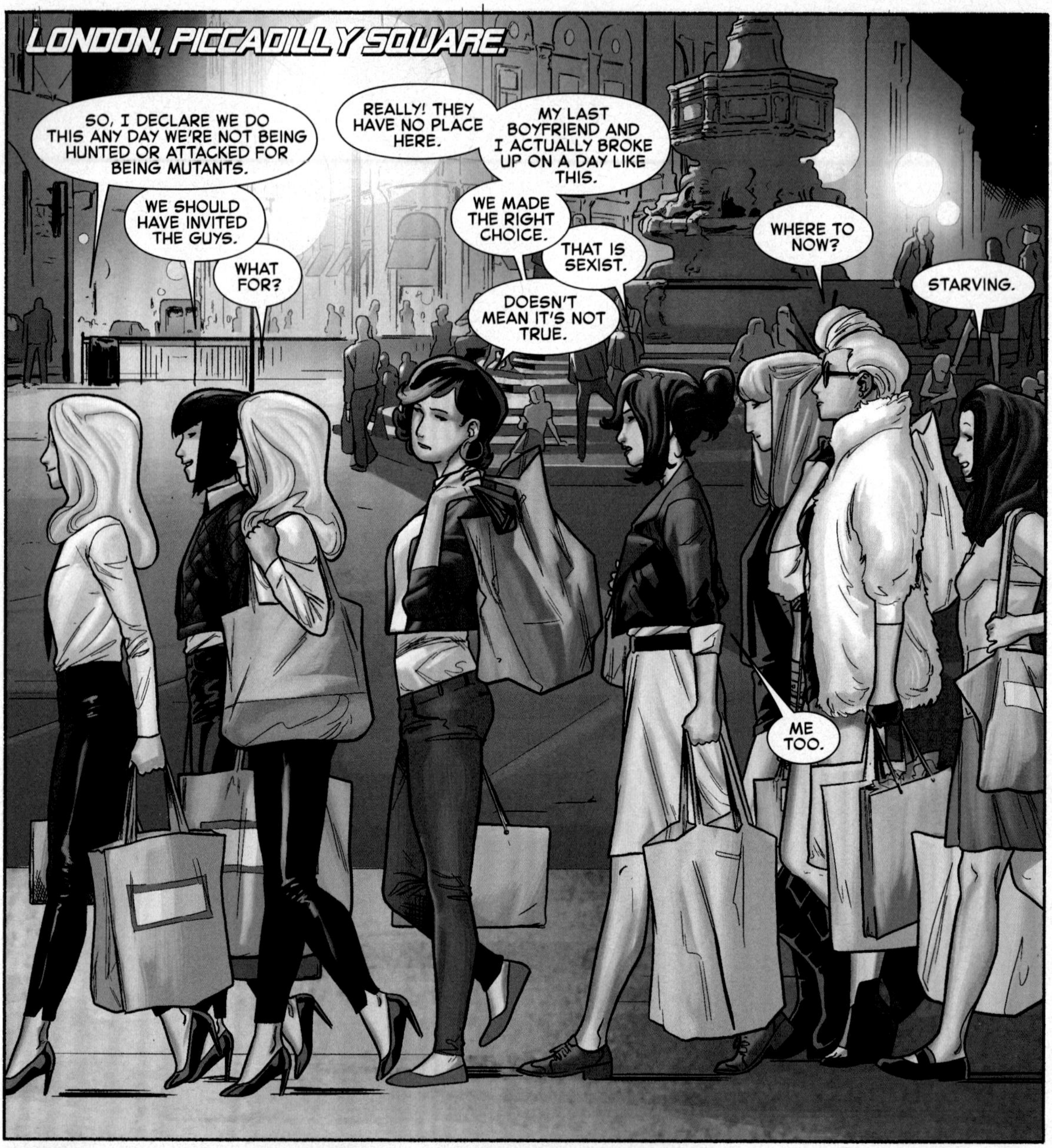
LONDON, PICCADILLY SQUARE.
SO, I DECLARE WE DO THIS ANY DAY WE'RE NOT BEING HUNTED OR ATTACKED FOR BEING MUTANTS.
WE SHOULD HAVE INVITED THE GUYS.
WHAT FOR?
REALLY! THEY HAVE NO PLACE HERE.
MY LAST BOYFRIEND AND I ACTUALLY BROKE UP ON A DAY LIKE THIS.
WE MADE THE RIGHT CHOICE.
THAT IS SEXIST.
DOESN'T MEAN IT'S NOT TRUE.
WHERE TO NOW?
STARVING.
ME TOO.

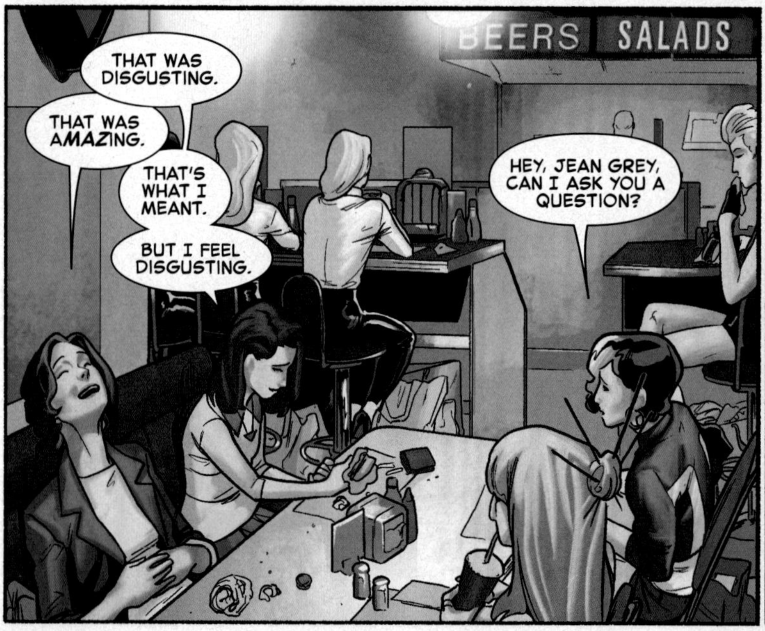
BEERS SALADS
THAT WAS DISGUSTING.
THAT WAS AMAZING.
THAT'S WHAT I MEANT.
BUT I FEEL DISGUSTING.
HEY, JEAN GREY, CAN I ASK YOU A QUESTION?

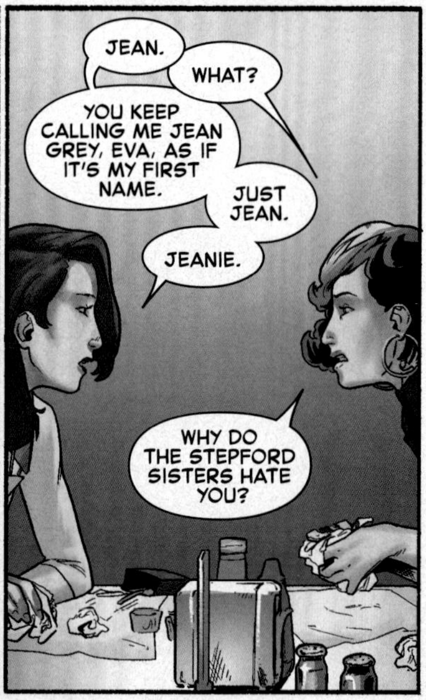
JEAN.
WHAT?
YOU KEEP CALLING ME JEAN GREY, EVA, AS IF IT'S MY FIRST NAME.
JUST JEAN.
JEANIE.
WHY DO THE STEPFORD SISTERS HATE YOU?

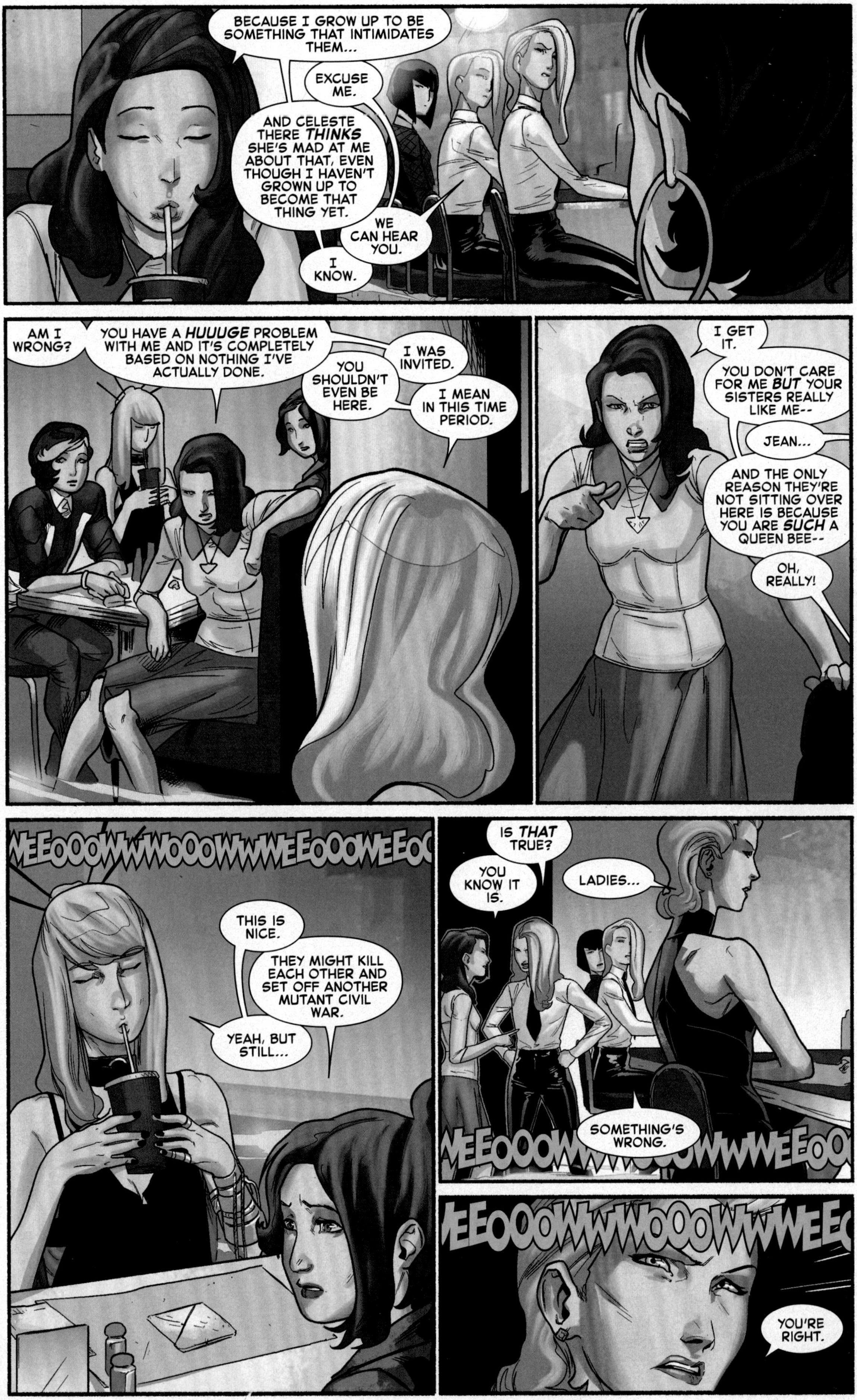
BECAUSE I GROW UP TO BE SOMETHING THAT INTIMIDATES THEM...
EXCUSE ME.
AND CELESTE THERE *THINKS* SHE'S MAD AT ME ABOUT THAT, EVEN THOUGH I HAVEN'T GROWN UP TO BECOME THAT THING YET.
WE CAN HEAR YOU.
I KNOW.
AM I WRONG?
YOU HAVE A *HUUUGE* PROBLEM WITH ME AND IT'S COMPLETELY BASED ON NOTHING I'VE ACTUALLY DONE.
YOU SHOULDN'T EVEN BE HERE.
I WAS INVITED.
I MEAN IN THIS TIME PERIOD.
I GET IT.
YOU DON'T CARE FOR ME *BUT* YOUR SISTERS REALLY LIKE ME--
JEAN...
AND THE ONLY REASON THEY'RE NOT SITTING OVER HERE IS BECAUSE YOU ARE *SUCH* A QUEEN BEE--
OH, REALLY!
WEEOOOWWWOOOWWWEEOOOWEEO
THIS IS NICE.
THEY MIGHT KILL EACH OTHER AND SET OFF ANOTHER MUTANT CIVIL WAR.
YEAH, BUT STILL...
IS *THAT* TRUE?
YOU KNOW IT IS.
LADIES...
SOMETHING'S WRONG.
WEEOOOWWWOOOWWWEEOO
WEEOOOWWWOOOWWWEE
YOU'RE RIGHT.

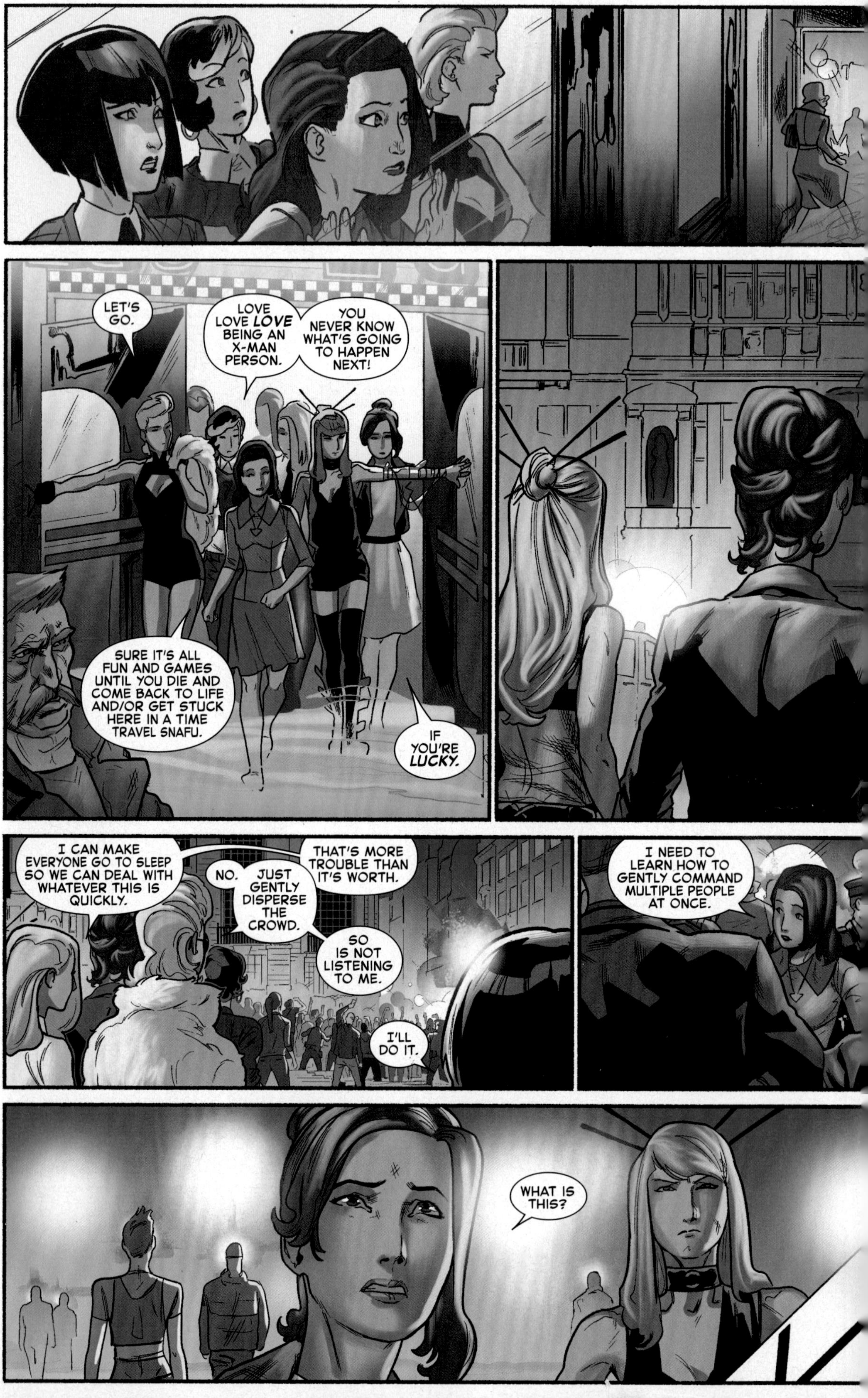
LET'S GO.
LOVE LOVE LOVE BEING AN X-MAN PERSON.
YOU NEVER KNOW WHAT'S GOING TO HAPPEN NEXT!
SURE IT'S ALL FUN AND GAMES UNTIL YOU DIE AND COME BACK TO LIFE AND/OR GET STUCK HERE IN A TIME TRAVEL SNAFU.
IF YOU'RE LUCKY.
I CAN MAKE EVERYONE GO TO SLEEP SO WE CAN DEAL WITH WHATEVER THIS IS QUICKLY.
THAT'S MORE TROUBLE THAN IT'S WORTH.
NO.
JUST GENTLY DISPERSE THE CROWD.
SO IS NOT LISTENING TO ME.
I'LL DO IT.
I NEED TO LEARN HOW TO GENTLY COMMAND MULTIPLE PEOPLE AT ONCE.
WHAT IS THIS?

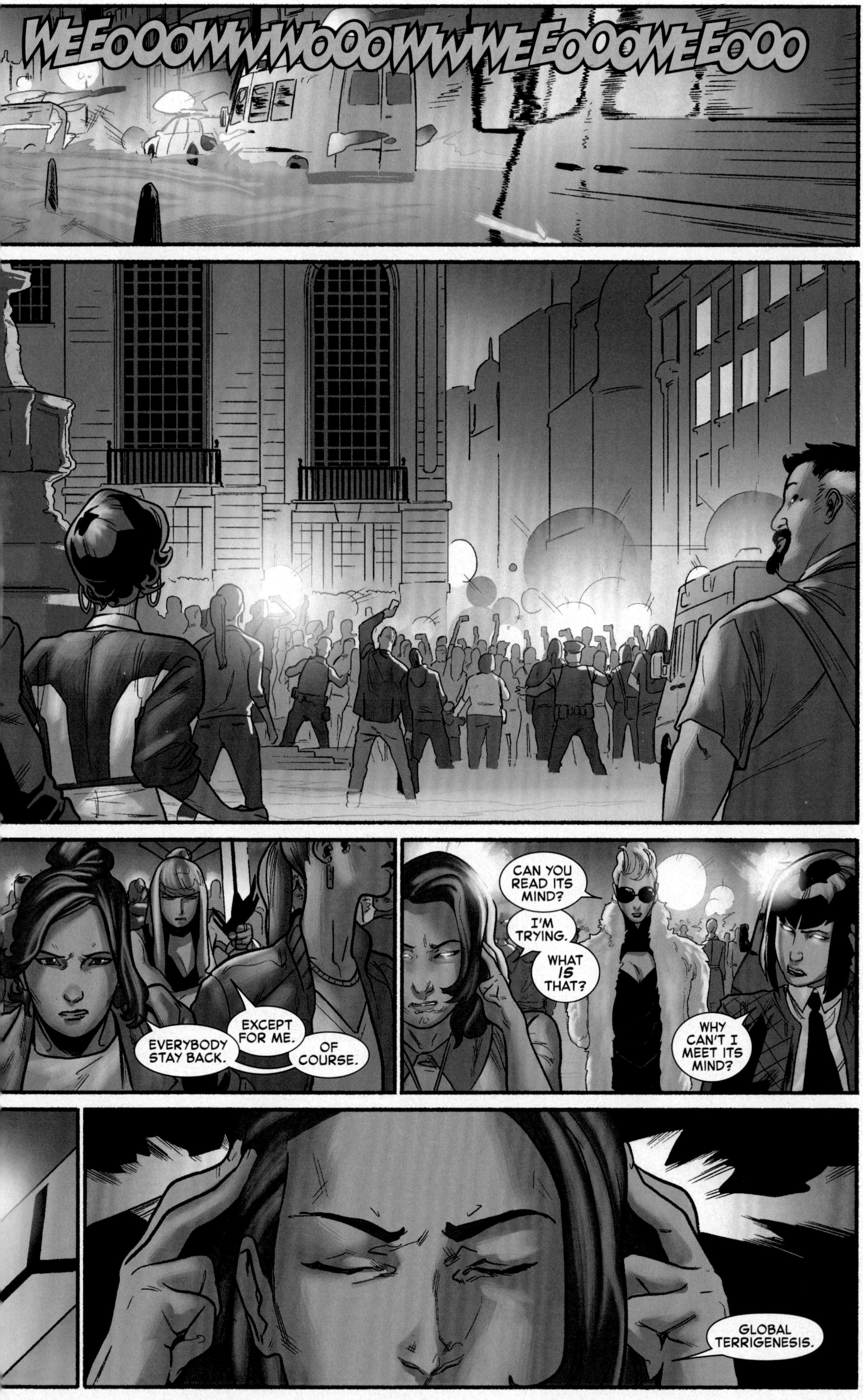
WEEOOOWWWOOOWWWEEOOOWEEOOO
EVERYBODY STAY BACK.
EXCEPT FOR ME.
OF COURSE.
CAN YOU READ ITS MIND?
I'M TRYING.
WHAT IS THAT?
WHY CAN'T I MEET ITS MIND?
GLOBAL TERRIGENESIS.

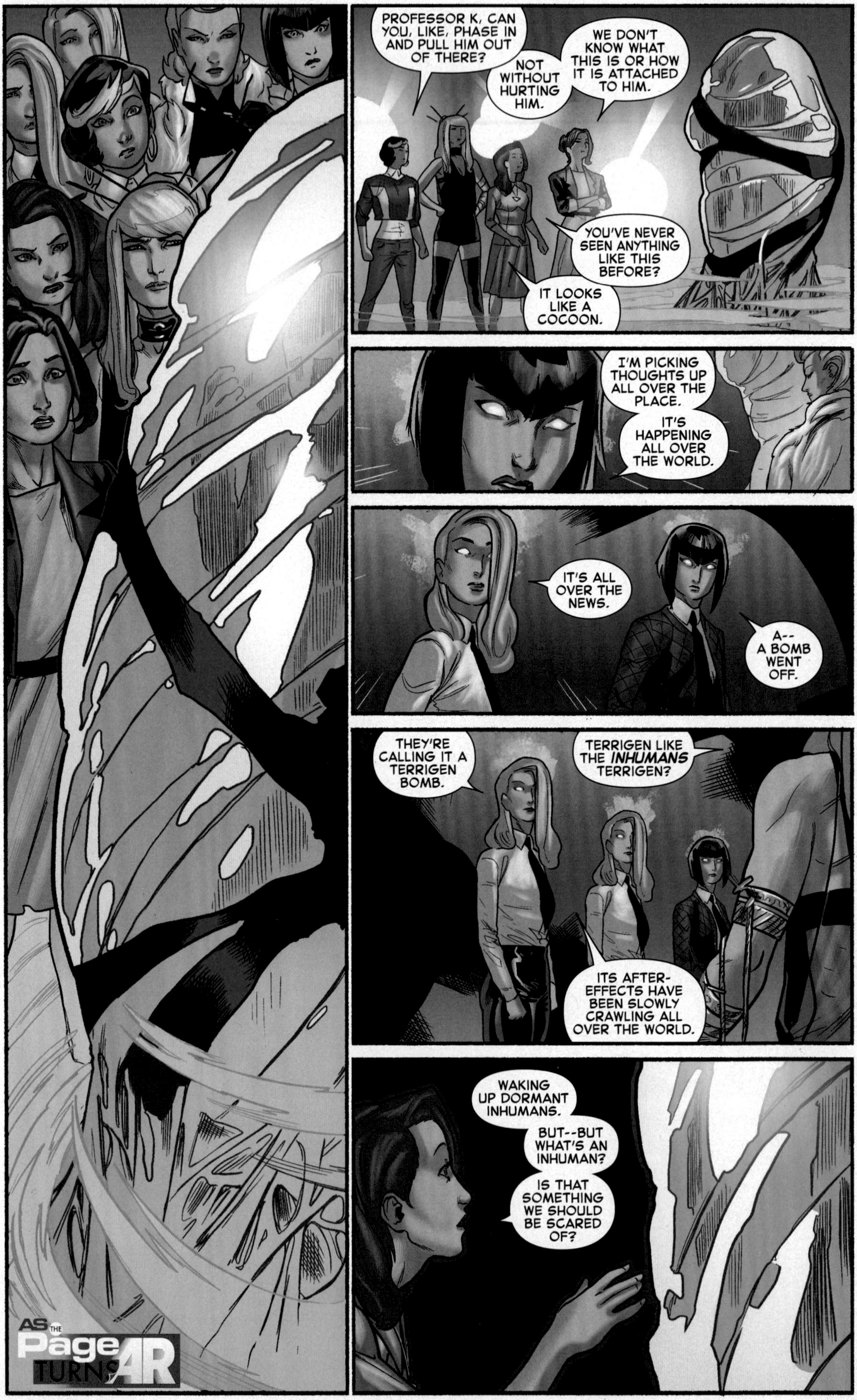
PROFESSOR K, CAN YOU, LIKE, PHASE IN AND PULL HIM OUT OF THERE?
NOT WITHOUT HURTING HIM.
WE DON'T KNOW WHAT THIS IS OR HOW IT IS ATTACHED TO HIM.
YOU'VE NEVER SEEN ANYTHING LIKE THIS BEFORE?
IT LOOKS LIKE A COCOON.
I'M PICKING THOUGHTS UP ALL OVER THE PLACE.
IT'S HAPPENING ALL OVER THE WORLD.
IT'S ALL OVER THE NEWS.
A-- A BOMB WENT OFF.
THEY'RE CALLING IT A TERRIGEN BOMB.
TERRIGEN LIKE THE *INHUMANS* TERRIGEN?
ITS AFTER-EFFECTS HAVE BEEN SLOWLY CRAWLING ALL OVER THE WORLD.
WAKING UP DORMANT INHUMANS.
BUT--BUT WHAT'S AN INHUMAN?
IS THAT SOMETHING WE SHOULD BE SCARED OF?
AS THE Page TURNS AR

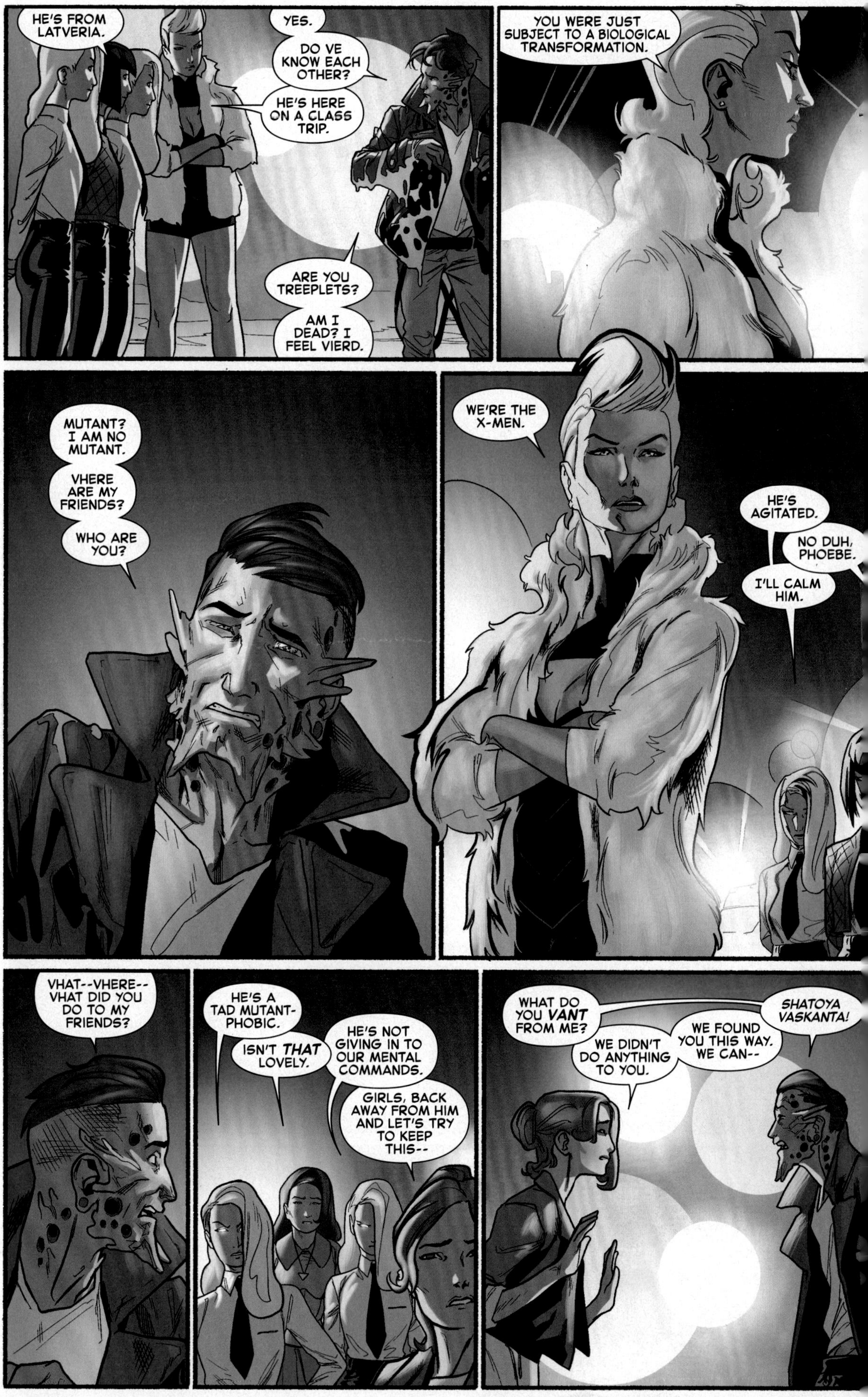
HE'S FROM LATVERIA.
YES.
DO VE KNOW EACH OTHER?
HE'S HERE ON A CLASS TRIP.
ARE YOU TREEPLETS?
AM I DEAD? I FEEL VIERD.
YOU WERE JUST SUBJECT TO A BIOLOGICAL TRANSFORMATION.
MUTANT? I AM NO MUTANT.
VHERE ARE MY FRIENDS?
WHO ARE YOU?
WE'RE THE X-MEN.
HE'S AGITATED.
NO DUH, PHOEBE.
I'LL CALM HIM.
VHAT--VHERE--VHAT DID YOU DO TO MY FRIENDS?
HE'S A TAD MUTANT-PHOBIC.
ISN'T THAT LOVELY.
HE'S NOT GIVING IN TO OUR MENTAL COMMANDS.
GIRLS, BACK AWAY FROM HIM AND LET'S TRY TO KEEP THIS--
WHAT DO YOU VANT FROM ME?
WE DIDN'T DO ANYTHING TO YOU.
WE FOUND YOU THIS WAY. WE CAN--
SHATOYA VASKANTA!

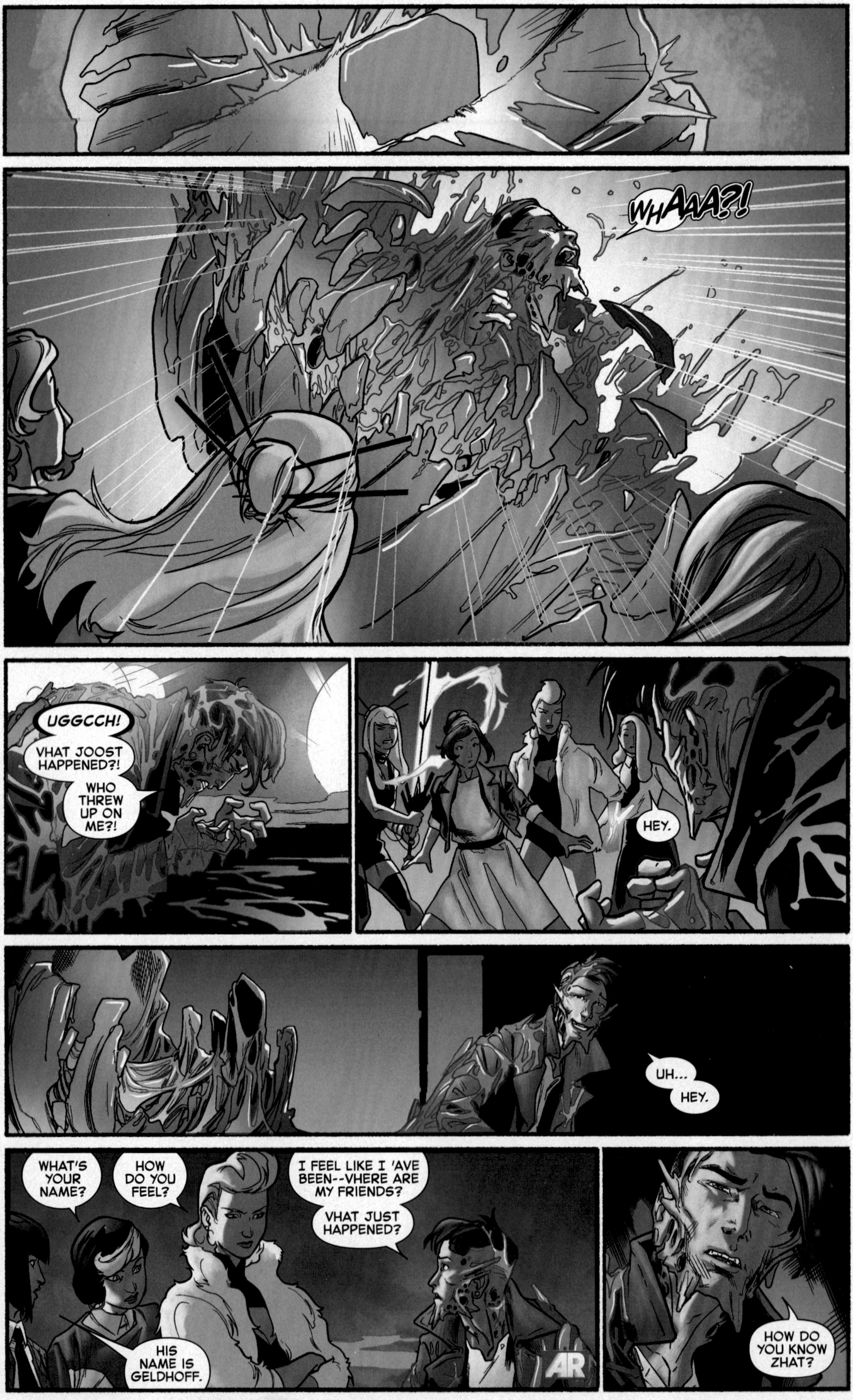
WHAAA?!
UGGCCH!
VHAT JOOST HAPPENED?!
WHO THREW UP ON ME?!
HEY.
UH...
HEY.
WHAT'S YOUR NAME?
HOW DO YOU FEEL?
I FEEL LIKE I 'AVE BEEN--VHERE ARE MY FRIENDS?
VHAT JUST HAPPENED?
HIS NAME IS GELDHOFF.
HOW DO YOU KNOW ZHAT?

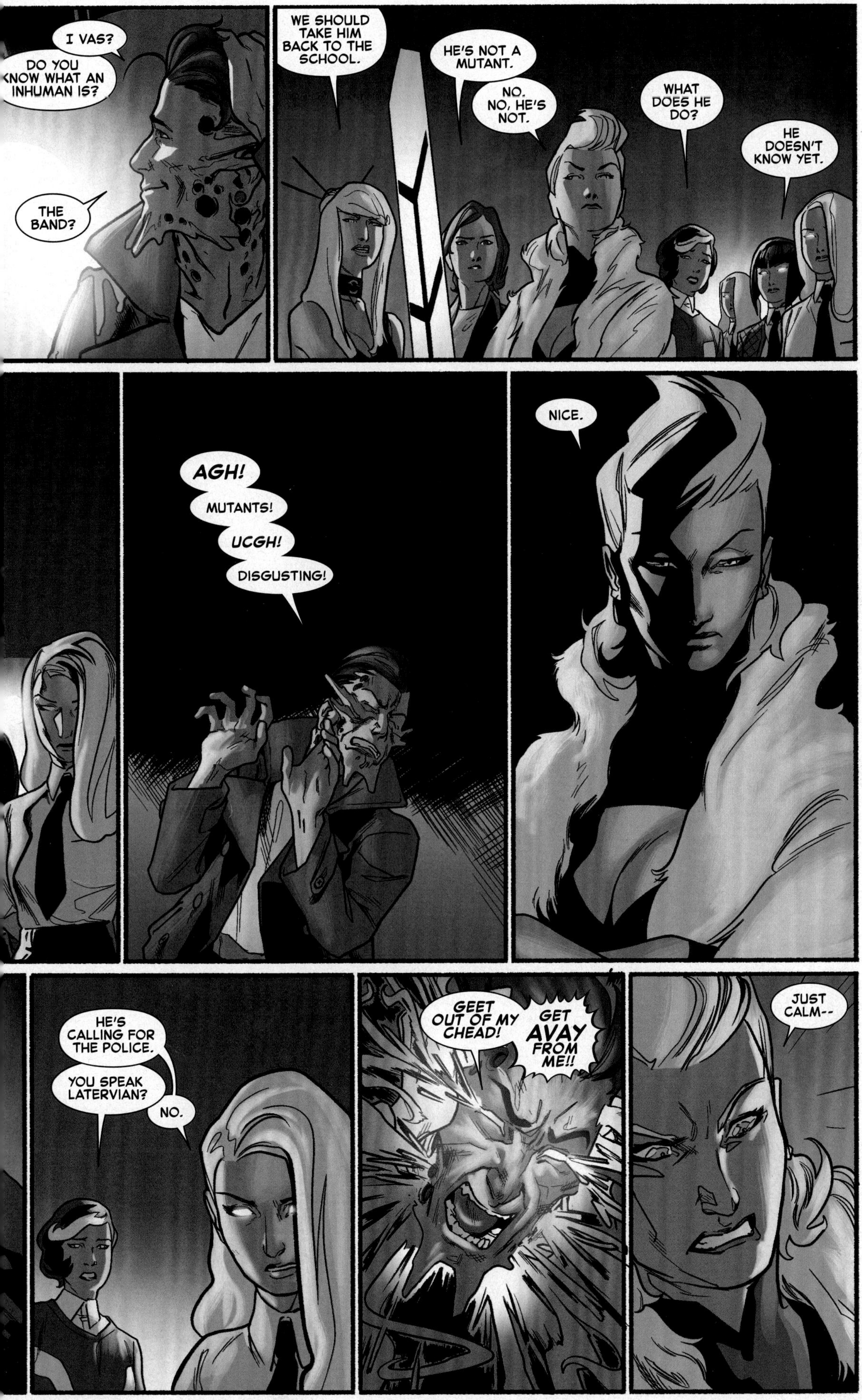
I VAS?
DO YOU KNOW WHAT AN INHUMAN IS?
THE BAND?
WE SHOULD TAKE HIM BACK TO THE SCHOOL.
HE'S NOT A MUTANT.
NO. NO, HE'S NOT.
WHAT DOES HE DO?
HE DOESN'T KNOW YET.
AGH!
MUTANTS!
UCGH!
DISGUSTING!
NICE.
HE'S CALLING FOR THE POLICE.
YOU SPEAK LATERVIAN?
NO.
GEET OUT OF MY CHEAD!
GET AVAY FROM ME!!
JUST CALM--

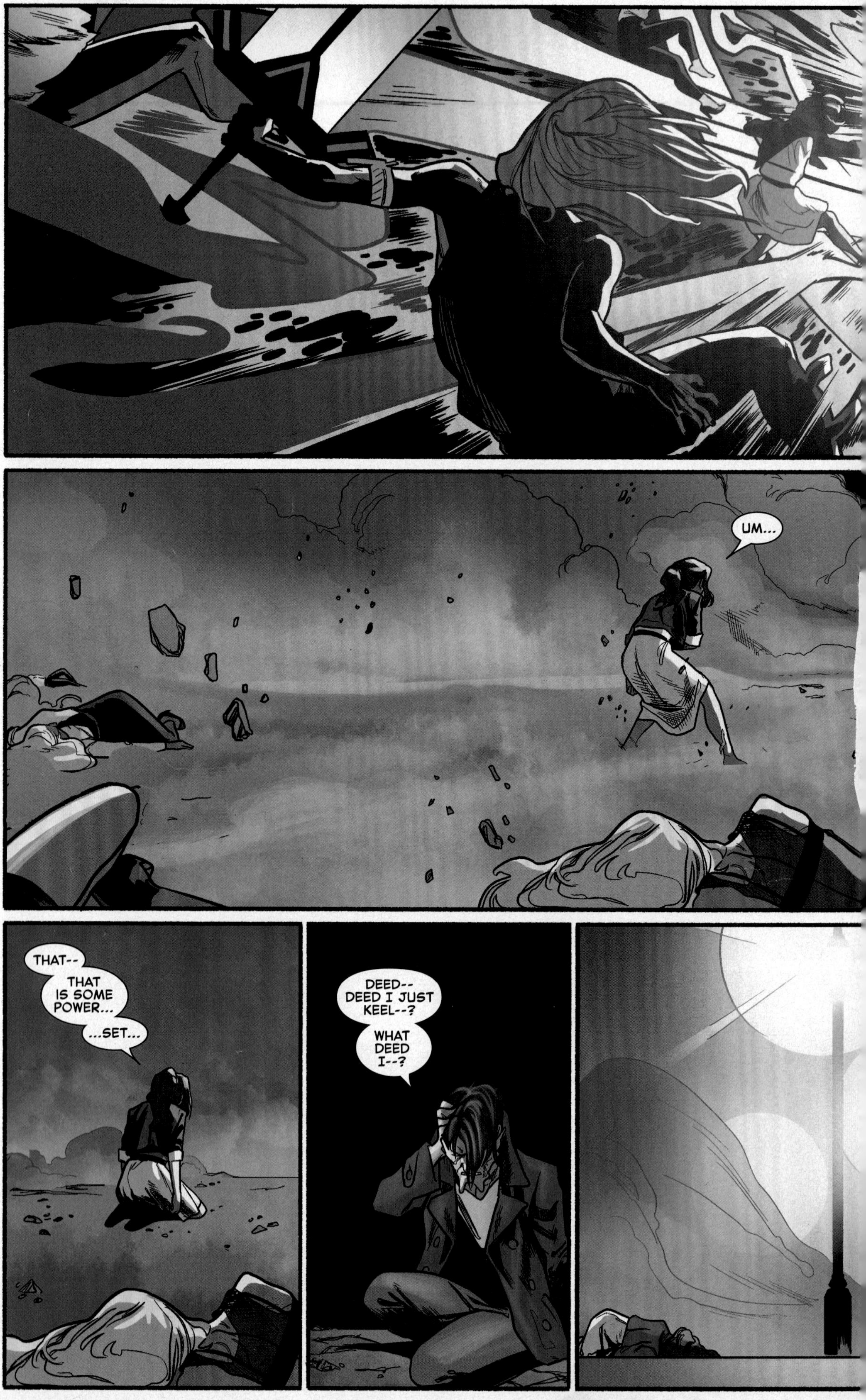
UM...
THAT--
THAT IS SOME POWER...
...SET...
DEED-- DEED I JUST KEEL--?
WHAT DEED I--?

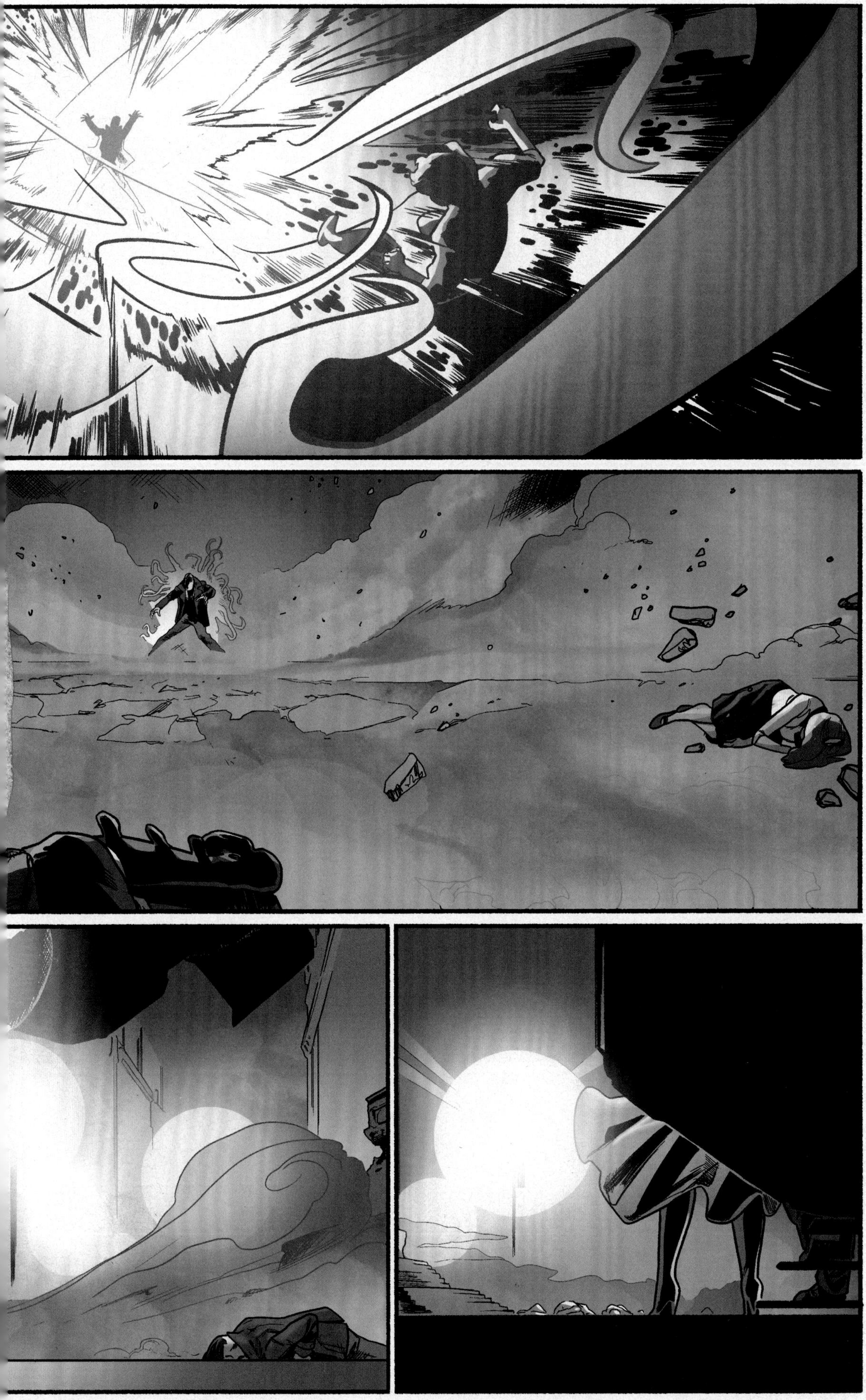

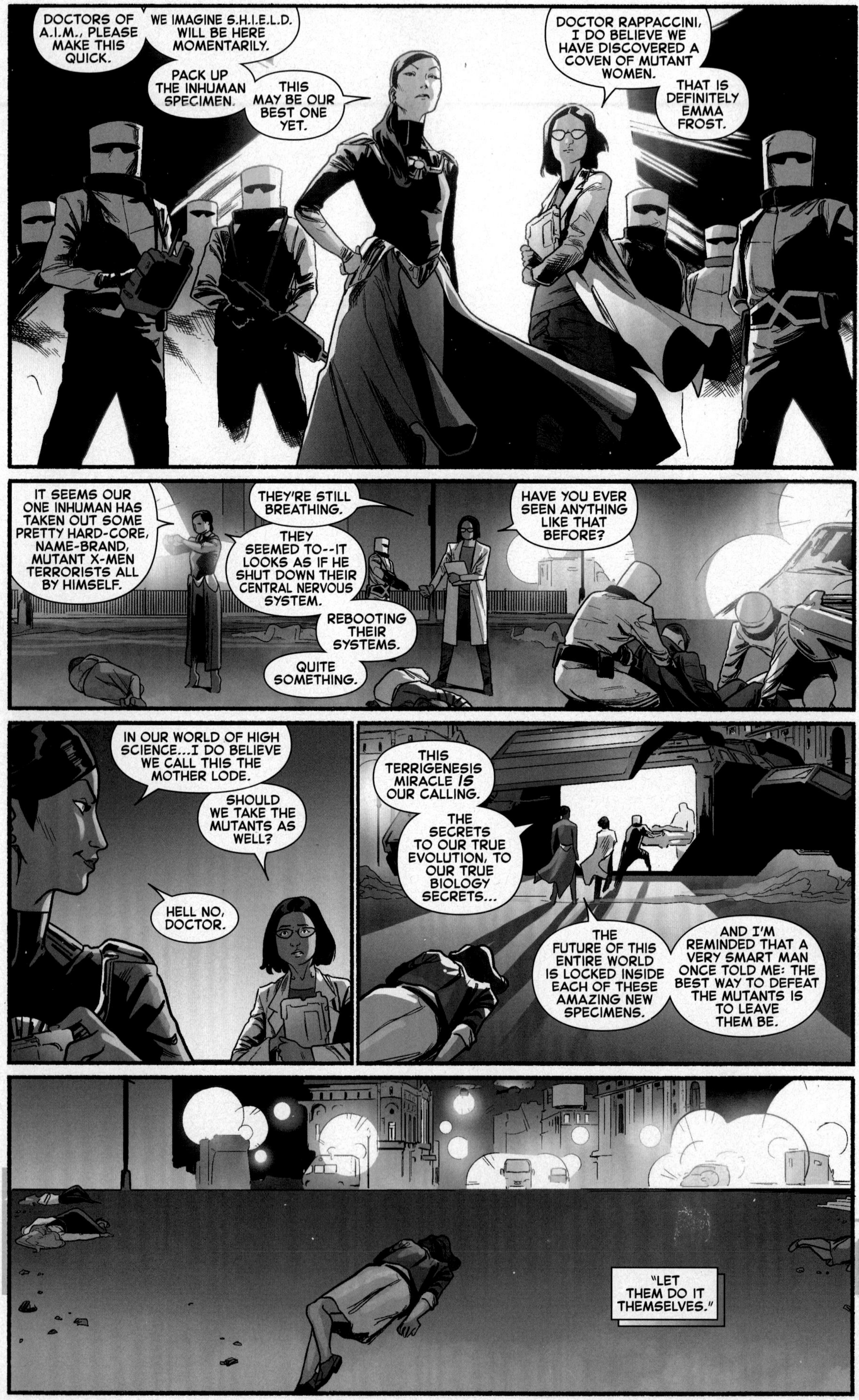

DOCTORS OF A.I.M., PLEASE MAKE THIS QUICK.
WE IMAGINE S.H.I.E.L.D. WILL BE HERE MOMENTARILY.
PACK UP THE INHUMAN SPECIMEN.
THIS MAY BE OUR BEST ONE YET.
DOCTOR RAPPACCINI, I DO BELIEVE WE HAVE DISCOVERED A COVEN OF MUTANT WOMEN.
THAT IS DEFINITELY EMMA FROST.
IT SEEMS OUR ONE INHUMAN HAS TAKEN OUT SOME PRETTY HARD-CORE, NAME-BRAND, MUTANT X-MEN TERRORISTS ALL BY HIMSELF.
THEY'RE STILL BREATHING.
THEY SEEMED TO--IT LOOKS AS IF HE SHUT DOWN THEIR CENTRAL NERVOUS SYSTEM.
REBOOTING THEIR SYSTEMS.
QUITE SOMETHING.
HAVE YOU EVER SEEN ANYTHING LIKE THAT BEFORE?
IN OUR WORLD OF HIGH SCIENCE...I DO BELIEVE WE CALL THIS THE MOTHER LODE.
SHOULD WE TAKE THE MUTANTS AS WELL?
HELL NO, DOCTOR.
THIS TERRIGENESIS MIRACLE *IS* OUR CALLING.
THE SECRETS TO OUR TRUE EVOLUTION, TO OUR TRUE BIOLOGY SECRETS...
THE FUTURE OF THIS ENTIRE WORLD IS LOCKED INSIDE EACH OF THESE AMAZING NEW SPECIMENS.
AND I'M REMINDED THAT A VERY SMART MAN ONCE TOLD ME: THE BEST WAY TO DEFEAT THE MUTANTS IS TO LEAVE THEM BE.
"LET THEM DO IT THEMSELVES."

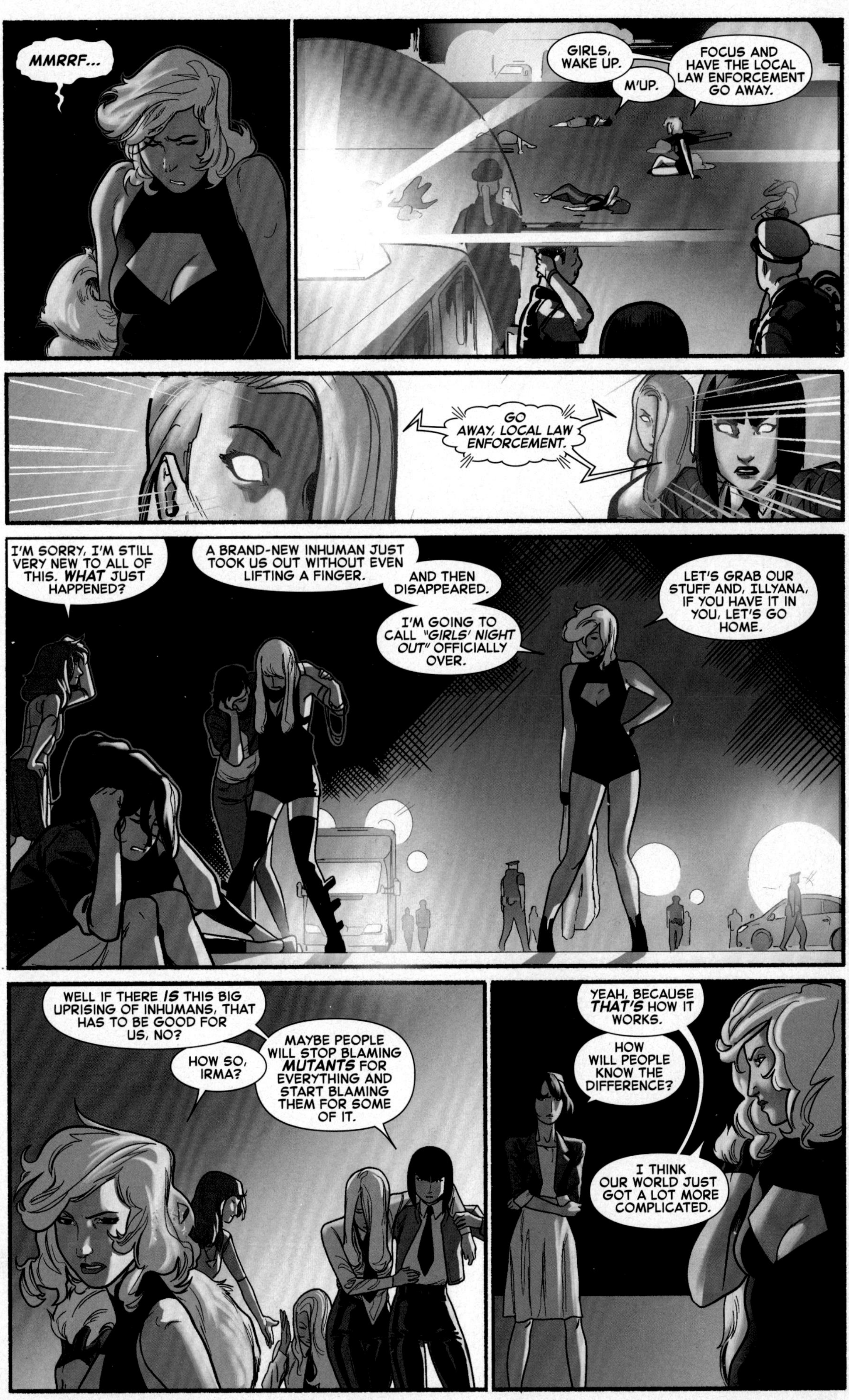
MMRRF...
GIRLS, WAKE UP.
M'UP.
FOCUS AND HAVE THE LOCAL LAW ENFORCEMENT GO AWAY.
GO AWAY, LOCAL LAW ENFORCEMENT.
I'M SORRY, I'M STILL VERY NEW TO ALL OF THIS. WHAT JUST HAPPENED?
A BRAND-NEW INHUMAN JUST TOOK US OUT WITHOUT EVEN LIFTING A FINGER.
AND THEN DISAPPEARED.
I'M GOING TO CALL "GIRLS' NIGHT OUT" OFFICIALLY OVER.
LET'S GRAB OUR STUFF AND, ILLYANA, IF YOU HAVE IT IN YOU, LET'S GO HOME.
WELL IF THERE IS THIS BIG UPRISING OF INHUMANS, THAT HAS TO BE GOOD FOR US, NO?
HOW SO, IRMA?
MAYBE PEOPLE WILL STOP BLAMING MUTANTS FOR EVERYTHING AND START BLAMING THEM FOR SOME OF IT.
YEAH, BECAUSE THAT'S HOW IT WORKS.
HOW WILL PEOPLE KNOW THE DIFFERENCE?
I THINK OUR WORLD JUST GOT A LOT MORE COMPLICATED.

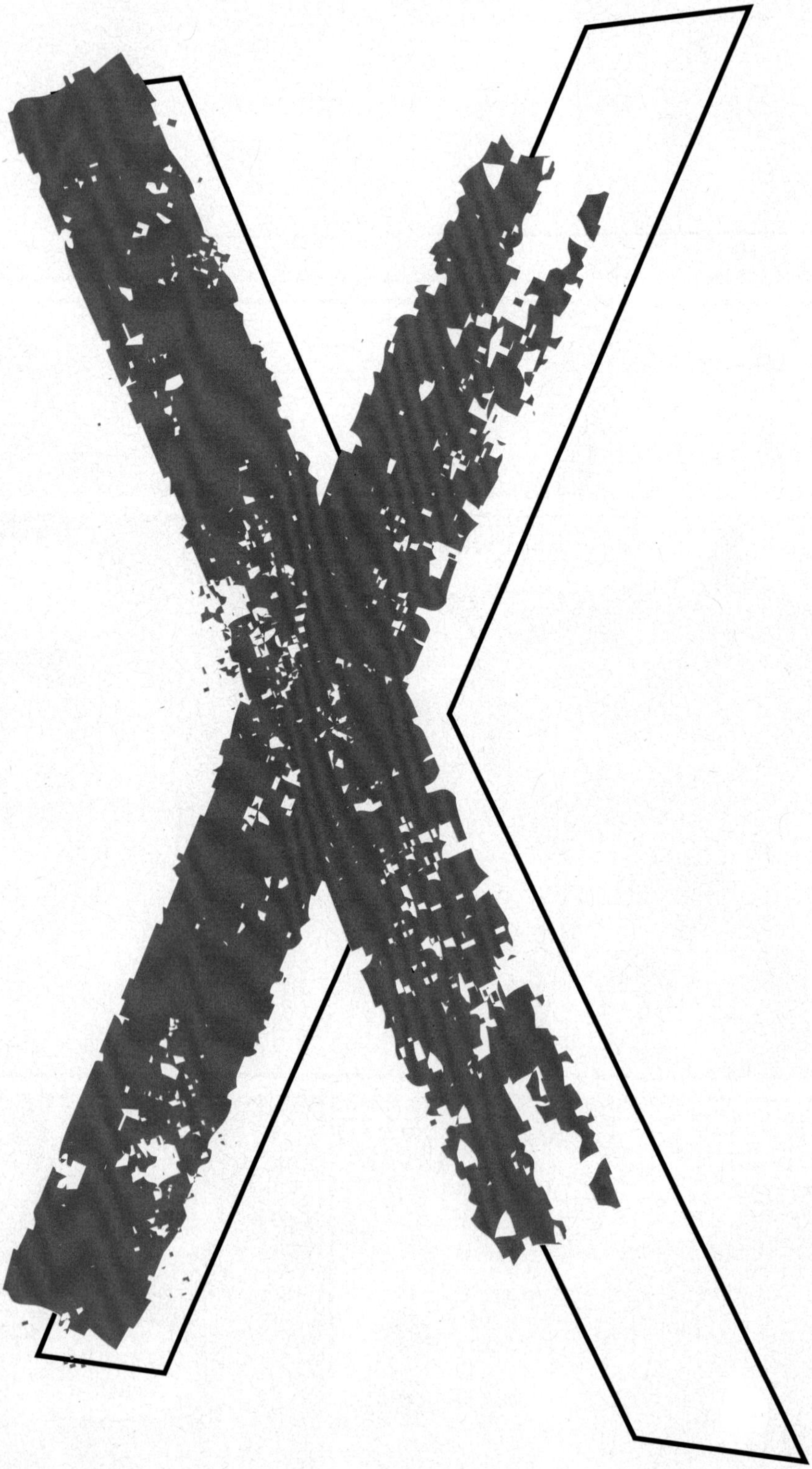

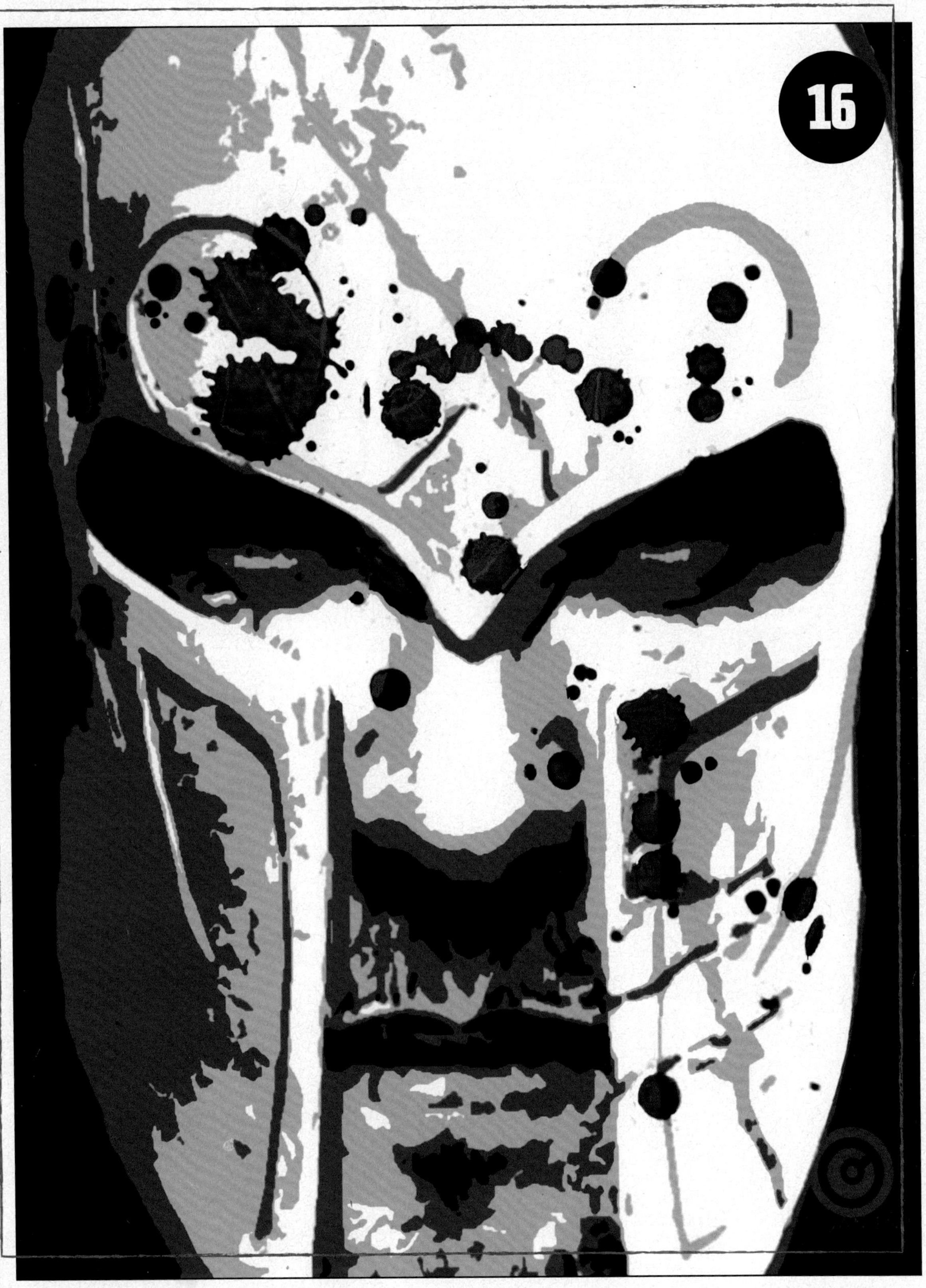
16

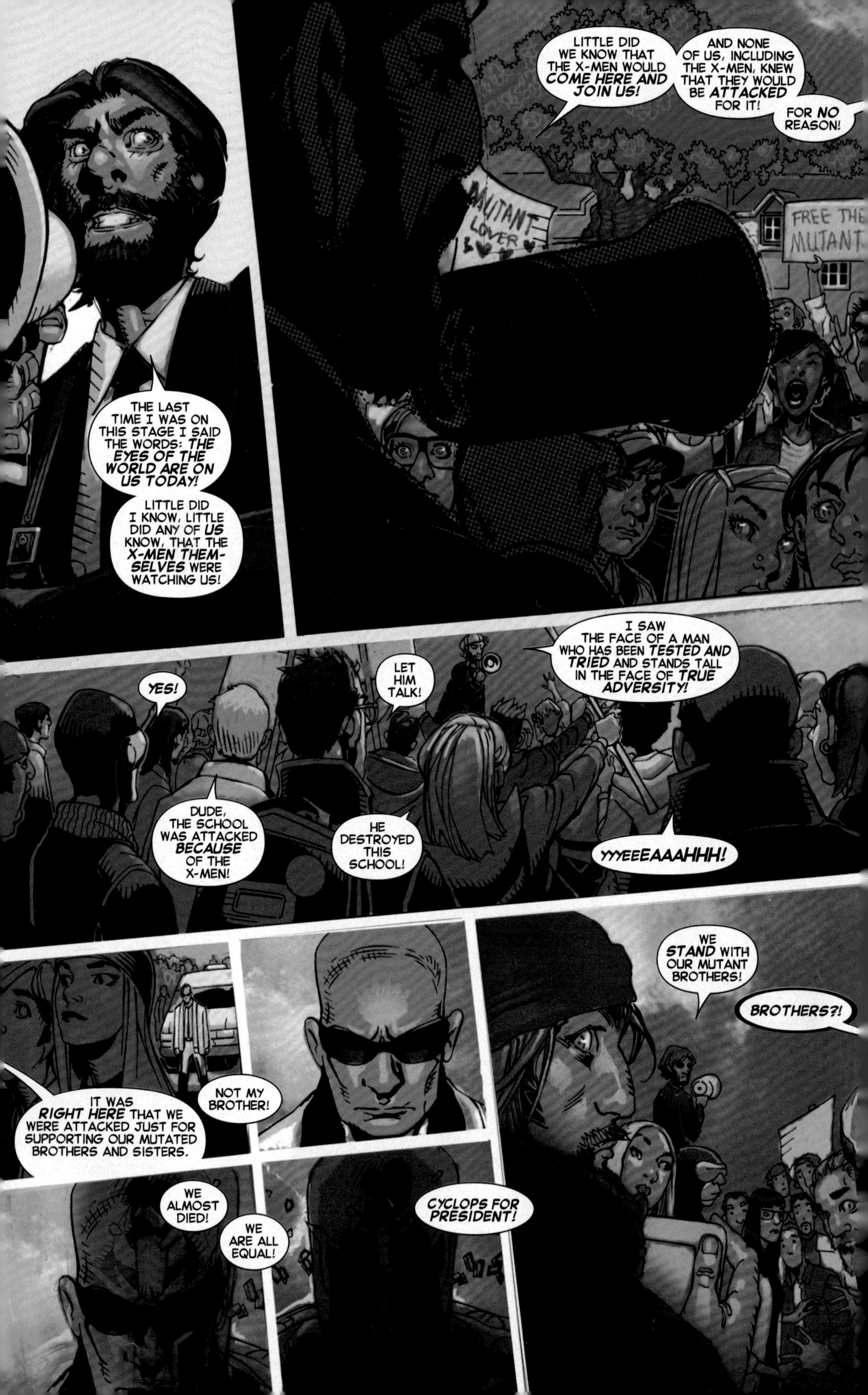
THE LAST TIME I WAS ON THIS STAGE I SAID THE WORDS: THE EYES OF THE WORLD ARE ON US TODAY!
LITTLE DID I KNOW, LITTLE DID ANY OF US KNOW, THAT THE X-MEN THEM-SELVES WERE WATCHING US!
LITTLE DID WE KNOW THAT THE X-MEN WOULD COME HERE AND JOIN US!
AND NONE OF US, INCLUDING THE X-MEN, KNEW THAT THEY WOULD BE ATTACKED FOR IT!
FOR NO REASON!
MUTANT LOVER
FREE THE MUTANT
YES!
LET HIM TALK!
I SAW THE FACE OF A MAN WHO HAS BEEN TESTED AND TRIED AND STANDS TALL IN THE FACE OF TRUE ADVERSITY!
DUDE, THE SCHOOL WAS ATTACKED BECAUSE OF THE X-MEN!
HE DESTROYED THIS SCHOOL!
YYYEEEAAAHHH!
IT WAS RIGHT HERE THAT WE WERE ATTACKED JUST FOR SUPPORTING OUR MUTATED BROTHERS AND SISTERS.
NOT MY BROTHER!
WE STAND WITH OUR MUTANT BROTHERS!
BROTHERS?!
WE ALMOST DIED!
WE ARE ALL EQUAL!
CYCLOPS FOR PRESIDENT!

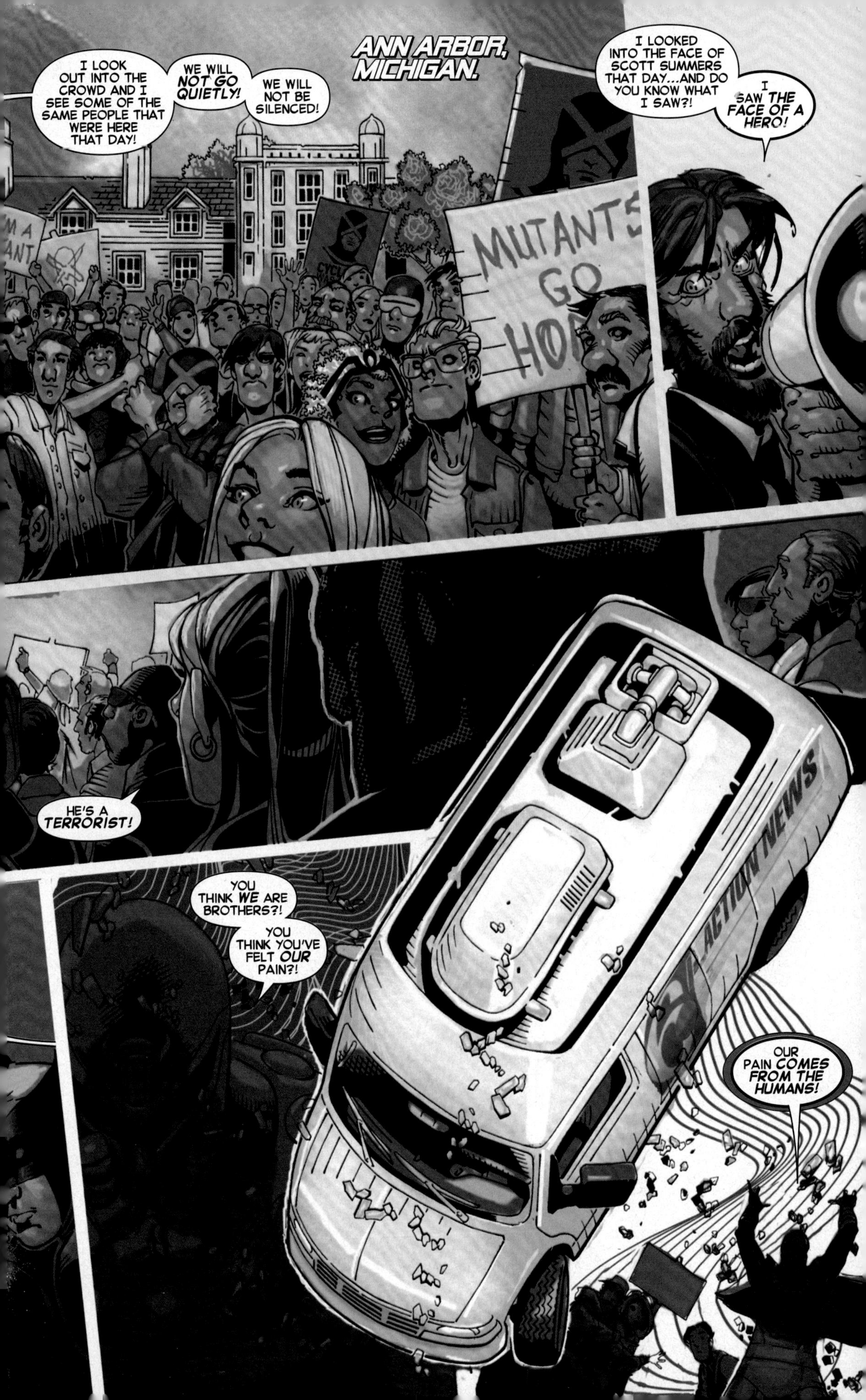
ANN ARBOR, MICHIGAN.
I LOOK OUT INTO THE CROWD AND I SEE SOME OF THE SAME PEOPLE THAT WERE HERE THAT DAY!
WE WILL NOT GO QUIETLY!
WE WILL NOT BE SILENCED!
I LOOKED INTO THE FACE OF SCOTT SUMMERS THAT DAY...AND DO YOU KNOW WHAT I SAW?!
I SAW THE FACE OF A HERO!
MUTANTS GO HO
HE'S A TERRORIST!
ACTION NEWS
YOU THINK WE ARE BROTHERS?!
YOU THINK YOU'VE FELT OUR PAIN?!
OUR PAIN COMES FROM THE HUMANS!

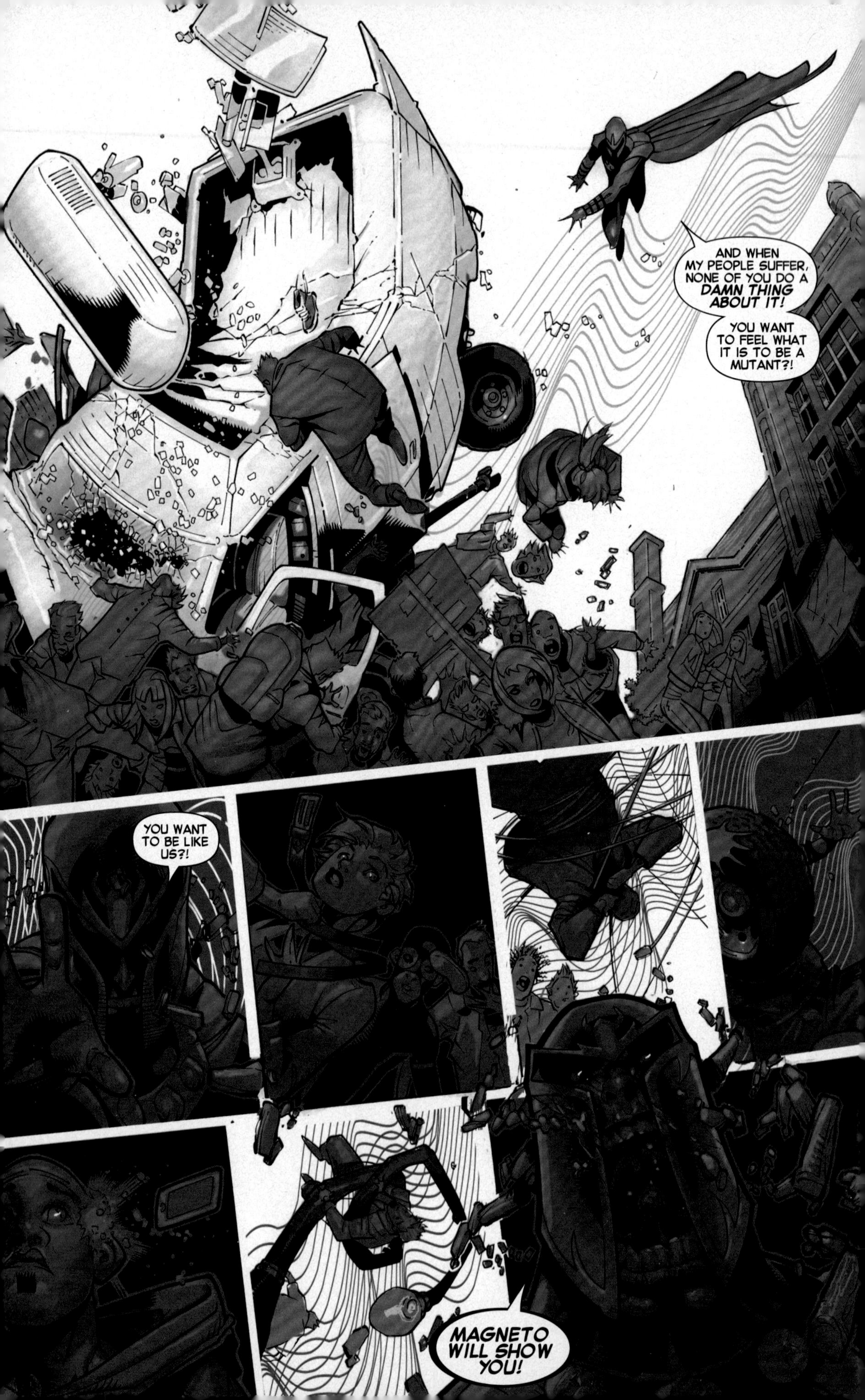
AND WHEN MY PEOPLE SUFFER, NONE OF YOU DO A DAMN THING ABOUT IT!
YOU WANT TO FEEL WHAT IT IS TO BE A MUTANT?!
YOU WANT TO BE LIKE US?!
MAGNETO WILL SHOW YOU!

WHY ISN'T THIS CAMPUS A CRIME SCENE, AGENT DAZZLER?

IT WAS.

NOW IT'S THIS.

I SAW THE FACE OF A MAN WHO HAS BEEN *TESTED* AND *TRIED* AND STANDS TALL IN THE FACE OF TRUE *ADVERSITY!*

ERIK... ...YOU CALLED?

IF S.H.I.E.L.D. AGENTS WERE ATTACKED HERE THIS PLACE WOULD BE UNDER A DOME WHILE YOUR PEOPLE COMBED IT FOR A TRACE OF A HINT OF A CLUE.

YOU ARE MY PEOPLE.

AND I AM SURE THEY DID ALL OF THOSE THINGS, ERIK.

SO DON'T GET SNIPPY.

THIS CROWD IS BIGGER THAN LAST TIME.

PEOPLE BE CRAZY.

WHY DID YOU CALL ME, ERIK?

MAGNETO.

WHAT DO YOU NEED, MAGNETO?

I NEED INFORMATION.

ABOUT THE MYSTERY SENTINELS THAT KEEP ATTACKING THE X-MEN.

YES.

IF I HAD ANY INFORMATION, YOU'D BE ONE OF THE FIRST TO KNOW.

OR YOU X-MEN COULD, I DON'T KNOW, *COOPERATE* WITH THE INVESTIGATION AND TELL US WHAT *YOU* KNOW.

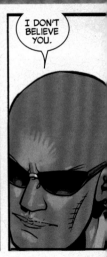

I DON'T BELIEVE YOU.

YOU THINK THAT I *WANT* INNOCENT MUTANTS AND HUMANS ATTACKED BY MUTANT-HUNTING ROBOTS?

YOU THINK I *WANT* THE JEAN GREY SCHOOL UNDER SIEGE?

I DON'T KNOW *WHAT* YOUR AGENDA IS ANYMORE, AGENT DAZZLER.

THAT'S FUNNY.

FUNNY?

THAT'S WHAT A LOT OF PEOPLE SAY ABOUT *YOU.*

ALMOST EXACTLY.

NO ONE KNOWS WHAT YOUR GOAL IS ANYMORE.

AT LEAST WHEN YOU WERE A BAT POOP CRAZY MUTANT TERRORIST YOU WERE VERY FOCUSED...

KILLING EVERYONE WHO DIDN'T AGREE WITH YOU.

BUT THERE IS ONE THEORY ABOUT YOU, MAGNETO...

THAT'S ENOUGH!

I HAVE A LETTER TO *THE PRESIDENT OF THE UNITED STATES* THAT I AM GOING TO READ TO YOU.

I WILL NOT BE SILENCED!

THAT WHATEVER THIS DRAMA THAT PLAYED OUT BETWEEN YOU AND CHARLES XAVIER AND SCOTT SUMMERS...

WHATEVER OR HOWEVER CHARLES XAVIER DIED...

IT MESSED YOU UP.

"EVERYBODY WAS SO FOCUSED ON HOW DAMAGING IT WAS TO SCOTT SUMMERS...

"NO ONE REALLY PAID ANY ATTENTION TO WHAT IT DID TO YOU."

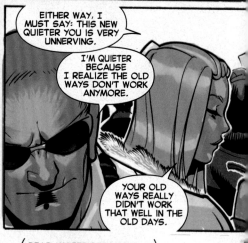

EITHER WAY, I MUST SAY: THIS NEW QUIETER YOU IS VERY UNNERVING.

I'M QUIETER BECAUSE I REALIZE THE OLD WAYS DON'T WORK ANYMORE.

YOUR OLD WAYS REALLY DIDN'T WORK THAT WELL IN THE OLD DAYS.

DEAR MISTER PRESIDENT, I SPEAK FOR *MILLIONS* WHEN I ASK: WHEN ARE YOU GOING TO STOP *PERSECUTING THE MUTANT PEOPLE?!*

DO YOU EVER WONDER IF MAYBE YOUR DRAMATIC POWER LOSS IS PSYCHOSOMATIC?

WHAT?

ARE YOU SAYING YOU'RE BETTER NOW?

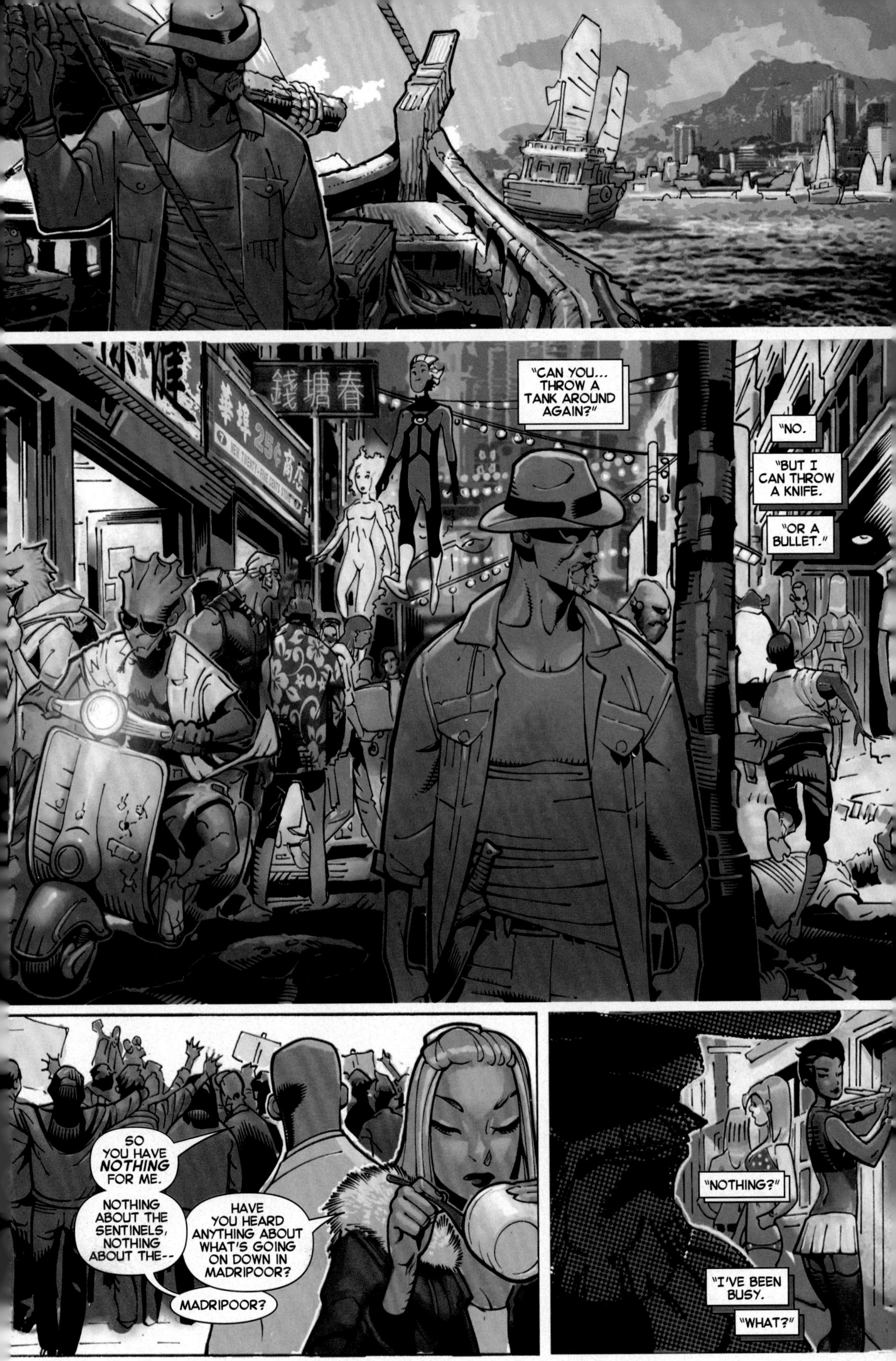
錢塘春
"CAN YOU... THROW A TANK AROUND AGAIN?"
"NO.
"BUT I CAN THROW A KNIFE.
"OR A BULLET."
SO YOU HAVE *NOTHING* FOR ME.
NOTHING ABOUT THE SENTINELS, NOTHING ABOUT THE--
HAVE YOU HEARD ANYTHING ABOUT WHAT'S GOING ON DOWN IN MADRIPOOR?
MADRIPOOR?
"NOTHING?"
"I'VE BEEN BUSY.
"WHAT?"

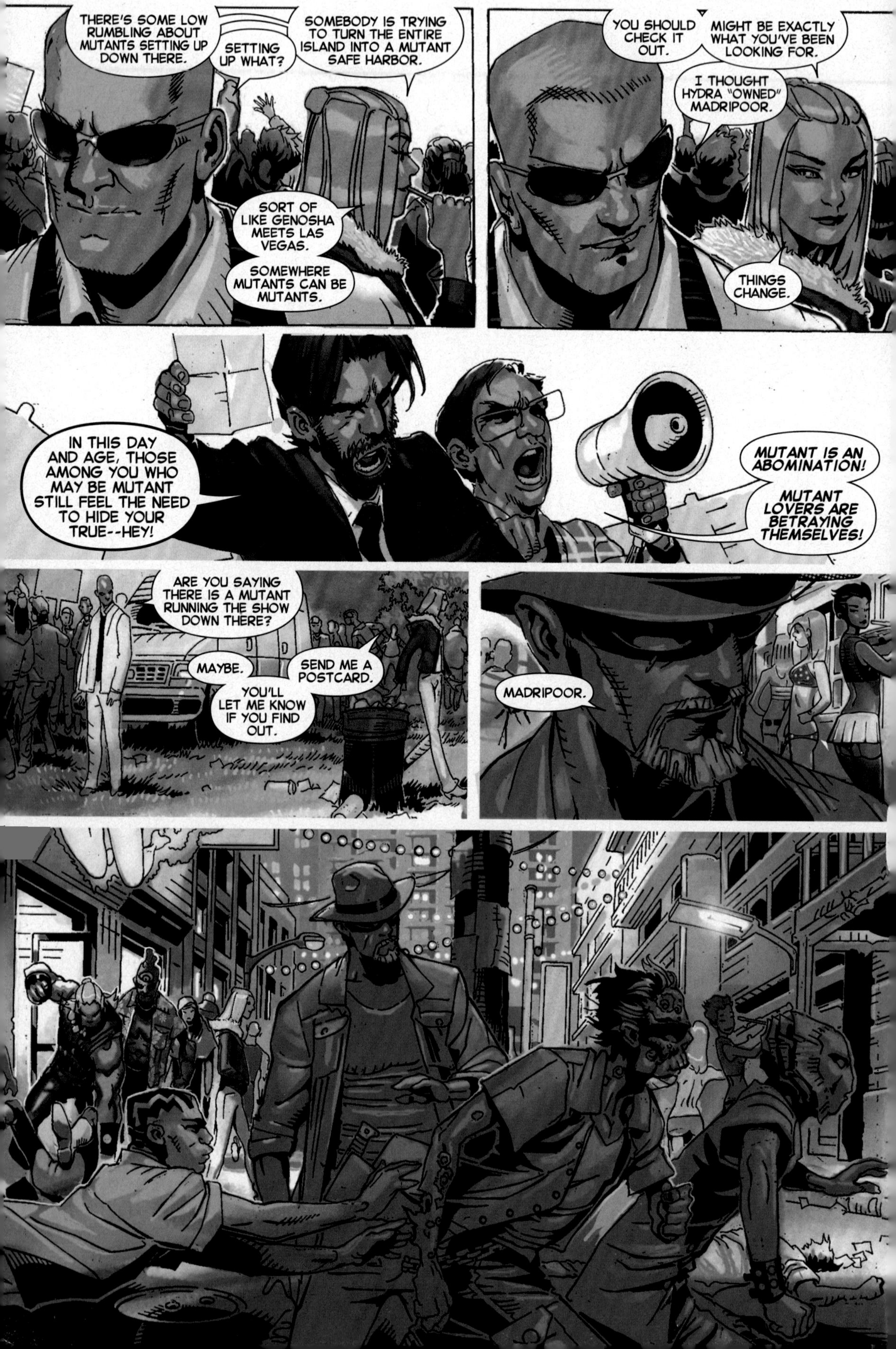
THERE'S SOME LOW RUMBLING ABOUT MUTANTS SETTING UP DOWN THERE.
SETTING UP WHAT?
SOMEBODY IS TRYING TO TURN THE ENTIRE ISLAND INTO A MUTANT SAFE HARBOR.
SORT OF LIKE GENOSHA MEETS LAS VEGAS.
SOMEWHERE MUTANTS CAN BE MUTANTS.
YOU SHOULD CHECK IT OUT.
MIGHT BE EXACTLY WHAT YOU'VE BEEN LOOKING FOR.
I THOUGHT HYDRA "OWNED" MADRIPOOR.
THINGS CHANGE.
IN THIS DAY AND AGE, THOSE AMONG YOU WHO MAY BE MUTANT STILL FEEL THE NEED TO HIDE YOUR TRUE--HEY!
MUTANT IS AN ABOMINATION!
MUTANT LOVERS ARE BETRAYING THEMSELVES!
ARE YOU SAYING THERE IS A MUTANT RUNNING THE SHOW DOWN THERE?
MAYBE.
SEND ME A POSTCARD.
YOU'LL LET ME KNOW IF YOU FIND OUT.
MADRIPOOR.

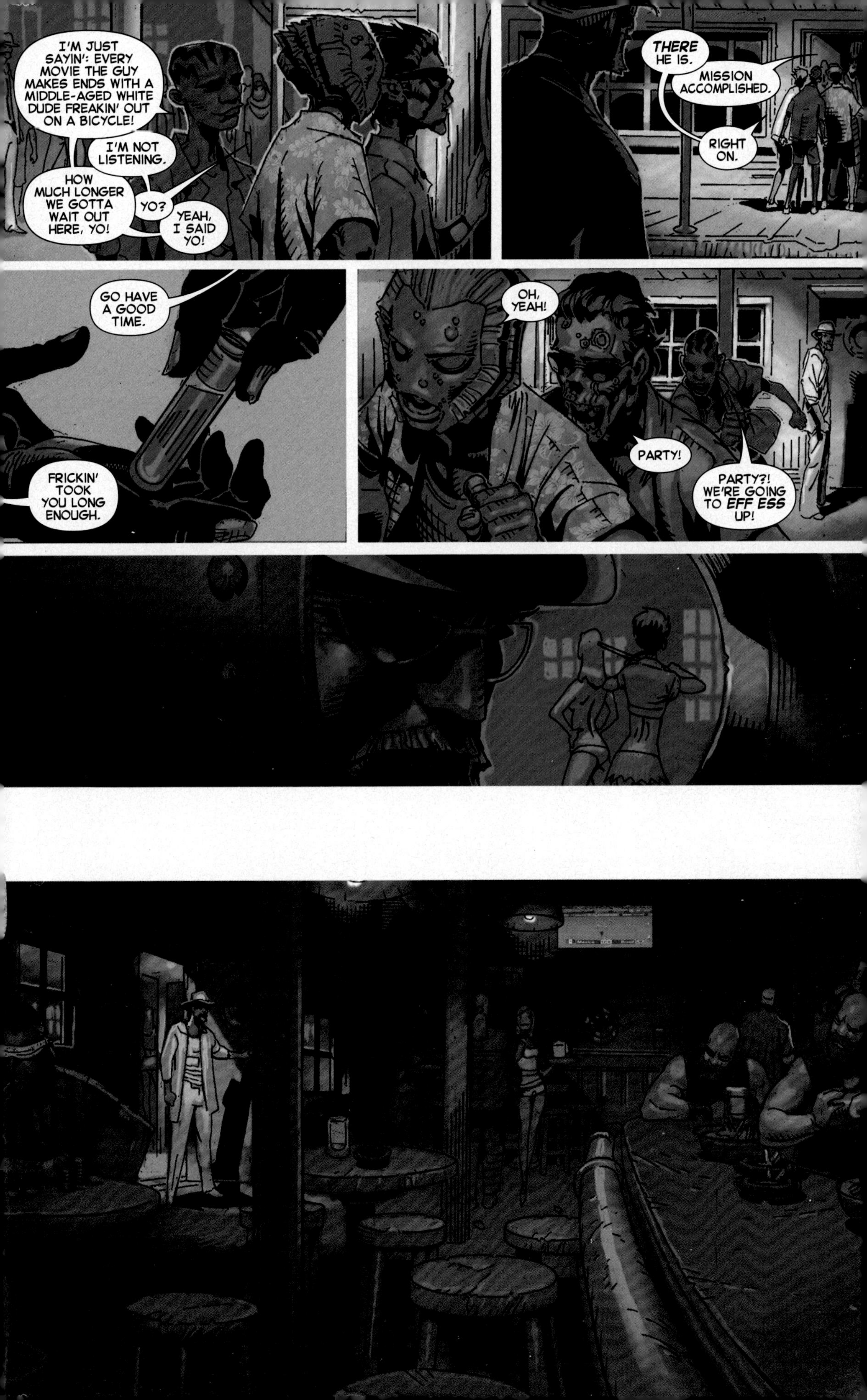
I'M JUST SAYIN': EVERY MOVIE THE GUY MAKES ENDS WITH A MIDDLE-AGED WHITE DUDE FREAKIN' OUT ON A BICYCLE!
I'M NOT LISTENING.
HOW MUCH LONGER WE GOTTA WAIT OUT HERE, YO!
YO?
YEAH, I SAID YO!
THERE HE IS.
MISSION ACCOMPLISHED.
RIGHT ON.
GO HAVE A GOOD TIME.
FRICKIN' TOOK YOU LONG ENOUGH.
OH, YEAH!
PARTY!
PARTY?! WE'RE GOING TO EFF ESS UP!

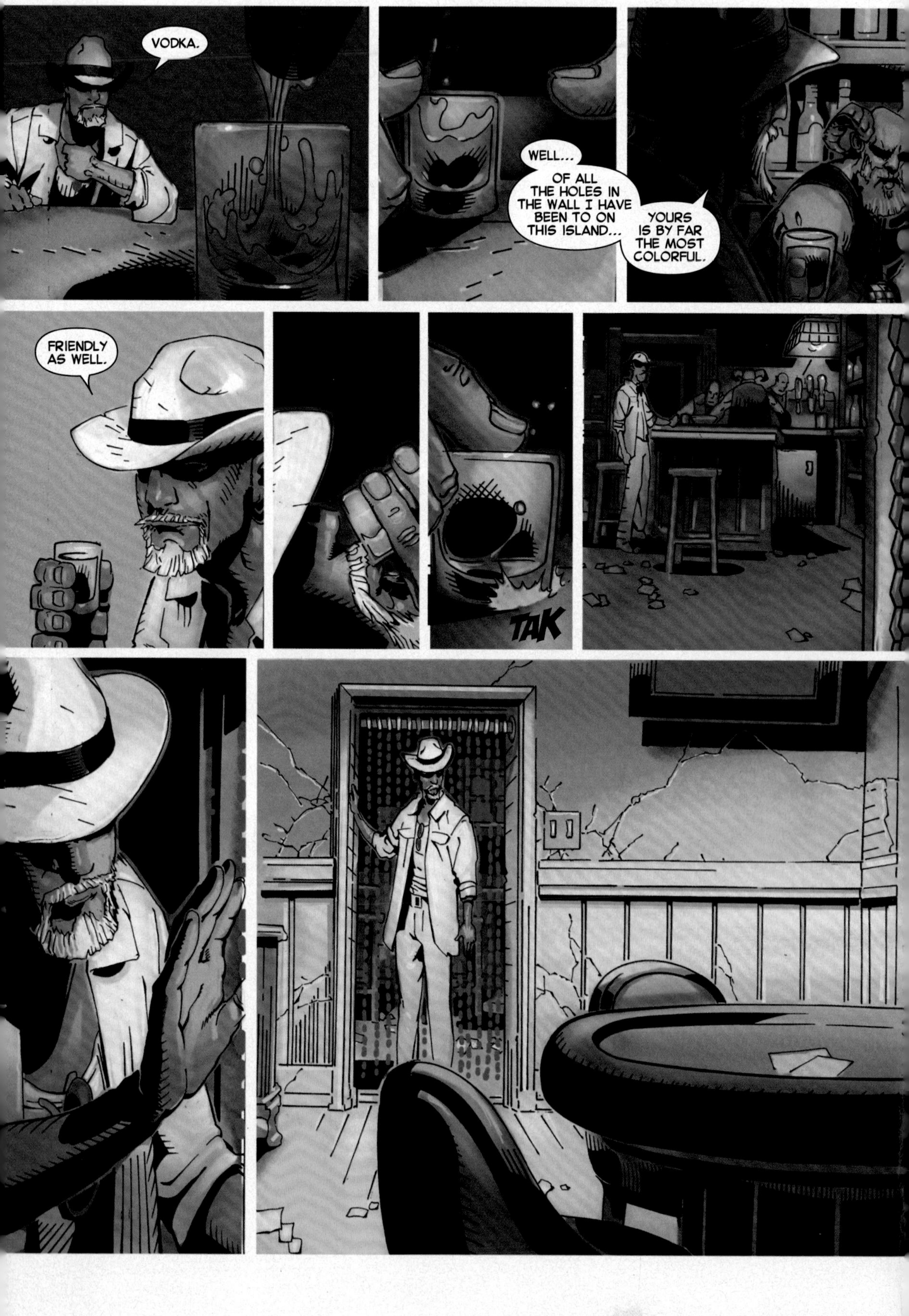
VODKA.
WELL...
OF ALL THE HOLES IN THE WALL I HAVE BEEN TO ON THIS ISLAND...
YOURS IS BY FAR THE MOST COLORFUL.
FRIENDLY AS WELL.
TAK

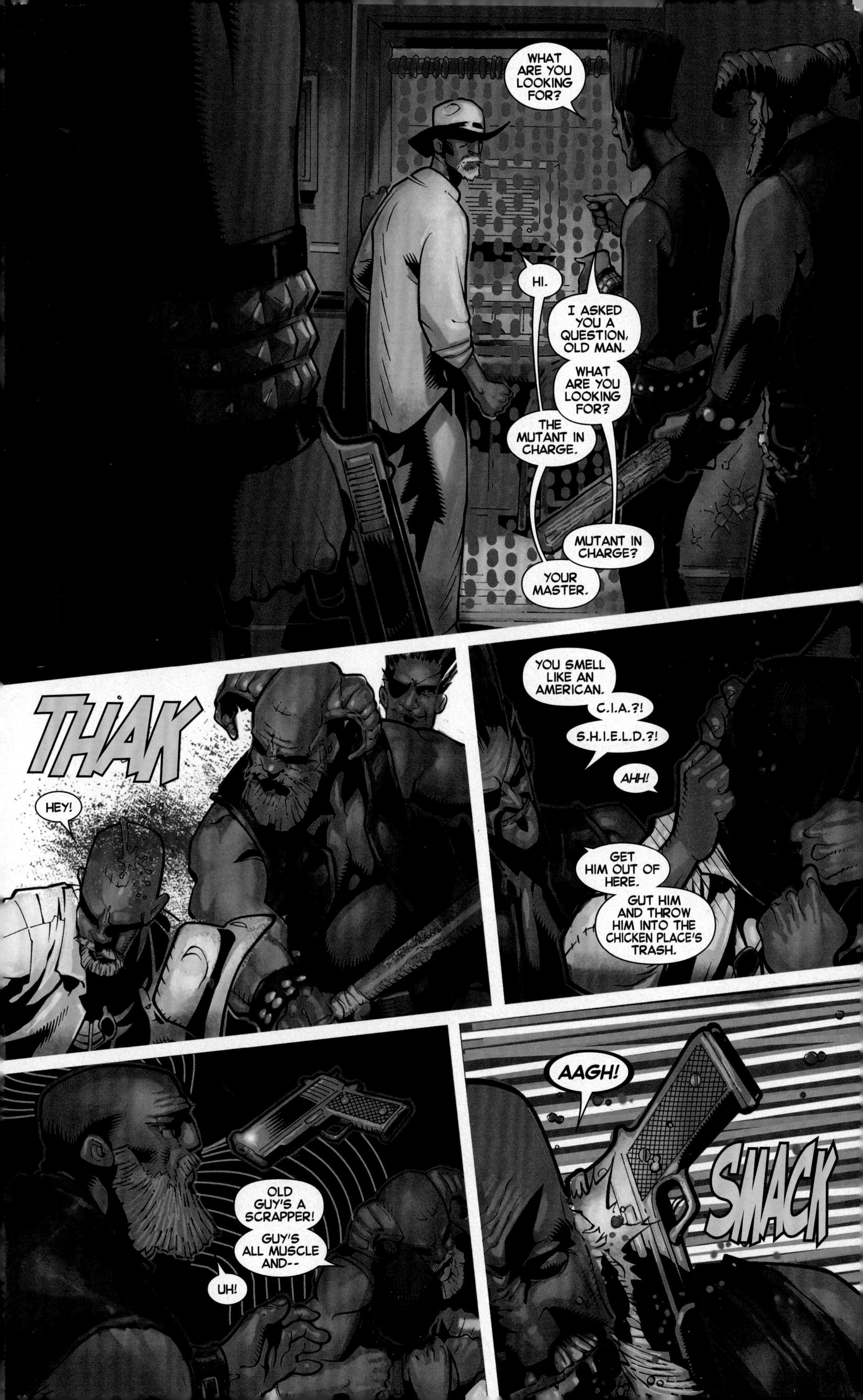
WHAT ARE YOU LOOKING FOR?
HI.
I ASKED YOU A QUESTION, OLD MAN.
WHAT ARE YOU LOOKING FOR?
THE MUTANT IN CHARGE.
MUTANT IN CHARGE?
YOUR MASTER.
THAK
HEY!
YOU SMELL LIKE AN AMERICAN.
C.I.A.?!
S.H.I.E.L.D.?!
AHH!
GET HIM OUT OF HERE.
GUT HIM AND THROW HIM INTO THE CHICKEN PLACE'S TRASH.
OLD GUY'S A SCRAPPER!
GUY'S ALL MUSCLE AND--
UH!
AAGH!
SMACK

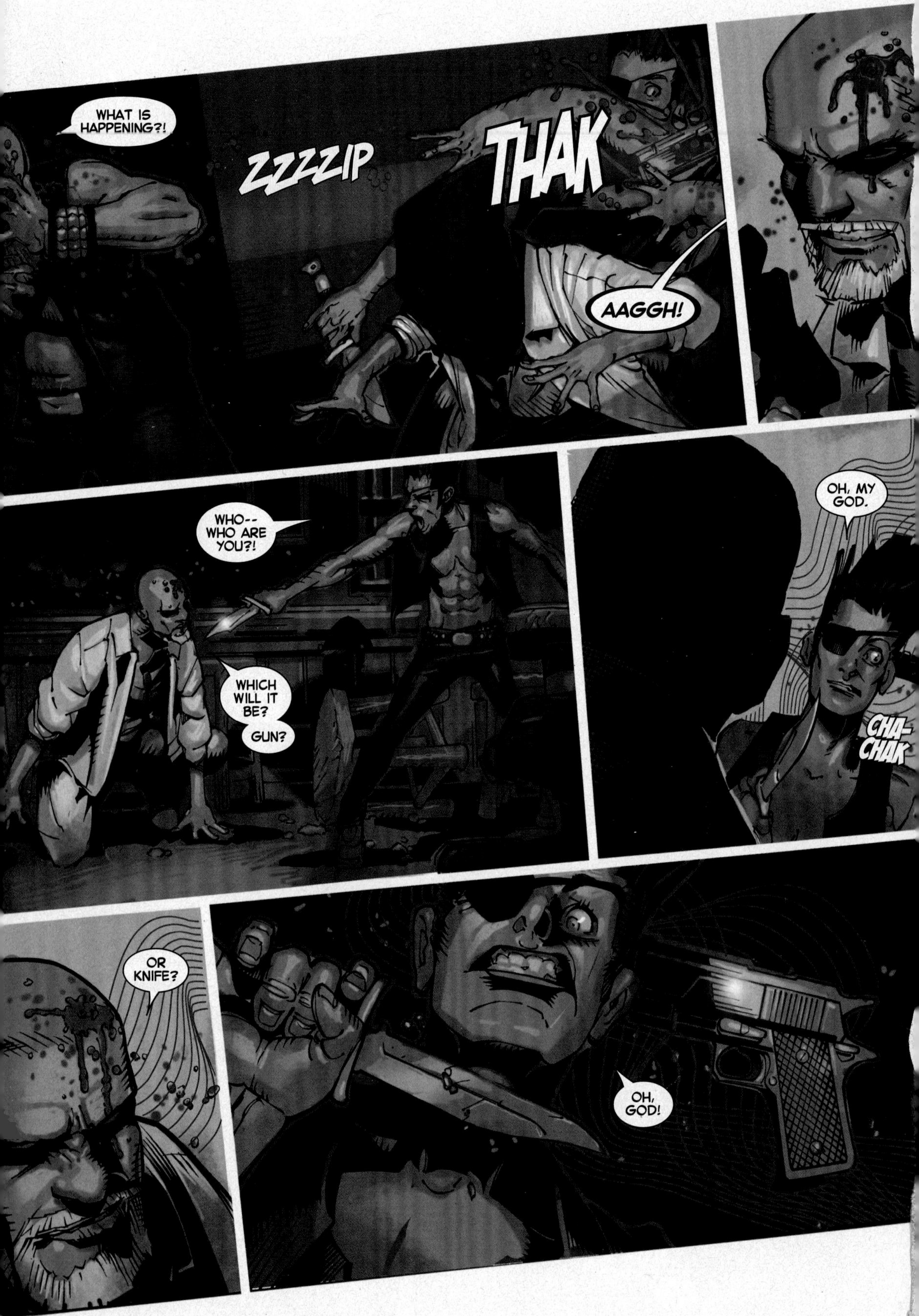
WHAT IS HAPPENING?!
ZZZZZIP
THAK
AAGGH!
WHO-- WHO ARE YOU?!
WHICH WILL IT BE?
GUN?
OH, MY GOD.
CHA-CHAK
OR KNIFE?
OH, GOD!

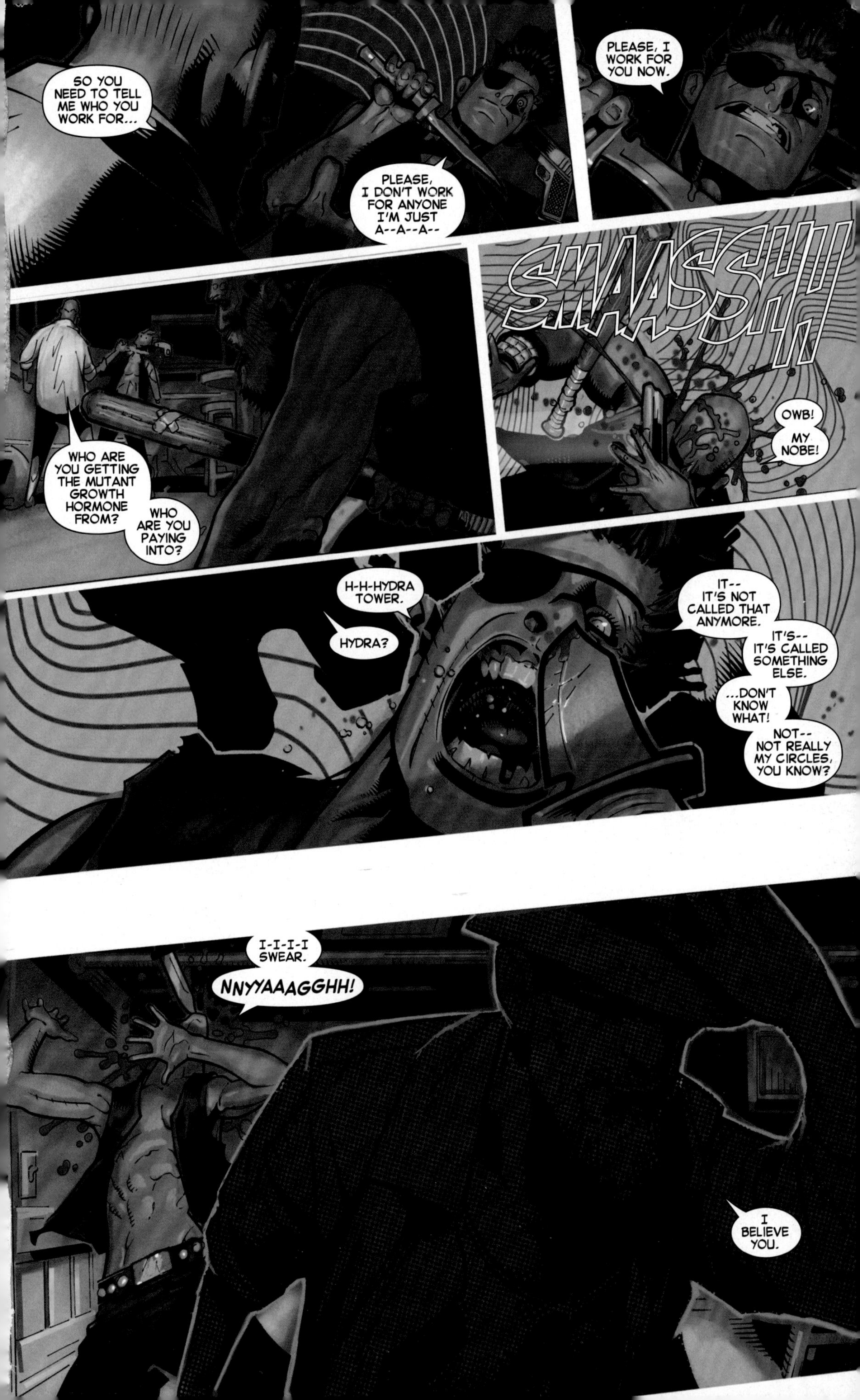
SO YOU NEED TO TELL ME WHO YOU WORK FOR...
PLEASE, I DON'T WORK FOR ANYONE I'M JUST A--A--A--
PLEASE, I WORK FOR YOU NOW.
WHO ARE YOU GETTING THE MUTANT GROWTH HORMONE FROM?
WHO ARE YOU PAYING INTO?
SWAASSHH
OWB!
MY NOBE!
H-H-HYDRA TOWER.
HYDRA?
IT-- IT'S NOT CALLED THAT ANYMORE.
IT'S-- IT'S CALLED SOMETHING ELSE.
...DON'T KNOW WHAT!
NOT-- NOT REALLY MY CIRCLES, YOU KNOW?
I-I-I-I SWEAR.
NNYYAAAGGHH!
I BELIEVE YOU.

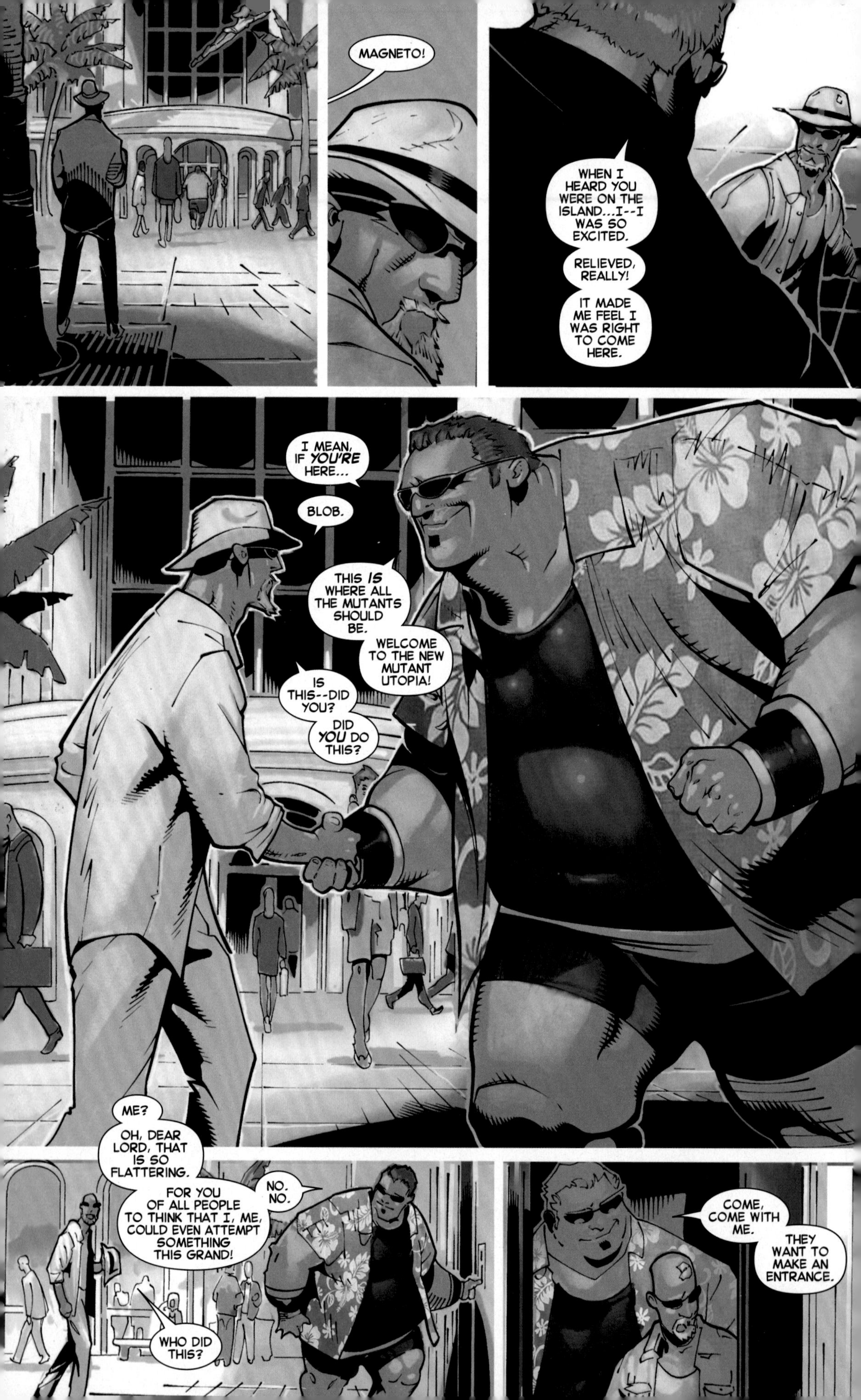
MAGNETO!
WHEN I HEARD YOU WERE ON THE ISLAND...I--I WAS SO EXCITED.
RELIEVED, REALLY!
IT MADE ME FEEL I WAS RIGHT TO COME HERE.
I MEAN, IF YOU'RE HERE...
BLOB.
THIS IS WHERE ALL THE MUTANTS SHOULD BE.
WELCOME TO THE NEW MUTANT UTOPIA!
IS THIS--DID YOU?
DID YOU DO THIS?
ME?
OH, DEAR LORD, THAT IS SO FLATTERING.
FOR YOU OF ALL PEOPLE TO THINK THAT I, ME, COULD EVEN ATTEMPT SOMETHING THIS GRAND!
NO. NO.
WHO DID THIS?
COME, COME WITH ME.
THEY WANT TO MAKE AN ENTRANCE.

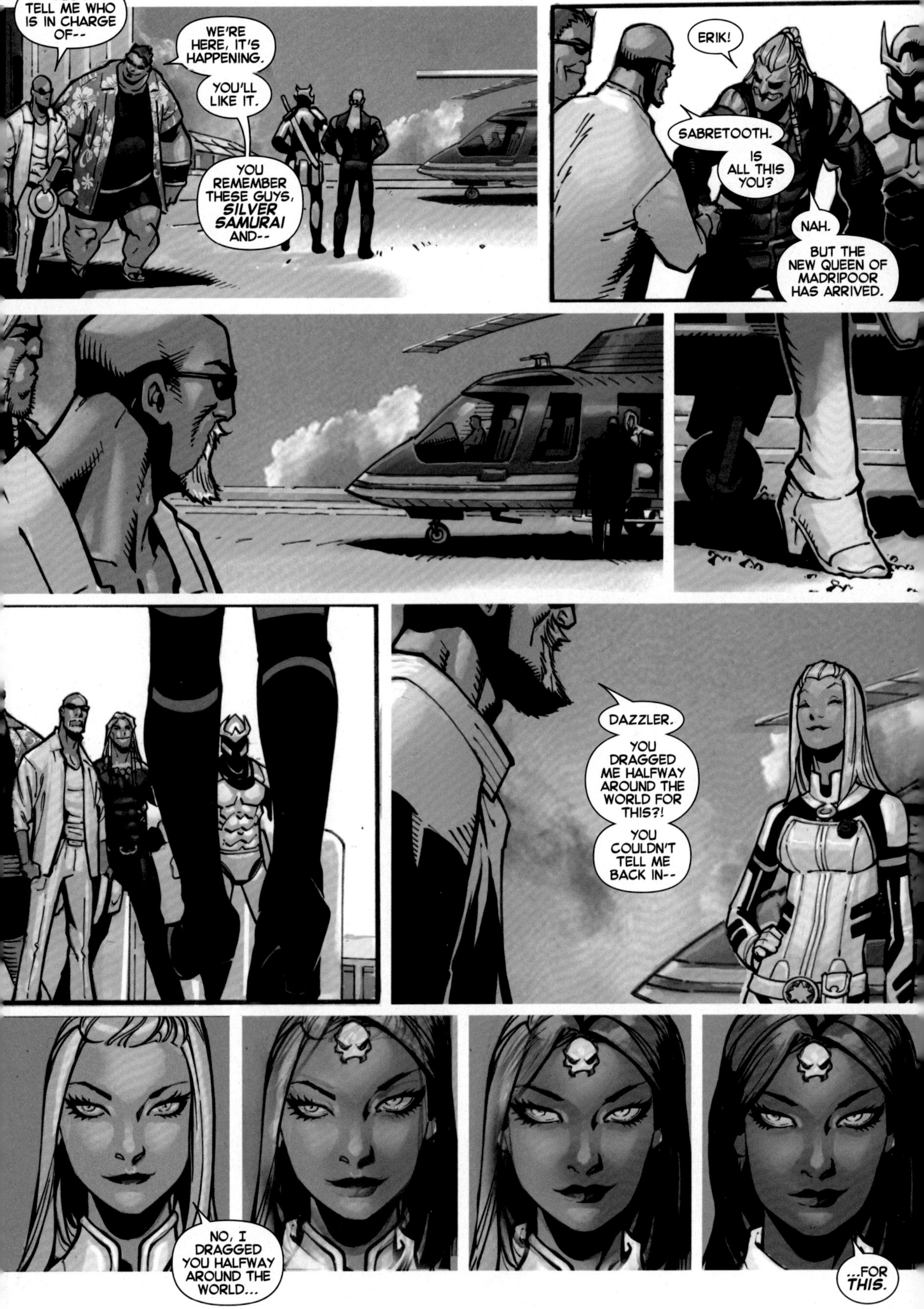
JUST TELL ME WHO IS IN CHARGE OF--
WE'RE HERE, IT'S HAPPENING.
YOU'LL LIKE IT.
YOU REMEMBER THESE GUYS, SILVER SAMURAI AND--
ERIK!
SABRETOOTH.
IS ALL THIS YOU?
NAH.
BUT THE NEW QUEEN OF MADRIPOOR HAS ARRIVED.
DAZZLER.
YOU DRAGGED ME HALFWAY AROUND THE WORLD FOR THIS?!
YOU COULDN'T TELL ME BACK IN--
NO, I DRAGGED YOU HALFWAY AROUND THE WORLD...
...FOR THIS.

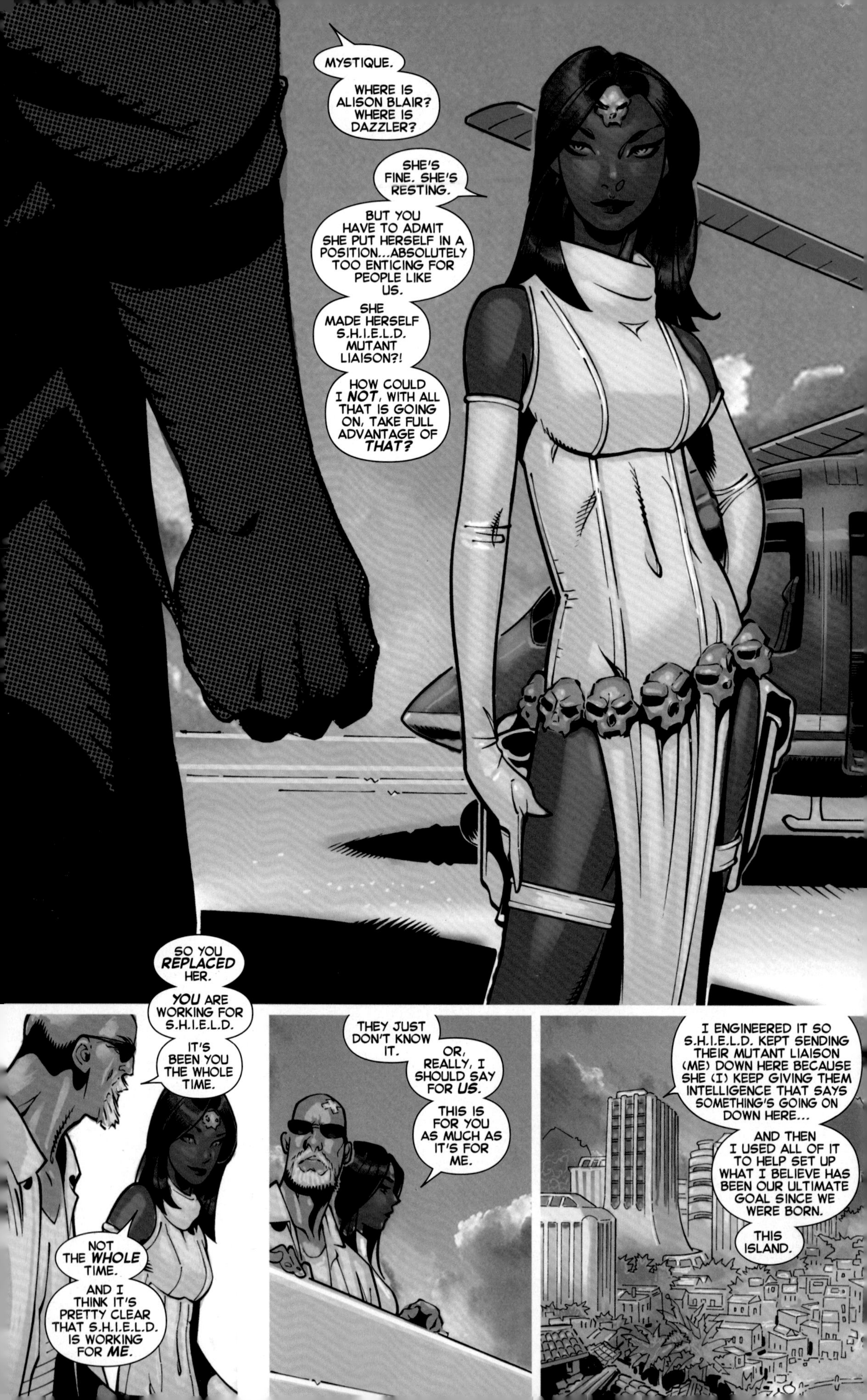
MYSTIQUE.
WHERE IS ALISON BLAIR? WHERE IS DAZZLER?
SHE'S FINE. SHE'S RESTING.
BUT YOU HAVE TO ADMIT SHE PUT HERSELF IN A POSITION...ABSOLUTELY TOO ENTICING FOR PEOPLE LIKE US.
SHE MADE HERSELF S.H.I.E.L.D. MUTANT LIAISON?!
HOW COULD I *NOT*, WITH ALL THAT IS GOING ON, TAKE FULL ADVANTAGE OF *THAT?*
SO YOU *REPLACED* HER.
YOU ARE WORKING FOR S.H.I.E.L.D.
IT'S BEEN YOU THE WHOLE TIME.
NOT THE *WHOLE* TIME.
AND I THINK IT'S PRETTY CLEAR THAT S.H.I.E.L.D. IS WORKING FOR *ME.*
THEY JUST DON'T KNOW IT.
OR, REALLY, I SHOULD SAY FOR *US.*
THIS IS FOR YOU AS MUCH AS IT'S FOR ME.
I ENGINEERED IT SO S.H.I.E.L.D. KEPT SENDING THEIR MUTANT LIAISON (ME) DOWN HERE BECAUSE SHE (I) KEEP GIVING THEM INTELLIGENCE THAT SAYS SOMETHING'S GOING ON DOWN HERE...
AND THEN I USED ALL OF IT TO HELP SET UP WHAT I BELIEVE HAS BEEN OUR ULTIMATE GOAL SINCE WE WERE BORN.
THIS ISLAND.

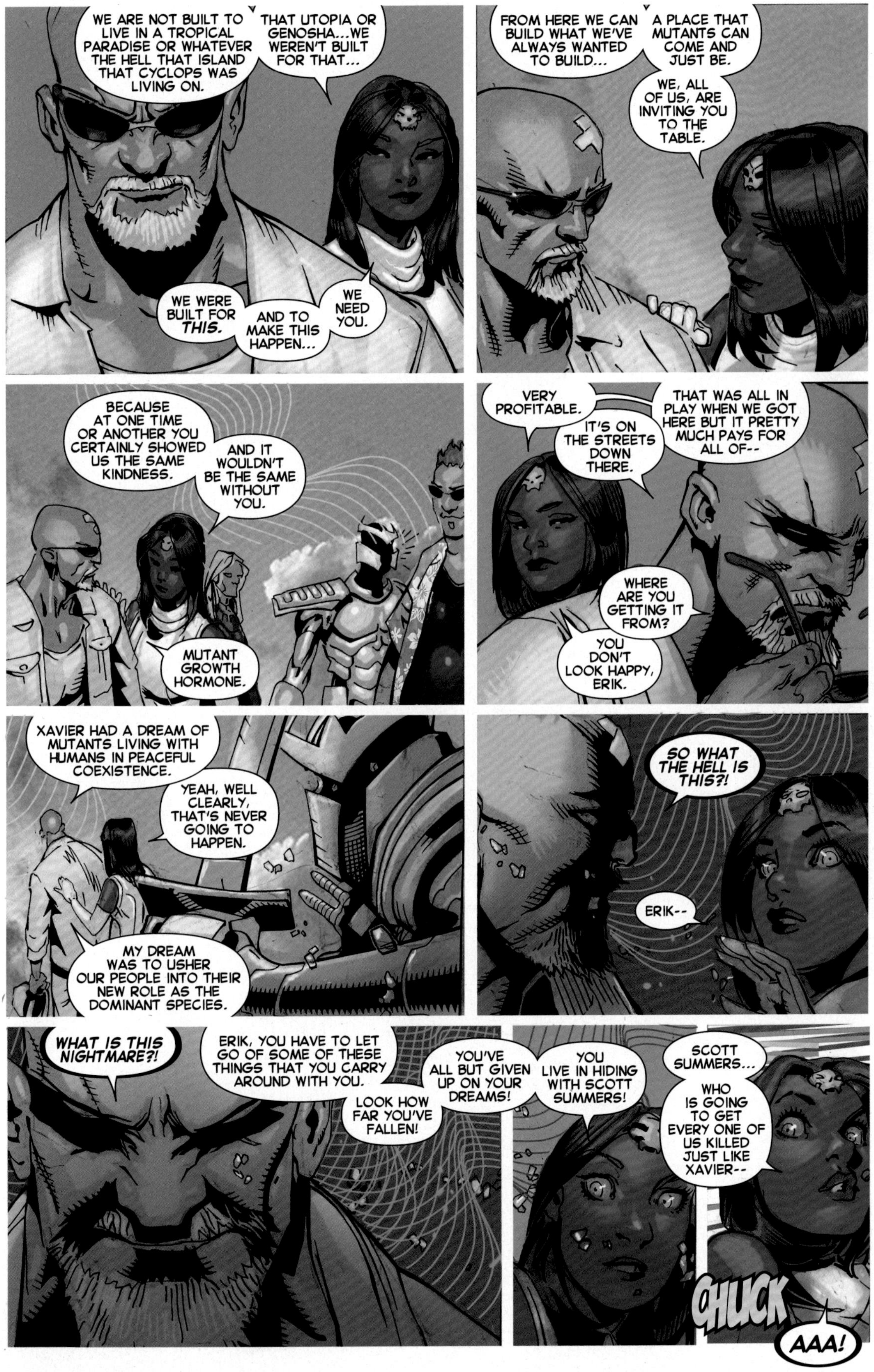
WE ARE NOT BUILT TO LIVE IN A TROPICAL PARADISE OR WHATEVER THE HELL THAT ISLAND THAT CYCLOPS WAS LIVING ON.
THAT UTOPIA OR GENOSHA...WE WEREN'T BUILT FOR THAT...
WE WERE BUILT FOR *THIS.*
AND TO MAKE THIS HAPPEN...
WE NEED YOU.
FROM HERE WE CAN BUILD WHAT WE'VE ALWAYS WANTED TO BUILD...
A PLACE THAT MUTANTS CAN COME AND JUST BE.
WE, ALL OF US, ARE INVITING YOU TO THE TABLE.
BECAUSE AT ONE TIME OR ANOTHER YOU CERTAINLY SHOWED US THE SAME KINDNESS.
AND IT WOULDN'T BE THE SAME WITHOUT YOU.
MUTANT GROWTH HORMONE.
VERY PROFITABLE.
IT'S ON THE STREETS DOWN THERE.
THAT WAS ALL IN PLAY WHEN WE GOT HERE BUT IT PRETTY MUCH PAYS FOR ALL OF--
WHERE ARE YOU GETTING IT FROM?
YOU DON'T LOOK HAPPY, ERIK.
XAVIER HAD A DREAM OF MUTANTS LIVING WITH HUMANS IN PEACEFUL COEXISTENCE.
YEAH, WELL CLEARLY, THAT'S NEVER GOING TO HAPPEN.
MY DREAM WAS TO USHER OUR PEOPLE INTO THEIR NEW ROLE AS THE DOMINANT SPECIES.
SO WHAT THE HELL IS THIS?!
ERIK--
WHAT IS THIS NIGHTMARE?!
ERIK, YOU HAVE TO LET GO OF SOME OF THESE THINGS THAT YOU CARRY AROUND WITH YOU.
LOOK HOW FAR YOU'VE FALLEN!
YOU'VE ALL BUT GIVEN UP ON YOUR DREAMS!
YOU LIVE IN HIDING WITH SCOTT SUMMERS!
SCOTT SUMMERS...
WHO IS GOING TO GET EVERY ONE OF US KILLED JUST LIKE XAVIER--
CHUCK
AAA!

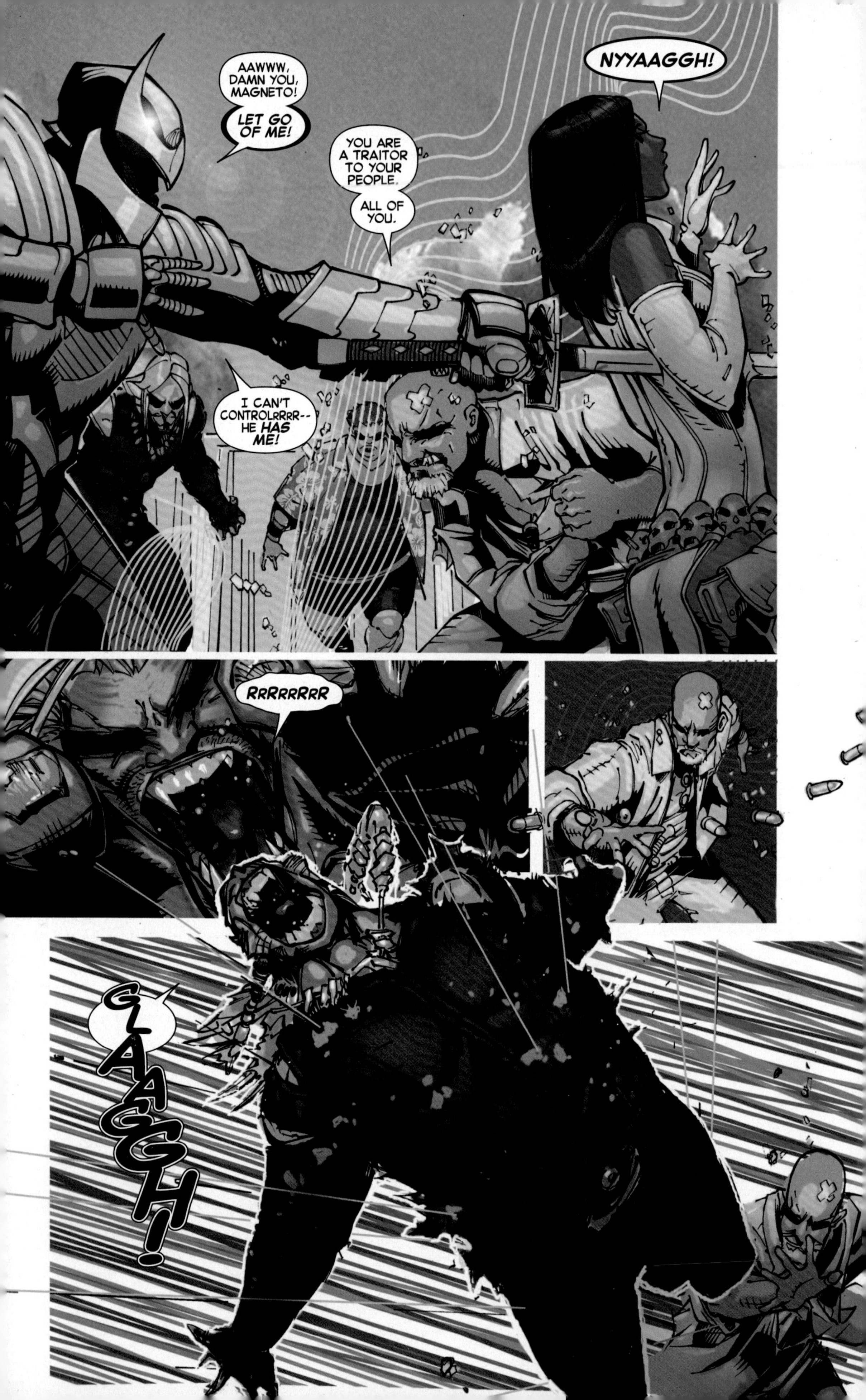
AAWWW, DAMN YOU, MAGNETO!
LET GO OF ME!
YOU ARE A TRAITOR TO YOUR PEOPLE.
ALL OF YOU.
NYYAAGGH!
I CAN'T CONTROLRRRR-- HE HAS ME!
RRRRRRRR
GLAAGGH!

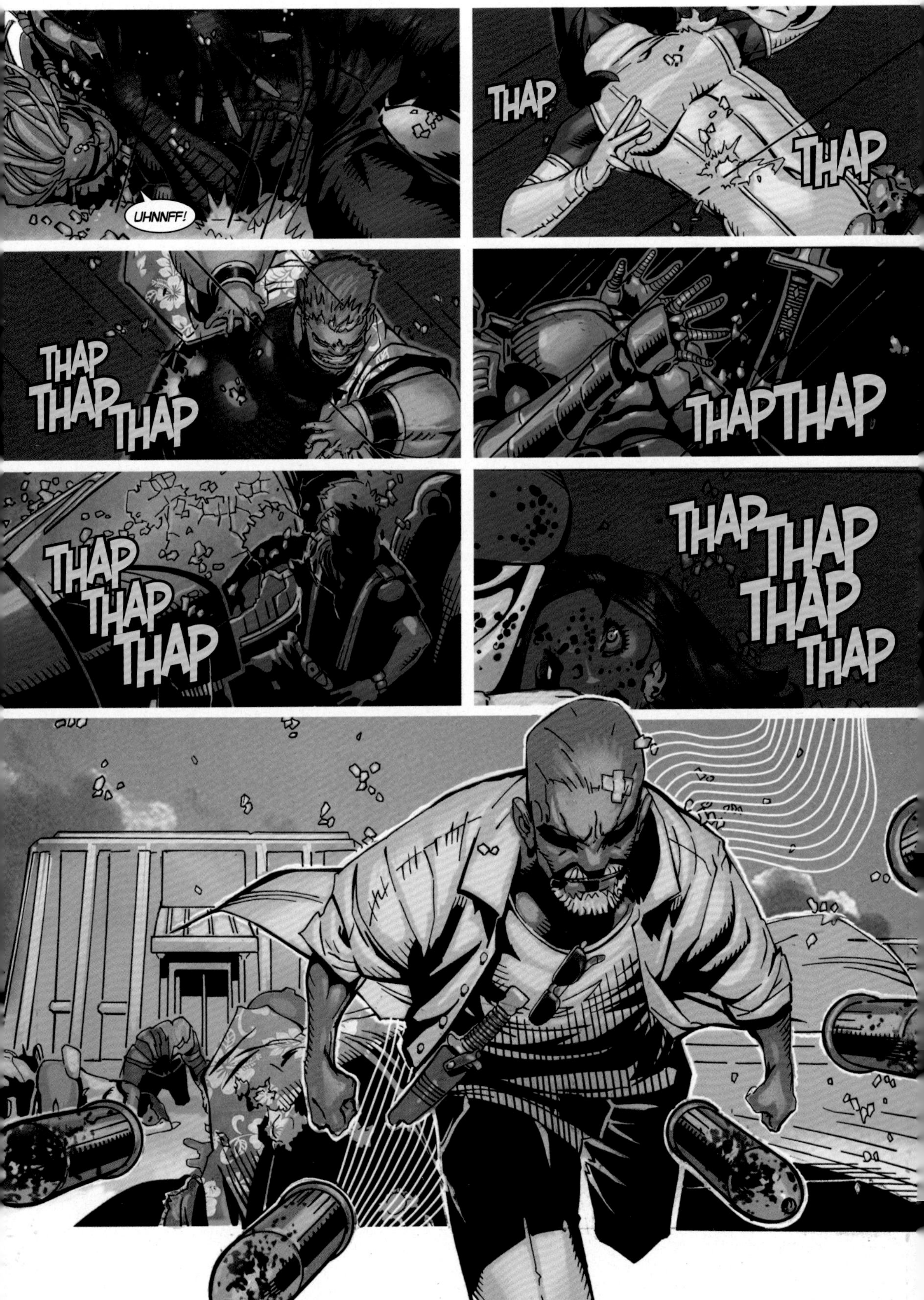
UHNNFF!
THAP
THAP
THAP THAP THAP
THAPTHAP
THAP THAP THAP
THAP THAP THAP THAP

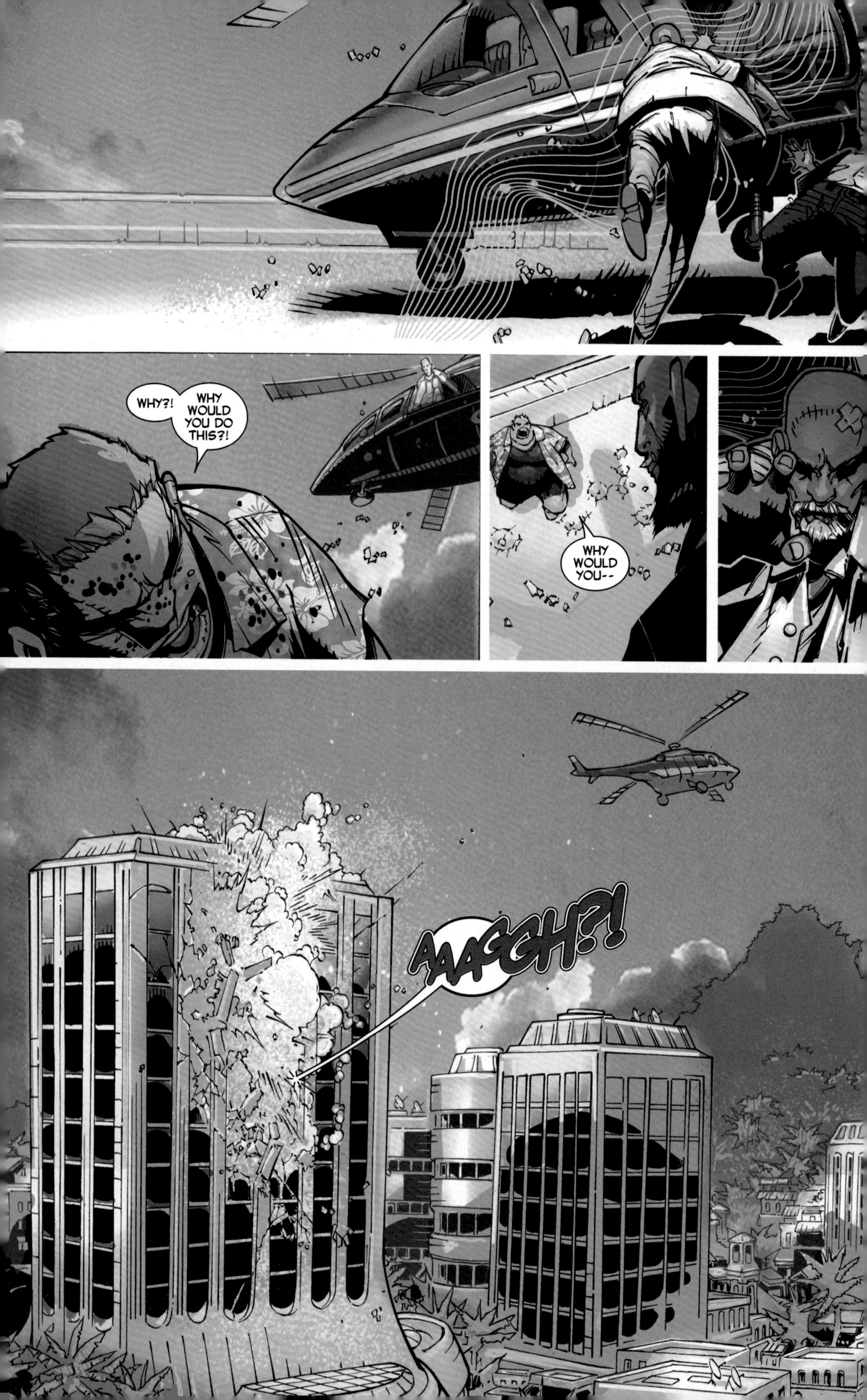
WHY?!
WHY WOULD YOU DO THIS?!
WHY WOULD YOU--
AAAGGH?!

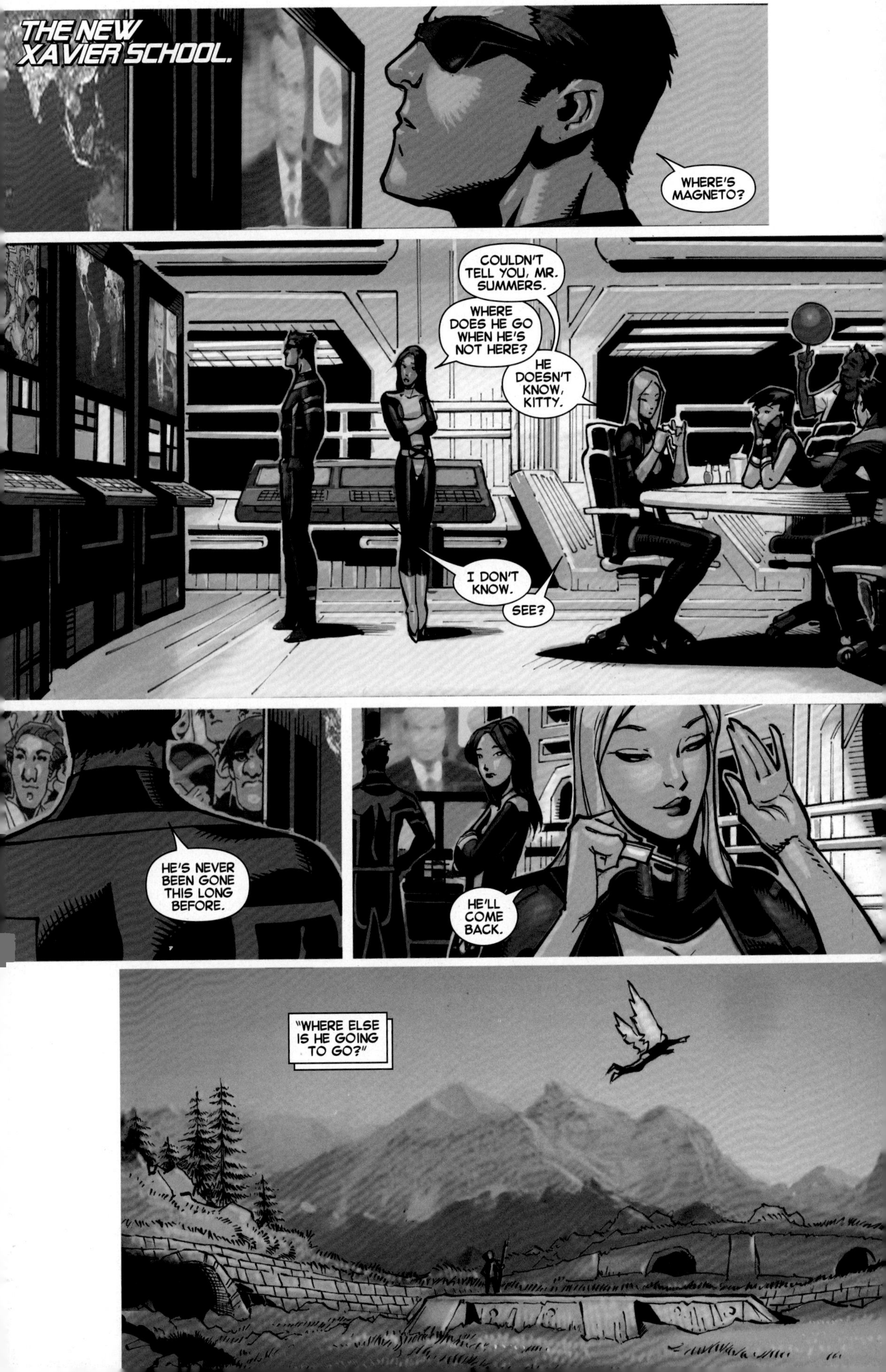
THE NEW XAVIER SCHOOL.
WHERE'S MAGNETO?
COULDN'T TELL YOU, MR. SUMMERS.
WHERE DOES HE GO WHEN HE'S NOT HERE?
HE DOESN'T KNOW, KITTY.
I DON'T KNOW.
SEE?
HE'S NEVER BEEN GONE THIS LONG BEFORE.
HE'LL COME BACK.
"WHERE ELSE IS HE GOING TO GO?"

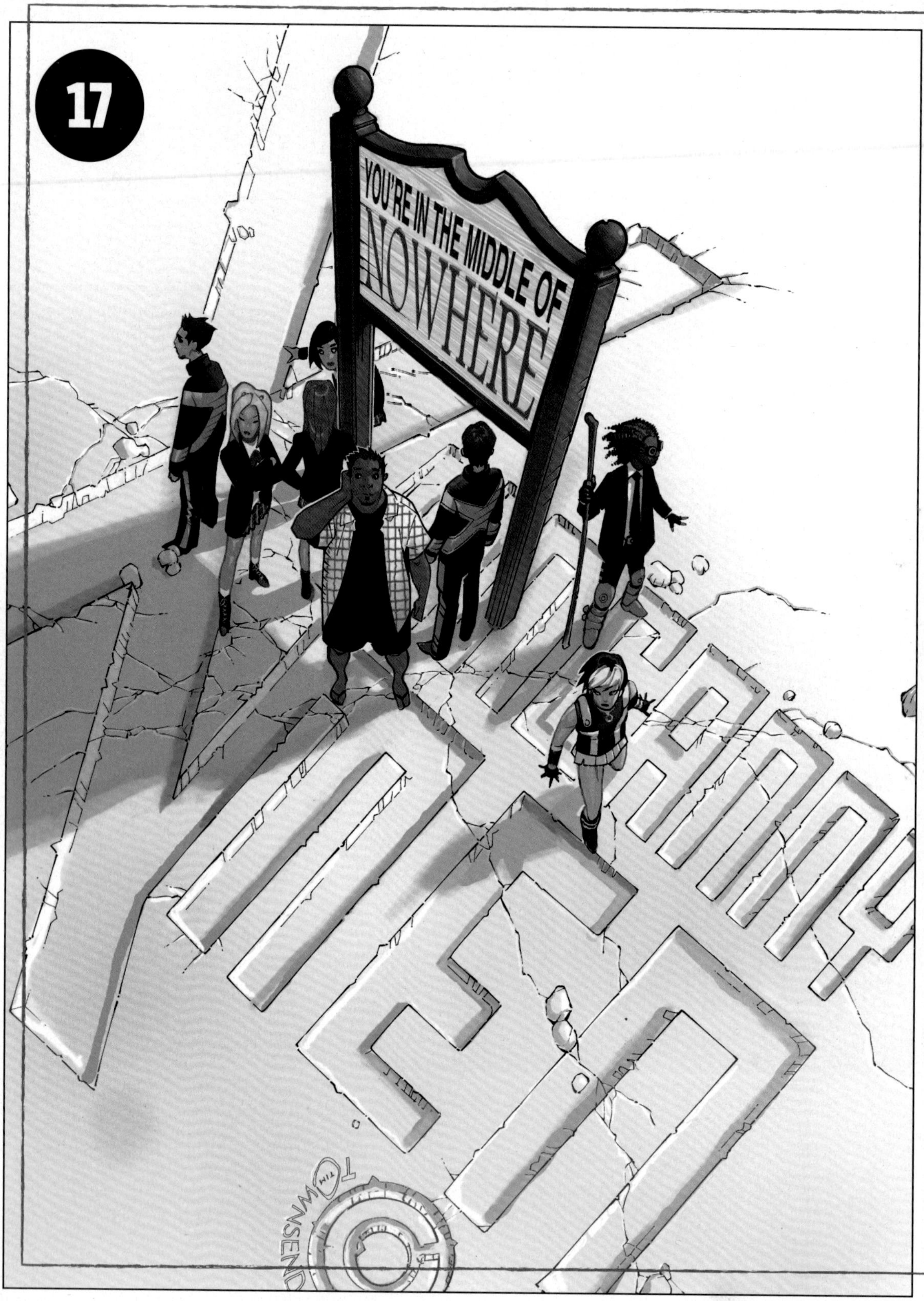
17
YOU'RE IN THE MIDDLE OF
NOWHERE

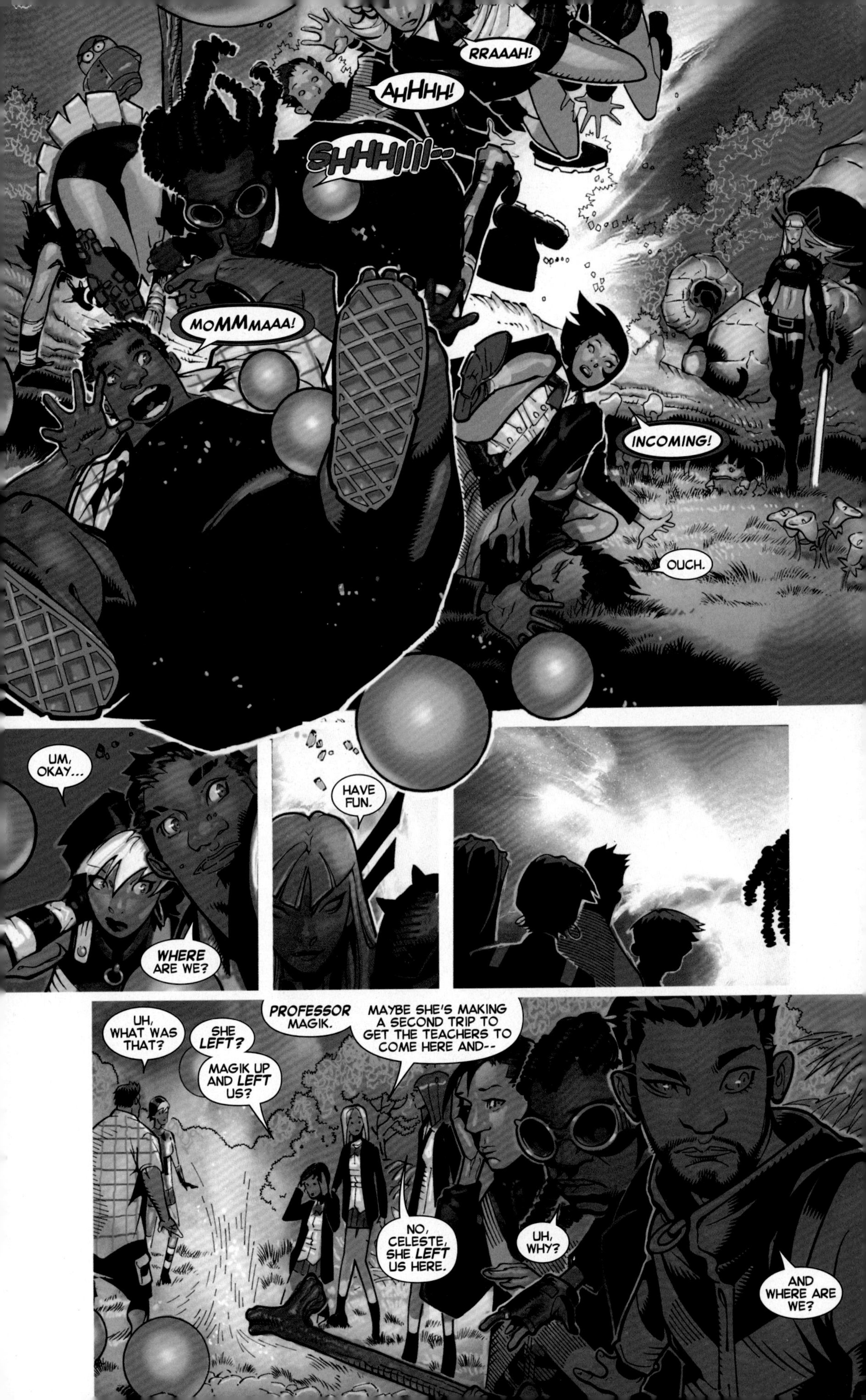
RRAAAH!
AHHHH!
SHHHIIII--
MOMMMAAA!
INCOMING!
OUCH.
UM, OKAY...
WHERE ARE WE?
HAVE FUN.
UH, WHAT WAS THAT?
SHE LEFT?
MAGIK UP AND LEFT US?
PROFESSOR MAGIK.
MAYBE SHE'S MAKING A SECOND TRIP TO GET THE TEACHERS TO COME HERE AND--
NO, CELESTE, SHE LEFT US HERE.
UH, WHY?
AND WHERE ARE WE?

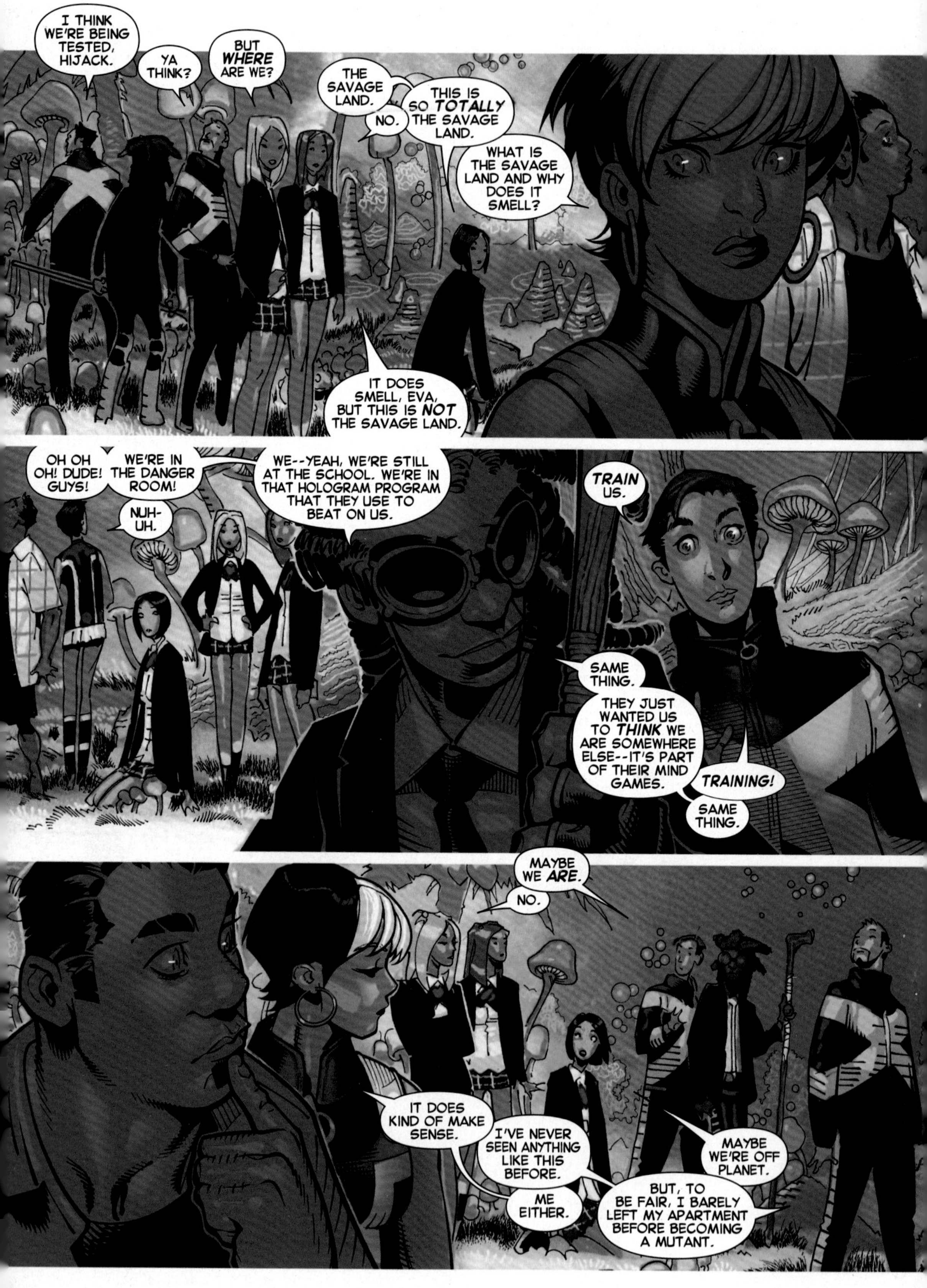
I THINK WE'RE BEING TESTED, HIJACK.
YA THINK?
BUT WHERE ARE WE?
THE SAVAGE LAND.
NO.
THIS IS SO TOTALLY THE SAVAGE LAND.
WHAT IS THE SAVAGE LAND AND WHY DOES IT SMELL?
IT DOES SMELL, EVA, BUT THIS IS NOT THE SAVAGE LAND.
OH OH OH! DUDE! GUYS!
WE'RE IN THE DANGER ROOM!
NUH-UH.
WE--YEAH, WE'RE STILL AT THE SCHOOL. WE'RE IN THAT HOLOGRAM PROGRAM THAT THEY USE TO BEAT ON US.
TRAIN US.
SAME THING.
THEY JUST WANTED US TO THINK WE ARE SOMEWHERE ELSE--IT'S PART OF THEIR MIND GAMES.
TRAINING!
SAME THING.
MAYBE WE ARE.
NO.
IT DOES KIND OF MAKE SENSE.
I'VE NEVER SEEN ANYTHING LIKE THIS BEFORE.
ME EITHER.
MAYBE WE'RE OFF PLANET.
BUT, TO BE FAIR, I BARELY LEFT MY APARTMENT BEFORE BECOMING A MUTANT.

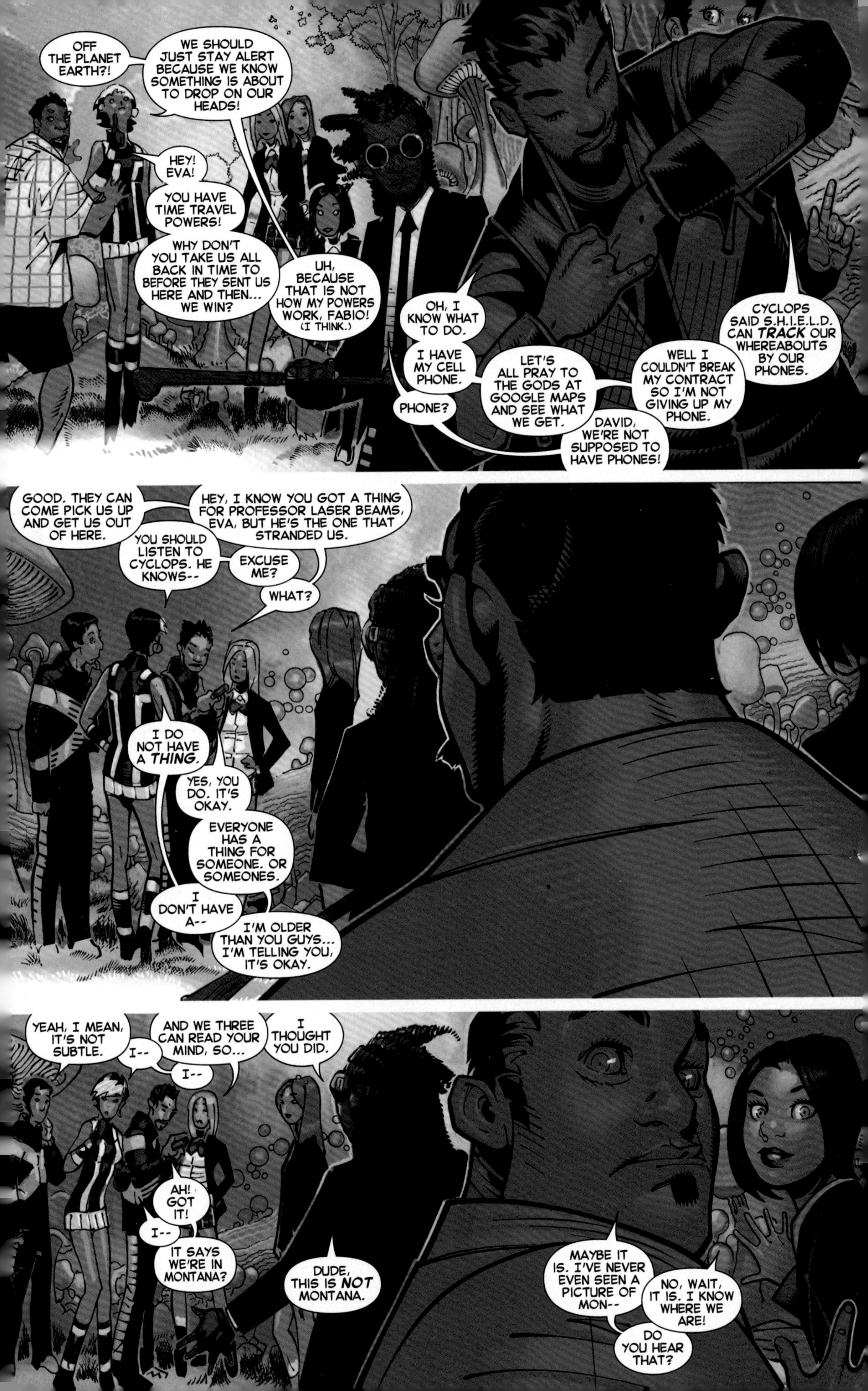

WE SHOULD JUST STAY ALERT BECAUSE WE KNOW SOMETHING IS ABOUT TO DROP ON OUR HEADS!
OFF THE PLANET EARTH?!
HEY! EVA!
YOU HAVE TIME TRAVEL POWERS!
WHY DON'T YOU TAKE US ALL BACK IN TIME TO BEFORE THEY SENT US HERE AND THEN... WE WIN?
UH, BECAUSE THAT IS NOT HOW MY POWERS WORK, FABIO! (I THINK.)
CYCLOPS SAID S.H.I.E.L.D. CAN TRACK OUR WHEREABOUTS BY OUR PHONES.
WELL I COULDN'T BREAK MY CONTRACT SO I'M NOT GIVING UP MY PHONE.
OH, I KNOW WHAT TO DO.
I HAVE MY CELL PHONE.
LET'S ALL PRAY TO THE GODS AT GOOGLE MAPS AND SEE WHAT WE GET.
PHONE?
DAVID, WE'RE NOT SUPPOSED TO HAVE PHONES!
GOOD. THEY CAN COME PICK US UP AND GET US OUT OF HERE.
HEY, I KNOW YOU GOT A THING FOR PROFESSOR LASER BEAMS, EVA, BUT HE'S THE ONE THAT STRANDED US.
YOU SHOULD LISTEN TO CYCLOPS. HE KNOWS--
EXCUSE ME?
WHAT?
I DO NOT HAVE A THING.
YES, YOU DO. IT'S OKAY.
EVERYONE HAS A THING FOR SOMEONE. OR SOMEONES.
I DON'T HAVE A--
I'M OLDER THAN YOU GUYS... I'M TELLING YOU, IT'S OKAY.
YEAH, I MEAN, IT'S NOT SUBTLE.
I--
AND WE THREE CAN READ YOUR MIND, SO...
I--
I THOUGHT YOU DID.
AH! GOT IT!
I--
IT SAYS WE'RE IN MONTANA?
DUDE, THIS IS NOT MONTANA.
MAYBE IT IS. I'VE NEVER EVEN SEEN A PICTURE OF MON--
NO, WAIT, IT IS. I KNOW WHERE WE ARE!
DO YOU HEAR THAT?

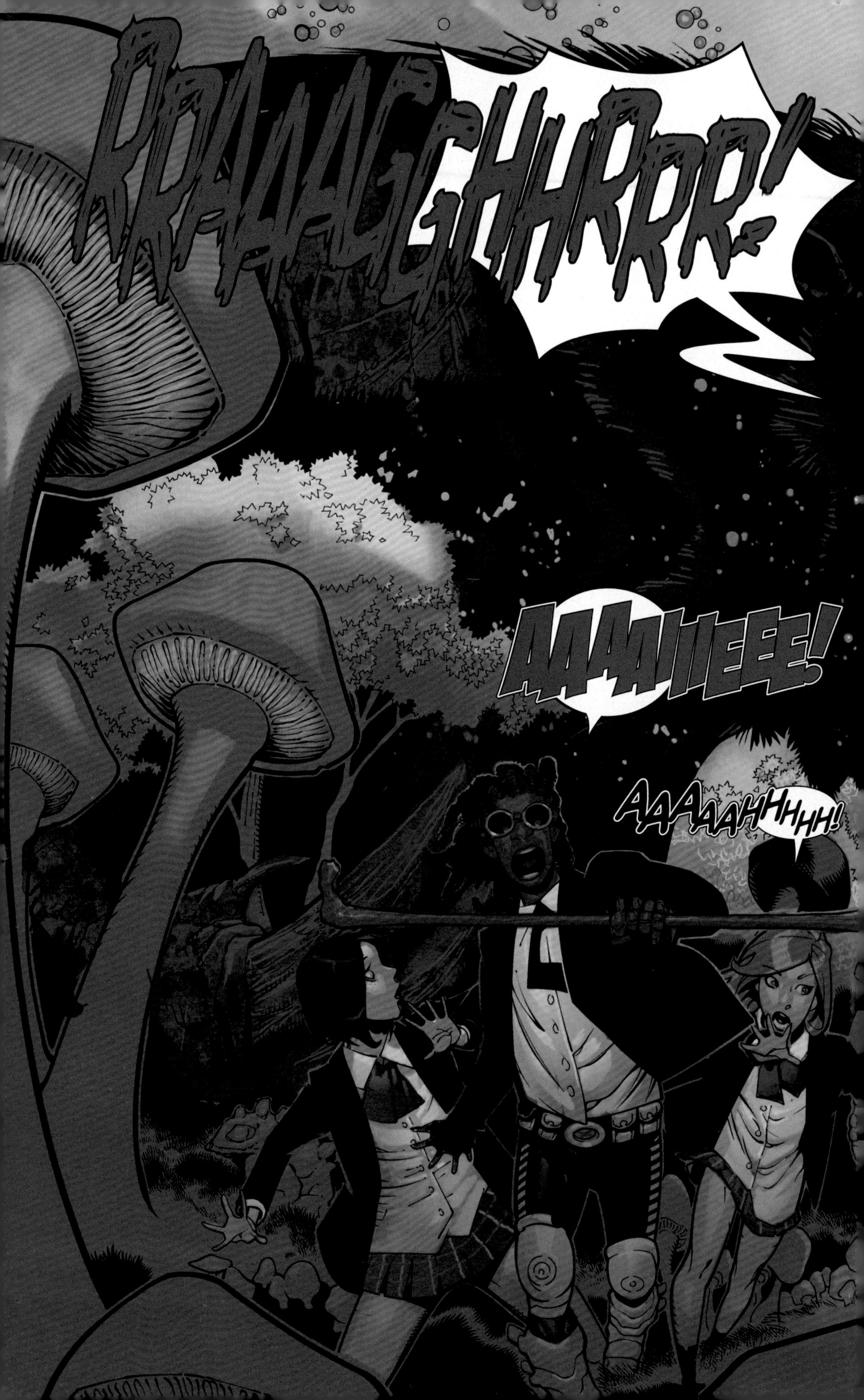
RRAAAGGHHRRRR!
AAAAIIIEEEE!
AAAAAHHHHH!

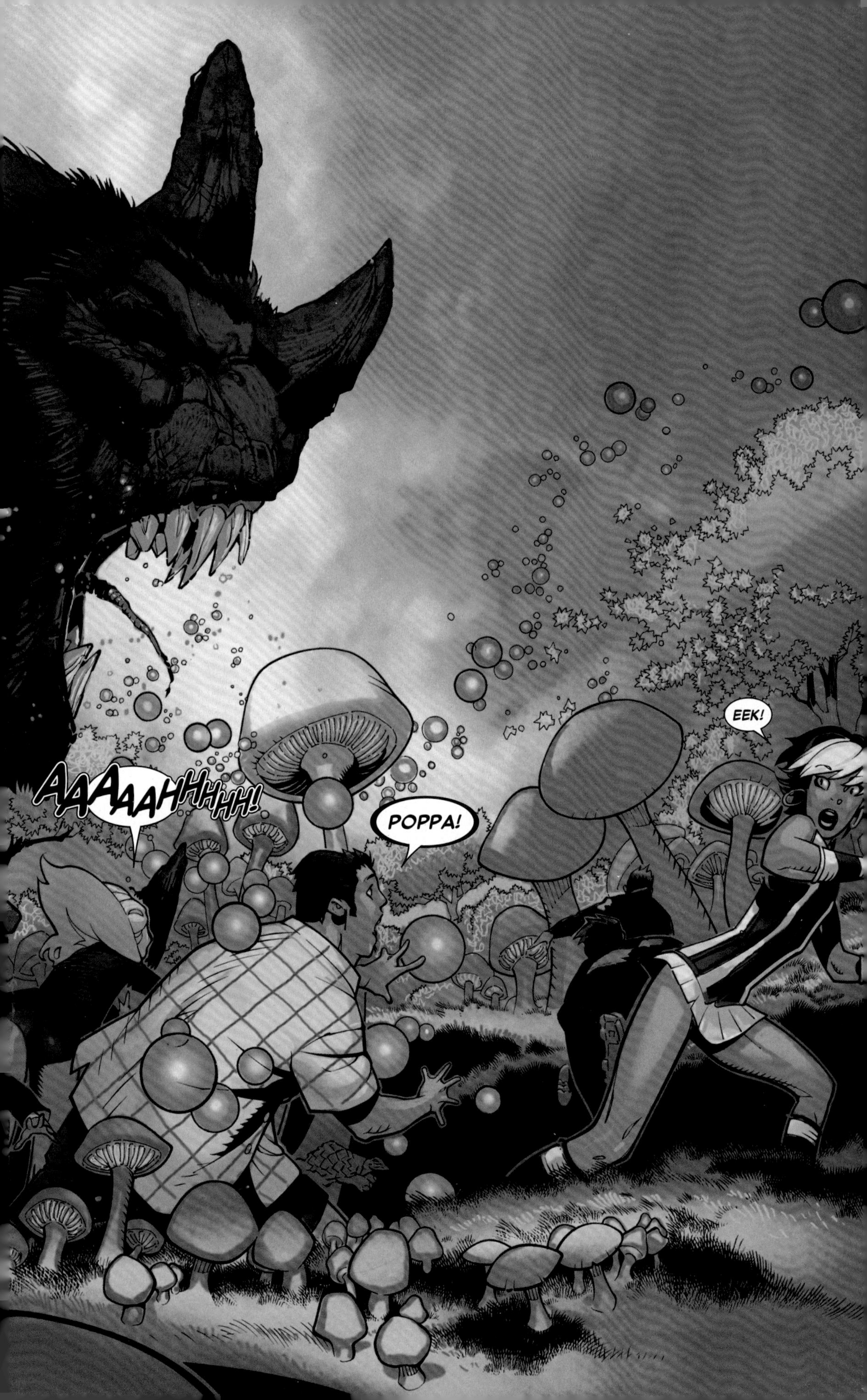
EEK!
AAAAAHHHHH!
POPPA!

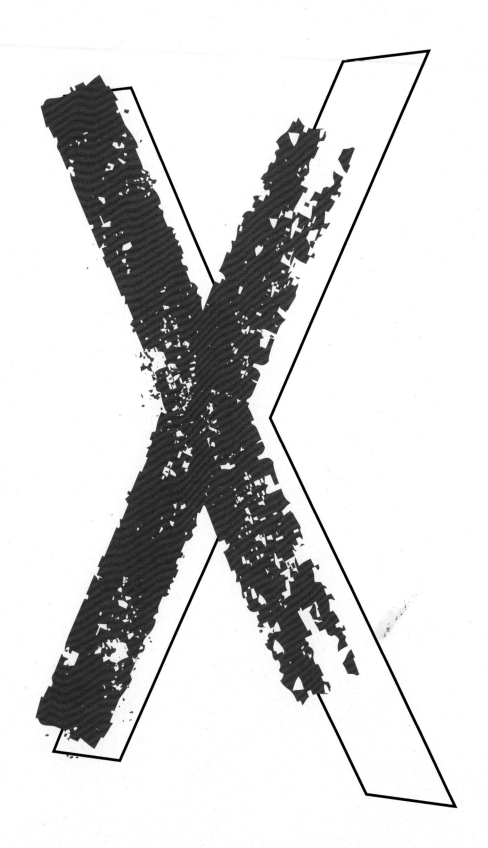

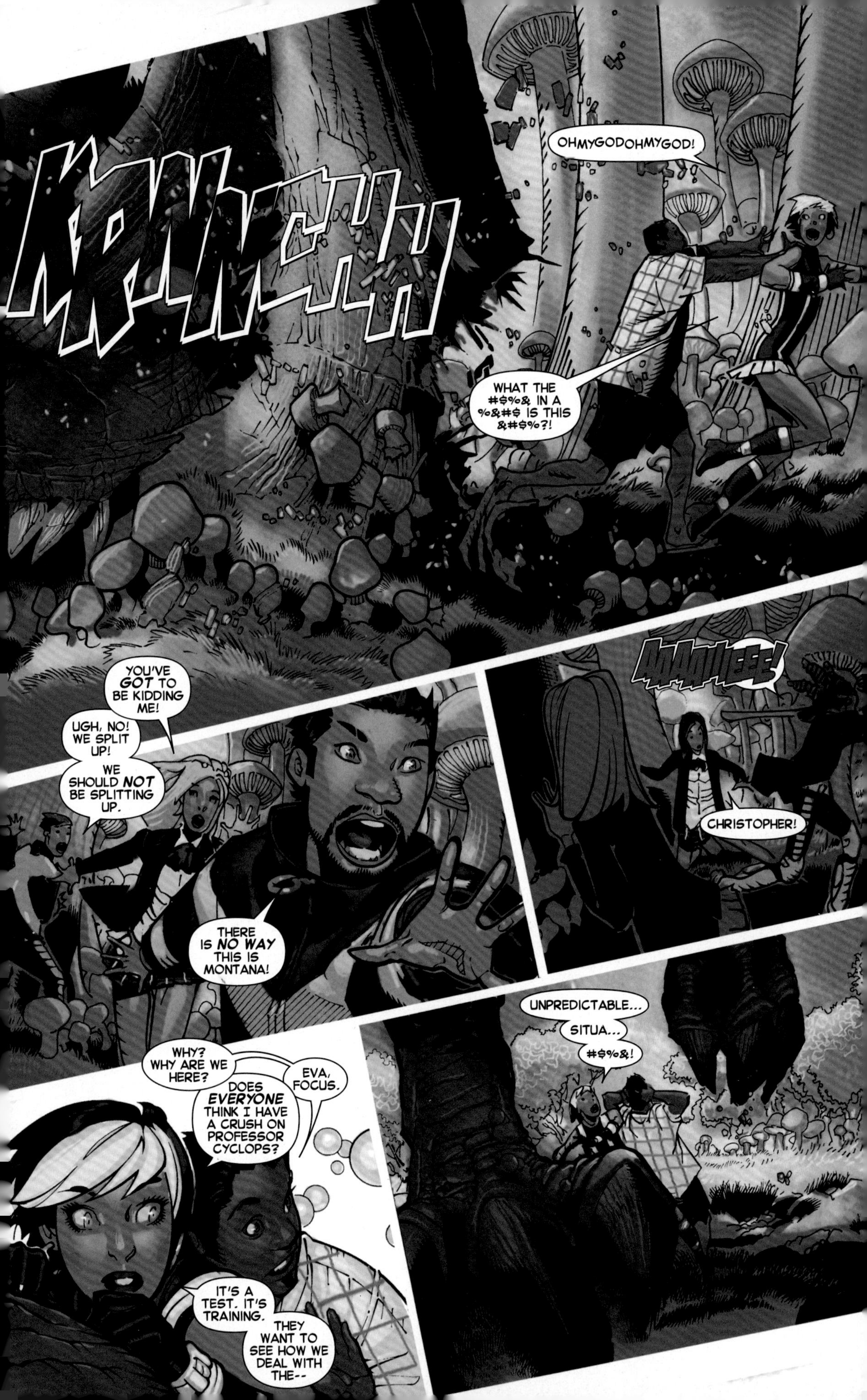
OHMYGODOHMYGOD!
WHAT THE #$%& IN A %&#$ IS THIS &#$%?!
YOU'VE **GOT** TO BE KIDDING ME!
UGH, NO! WE SPLIT UP!
WE SHOULD **NOT** BE SPLITTING UP.
THERE IS **NO WAY** THIS IS MONTANA!
CHRISTOPHER!
WHY? WHY ARE WE HERE?
EVA, FOCUS.
DOES **EVERYONE** THINK I HAVE A CRUSH ON PROFESSOR CYCLOPS?
IT'S A TEST. IT'S TRAINING.
THEY WANT TO SEE HOW WE DEAL WITH THE--
UNPREDICTABLE...
SITUA...
#$%&!

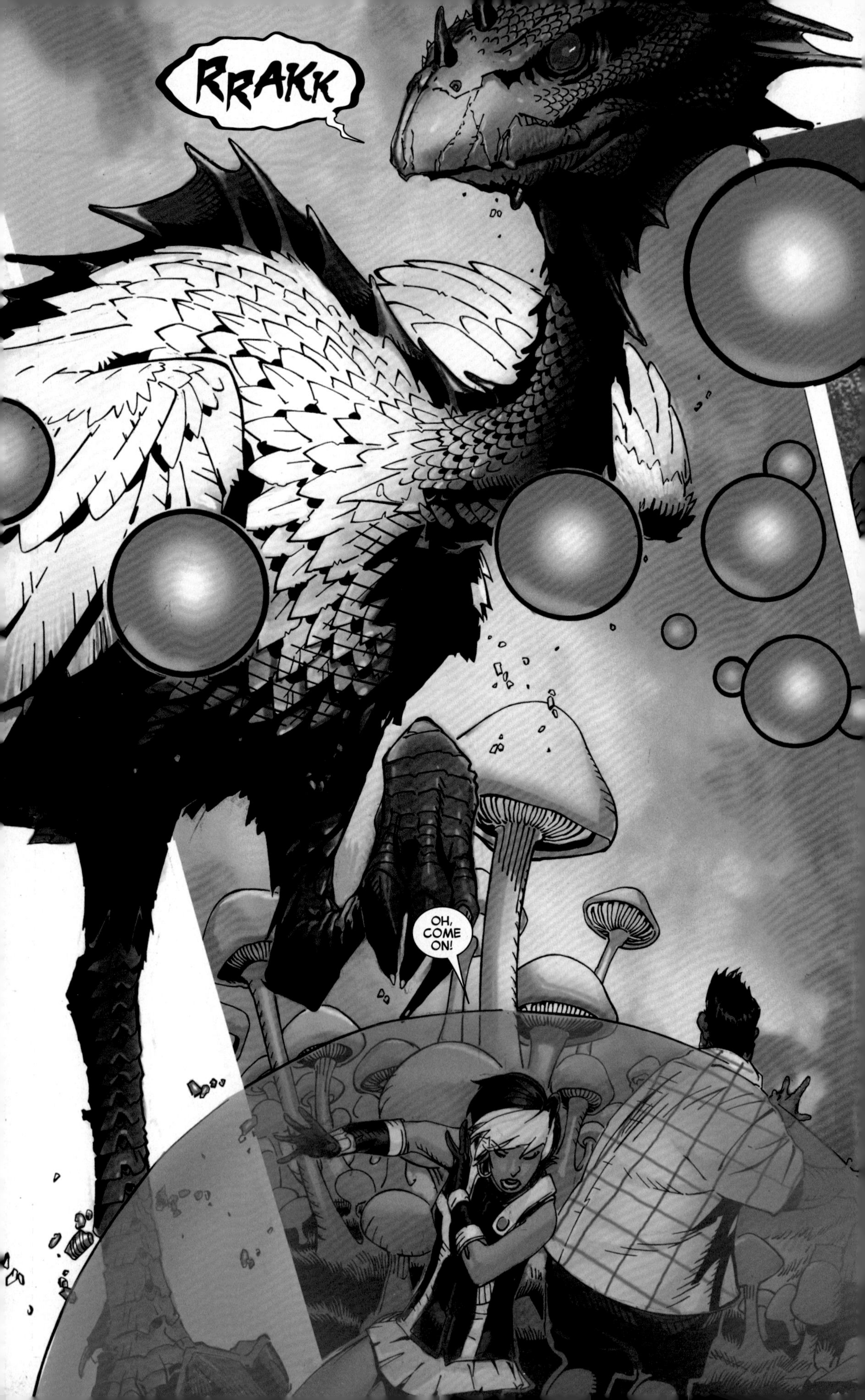
RRAKK
OH, COME ON!

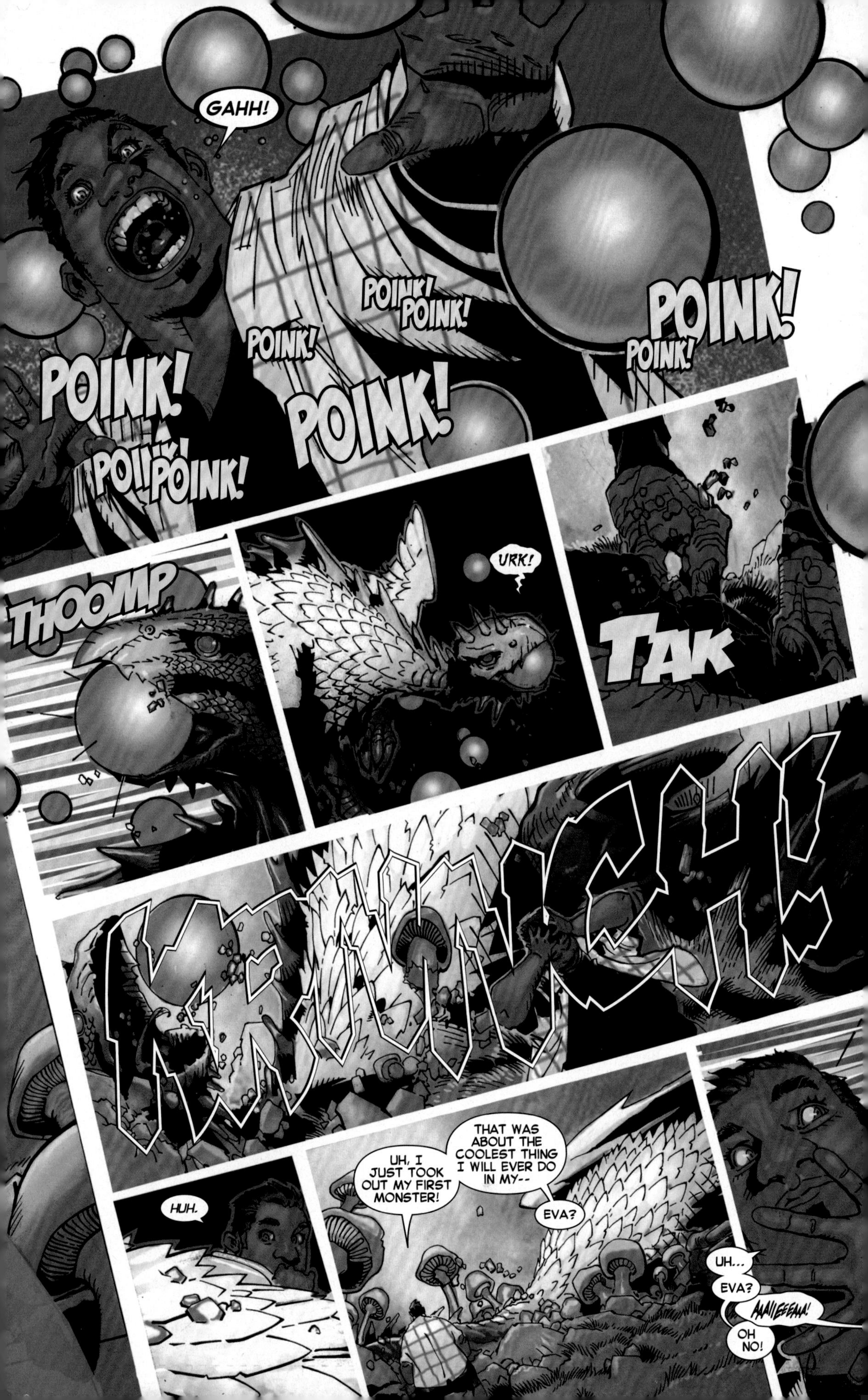

GAHH!
POINK!
POINK! POINK!
POINK!
POINK!
POINK!
POINK!
POINK!
THOOMP
URK!
TAK
HUH.
UH, I JUST TOOK OUT MY FIRST MONSTER!
THAT WAS ABOUT THE COOLEST THING I WILL EVER DO IN MY--
EVA?
UH...
EVA?
AAAIIEEEAA!
OH NO!

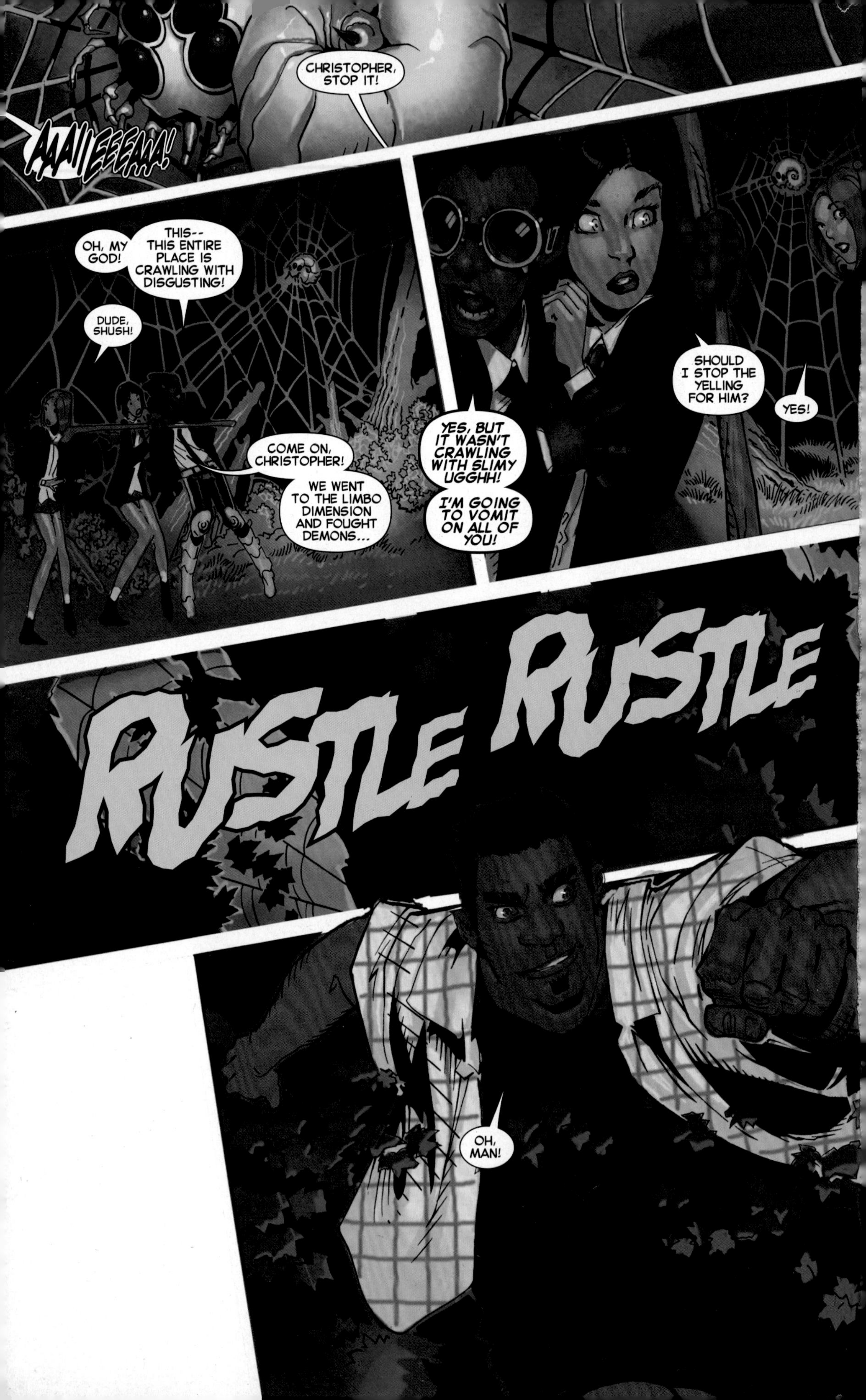
CHRISTOPHER, STOP IT!
AAAIIEEEAAA!
OH, MY GOD!
THIS-- THIS ENTIRE PLACE IS CRAWLING WITH DISGUSTING!
DUDE, SHUSH!
COME ON, CHRISTOPHER!
WE WENT TO THE LIMBO DIMENSION AND FOUGHT DEMONS...
YES, BUT IT WASN'T CRAWLING WITH SLIMY UGGHH!
I'M GOING TO VOMIT ON ALL OF YOU!
SHOULD I STOP THE YELLING FOR HIM?
YES!
RUSTLE RUSTLE
OH, MAN!

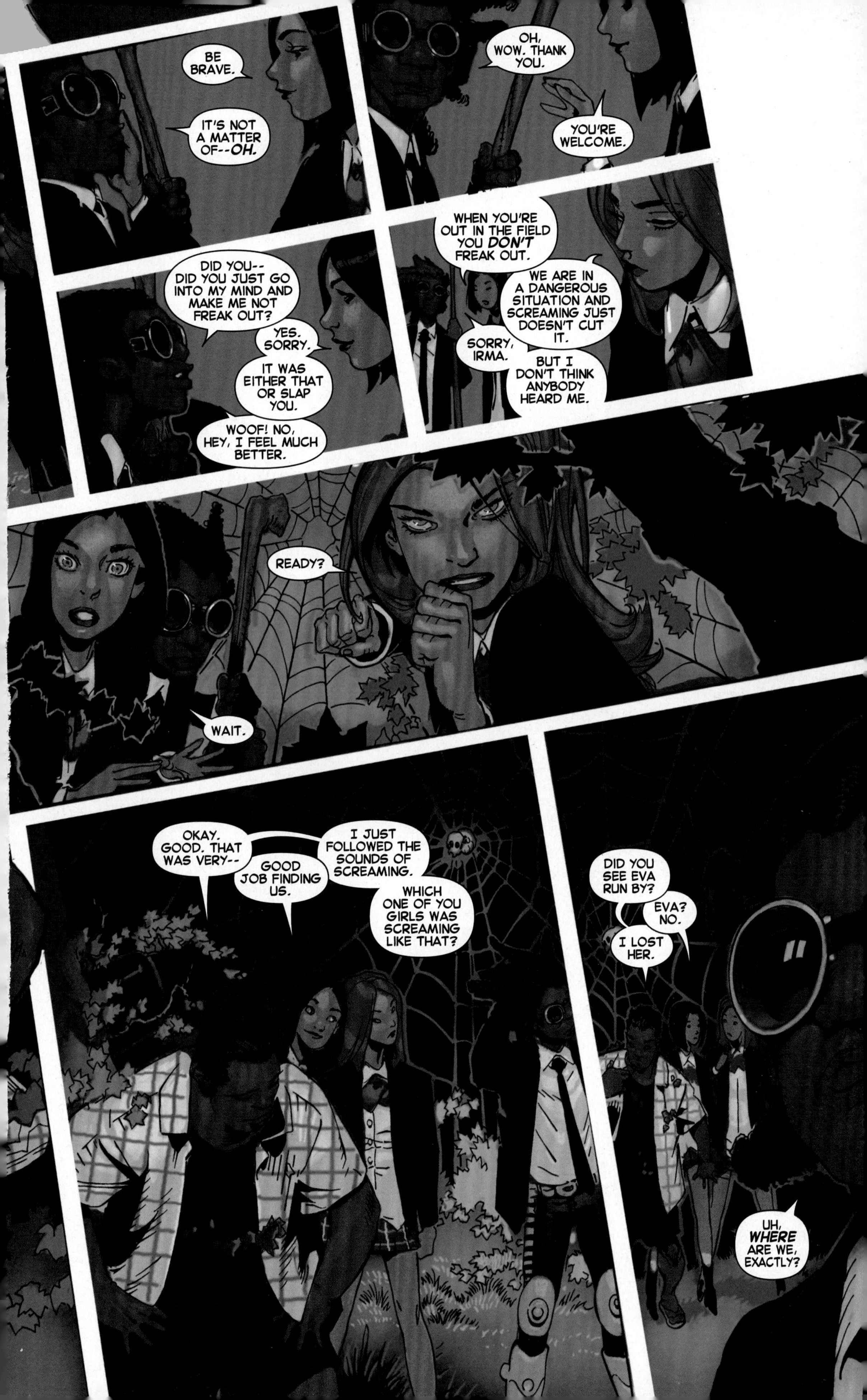
BE BRAVE.
IT'S NOT A MATTER OF--OH.
OH, WOW. THANK YOU.
YOU'RE WELCOME.
DID YOU-- DID YOU JUST GO INTO MY MIND AND MAKE ME NOT FREAK OUT?
YES. SORRY.
IT WAS EITHER THAT OR SLAP YOU.
WOOF! NO, HEY, I FEEL MUCH BETTER.
WHEN YOU'RE OUT IN THE FIELD YOU DON'T FREAK OUT.
WE ARE IN A DANGEROUS SITUATION AND SCREAMING JUST DOESN'T CUT IT.
SORRY, IRMA.
BUT I DON'T THINK ANYBODY HEARD ME.
READY?
WAIT.
OKAY. GOOD. THAT WAS VERY--
I JUST FOLLOWED THE SOUNDS OF SCREAMING.
GOOD JOB FINDING US.
WHICH ONE OF YOU GIRLS WAS SCREAMING LIKE THAT?
DID YOU SEE EVA RUN BY?
EVA? NO.
I LOST HER.
UH, WHERE ARE WE, EXACTLY?

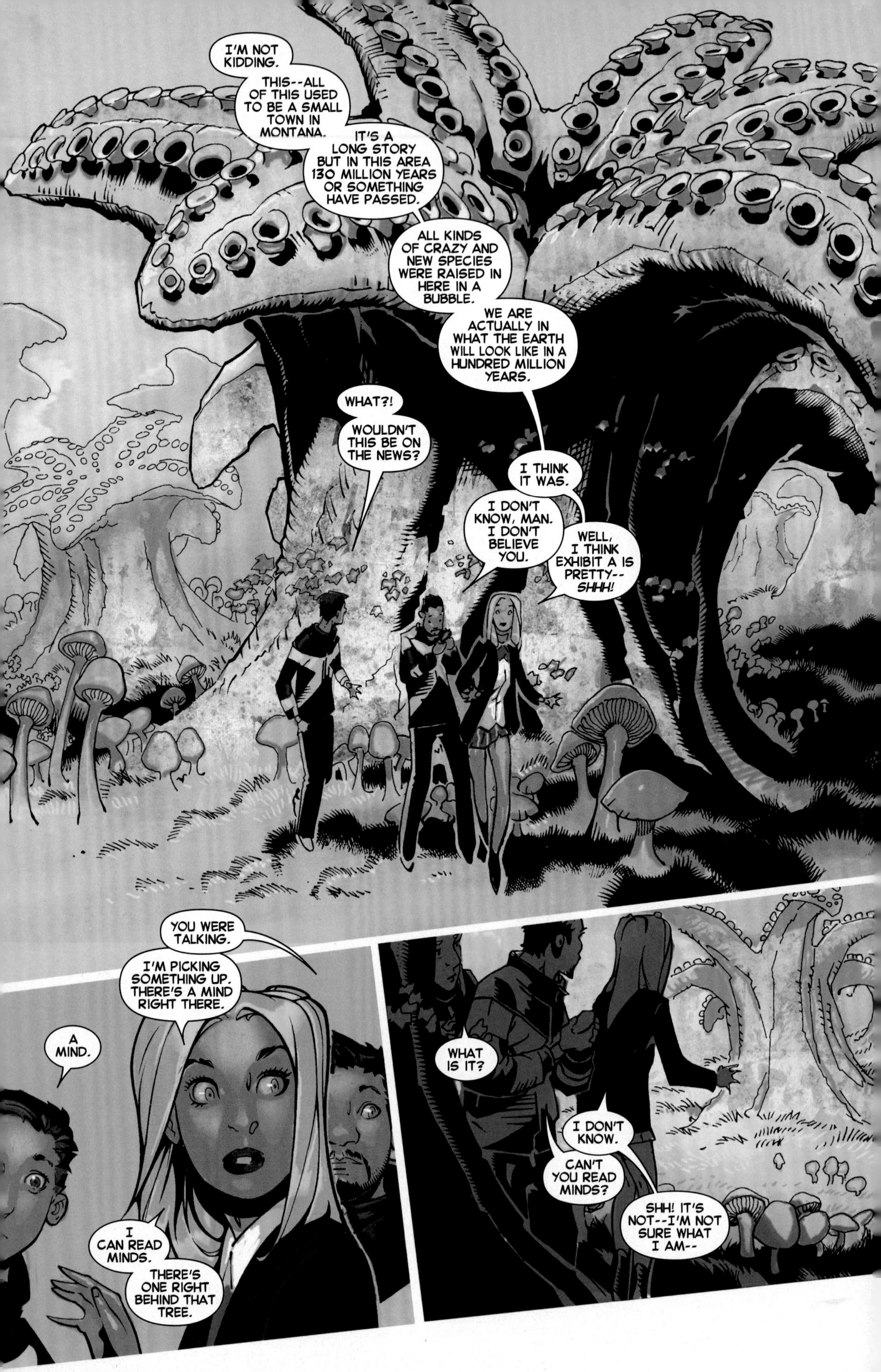
I'M NOT KIDDING.
THIS--ALL OF THIS USED TO BE A SMALL TOWN IN MONTANA.
IT'S A LONG STORY BUT IN THIS AREA 130 MILLION YEARS OR SOMETHING HAVE PASSED.
ALL KINDS OF CRAZY AND NEW SPECIES WERE RAISED IN HERE IN A BUBBLE.
WE ARE ACTUALLY IN WHAT THE EARTH WILL LOOK LIKE IN A HUNDRED MILLION YEARS.
WHAT?!
WOULDN'T THIS BE ON THE NEWS?
I THINK IT WAS.
I DON'T KNOW, MAN. I DON'T BELIEVE YOU.
WELL, I THINK EXHIBIT A IS PRETTY--
SHHH!
YOU WERE TALKING.
I'M PICKING SOMETHING UP. THERE'S A MIND RIGHT THERE.
A MIND.
I CAN READ MINDS.
THERE'S ONE RIGHT BEHIND THAT TREE.
WHAT IS IT?
I DON'T KNOW.
CAN'T YOU READ MINDS?
SHH! IT'S NOT--I'M NOT SURE WHAT I AM--

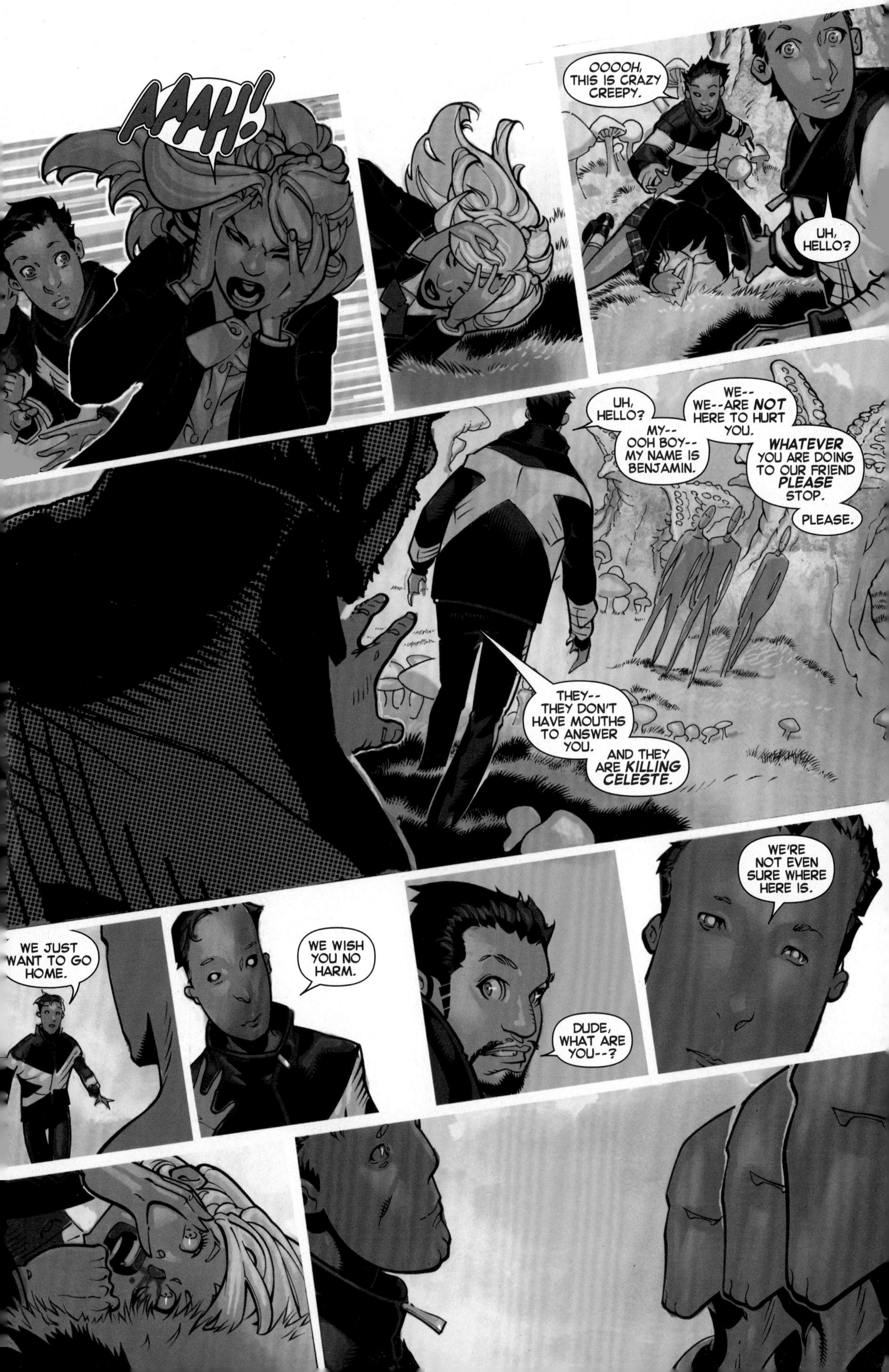
AAAH!
OOOOH, THIS IS CRAZY CREEPY.
UH, HELLO?
UH, HELLO?
MY-- OOH BOY-- MY NAME IS BENJAMIN.
WE-- WE--ARE NOT HERE TO HURT YOU.
WHATEVER YOU ARE DOING TO OUR FRIEND PLEASE STOP.
PLEASE.
THEY-- THEY DON'T HAVE MOUTHS TO ANSWER YOU.
AND THEY ARE KILLING CELESTE.
WE JUST WANT TO GO HOME.
WE WISH YOU NO HARM.
DUDE, WHAT ARE YOU--?
WE'RE NOT EVEN SURE WHERE HERE IS.

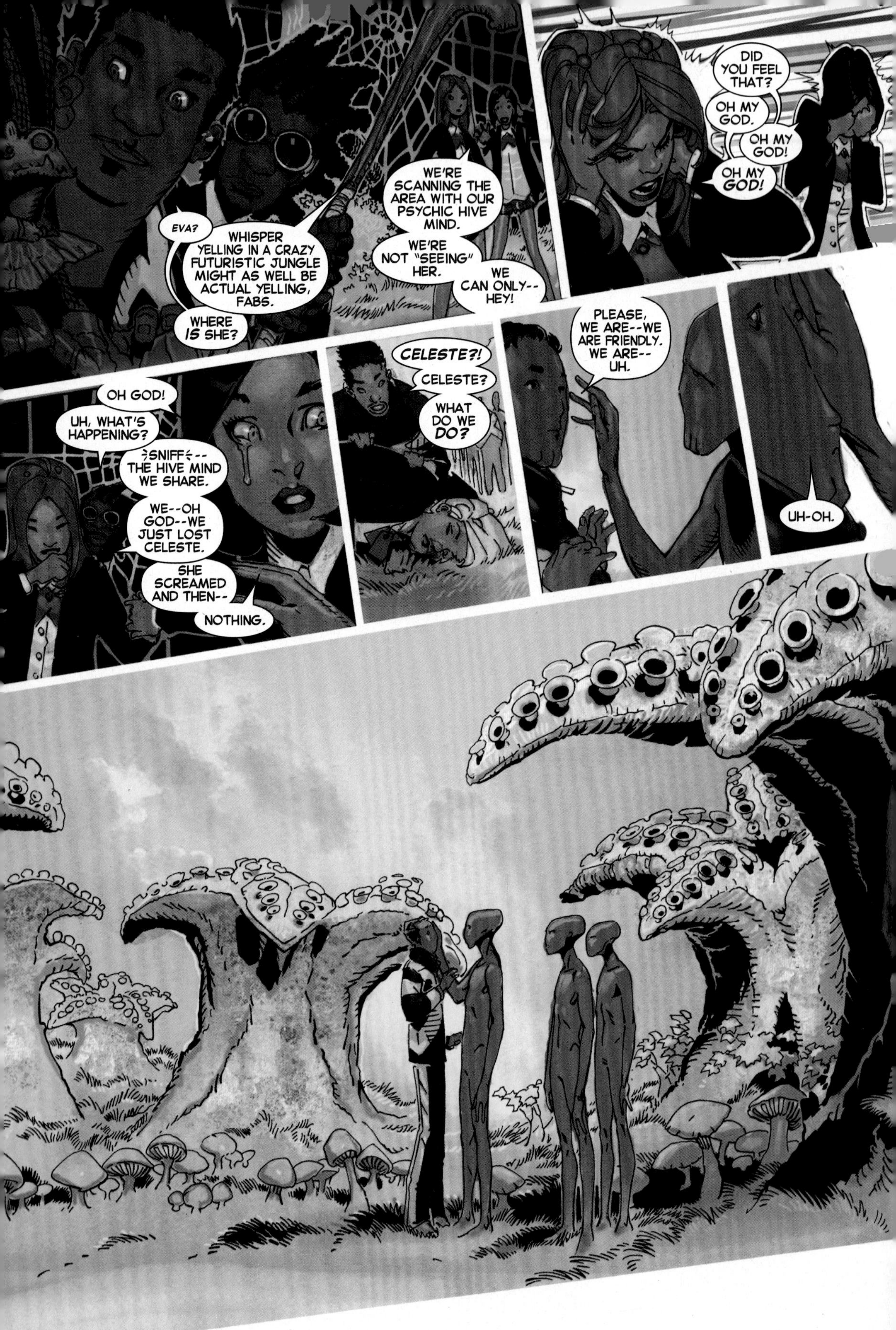
EVA?
WHISPER YELLING IN A CRAZY FUTURISTIC JUNGLE MIGHT AS WELL BE ACTUAL YELLING, FABS.
WHERE IS SHE?
WE'RE SCANNING THE AREA WITH OUR PSYCHIC HIVE MIND.
WE'RE NOT "SEEING" HER.
WE CAN ONLY--HEY!
DID YOU FEEL THAT?
OH MY GOD.
OH MY GOD!
OH MY GOD!
OH GOD!
UH, WHAT'S HAPPENING?
SNIFF--THE HIVE MIND WE SHARE.
WE--OH GOD--WE JUST LOST CELESTE.
SHE SCREAMED AND THEN--
NOTHING.
CELESTE?!
CELESTE?
WHAT DO WE DO?
PLEASE, WE ARE--WE ARE FRIENDLY. WE ARE--UH.
UH-OH.

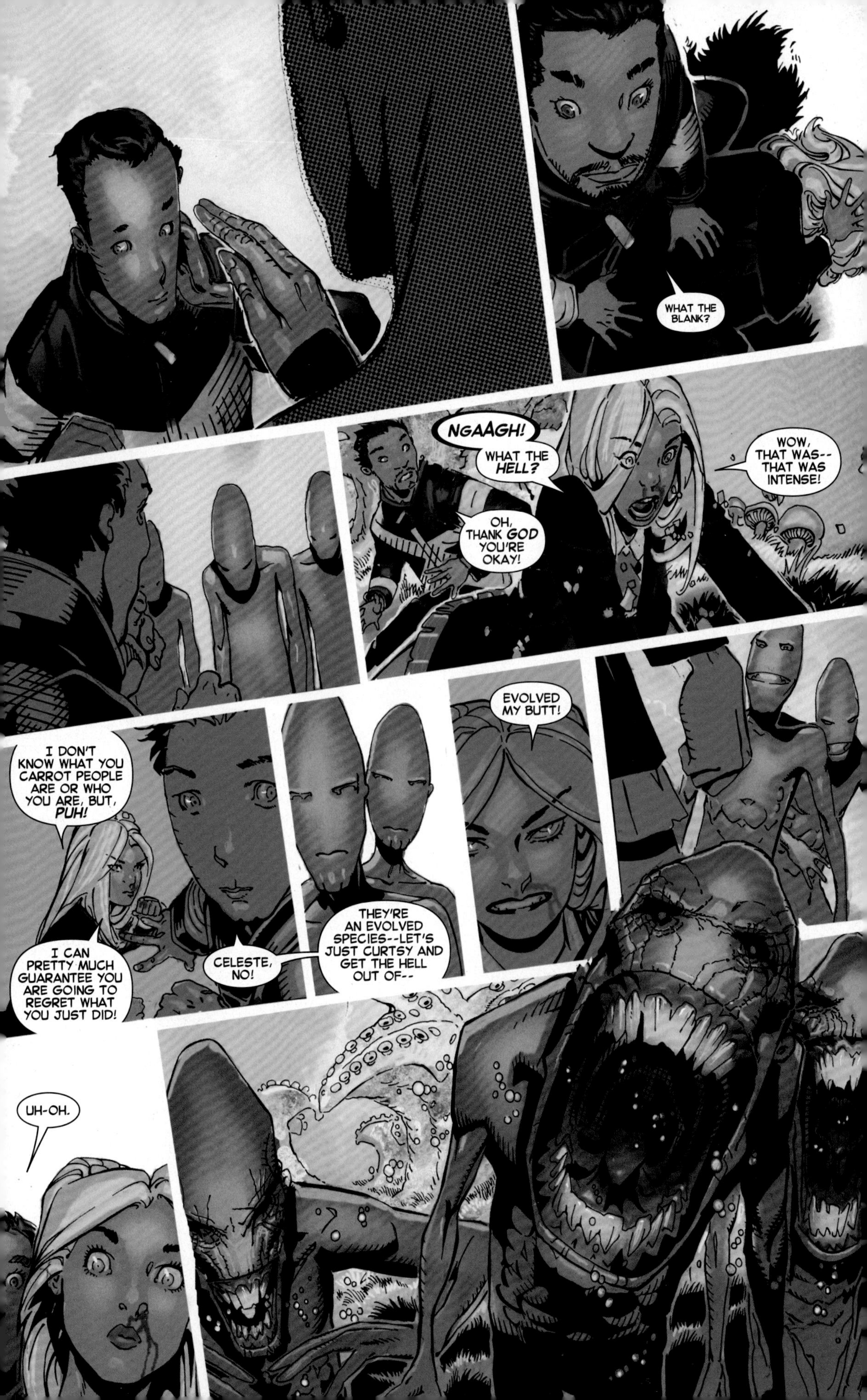

WHAT THE BLANK?
NGAAGH!
WHAT THE HELL?
OH, THANK GOD YOU'RE OKAY!
WOW, THAT WAS-- THAT WAS INTENSE!
I DON'T KNOW WHAT YOU CARROT PEOPLE ARE OR WHO YOU ARE, BUT, PUH!
I CAN PRETTY MUCH GUARANTEE YOU ARE GOING TO REGRET WHAT YOU JUST DID!
CELESTE, NO!
THEY'RE AN EVOLVED SPECIES--LET'S JUST CURTSY AND GET THE HELL OUT OF--
EVOLVED MY BUTT!
UH-OH.

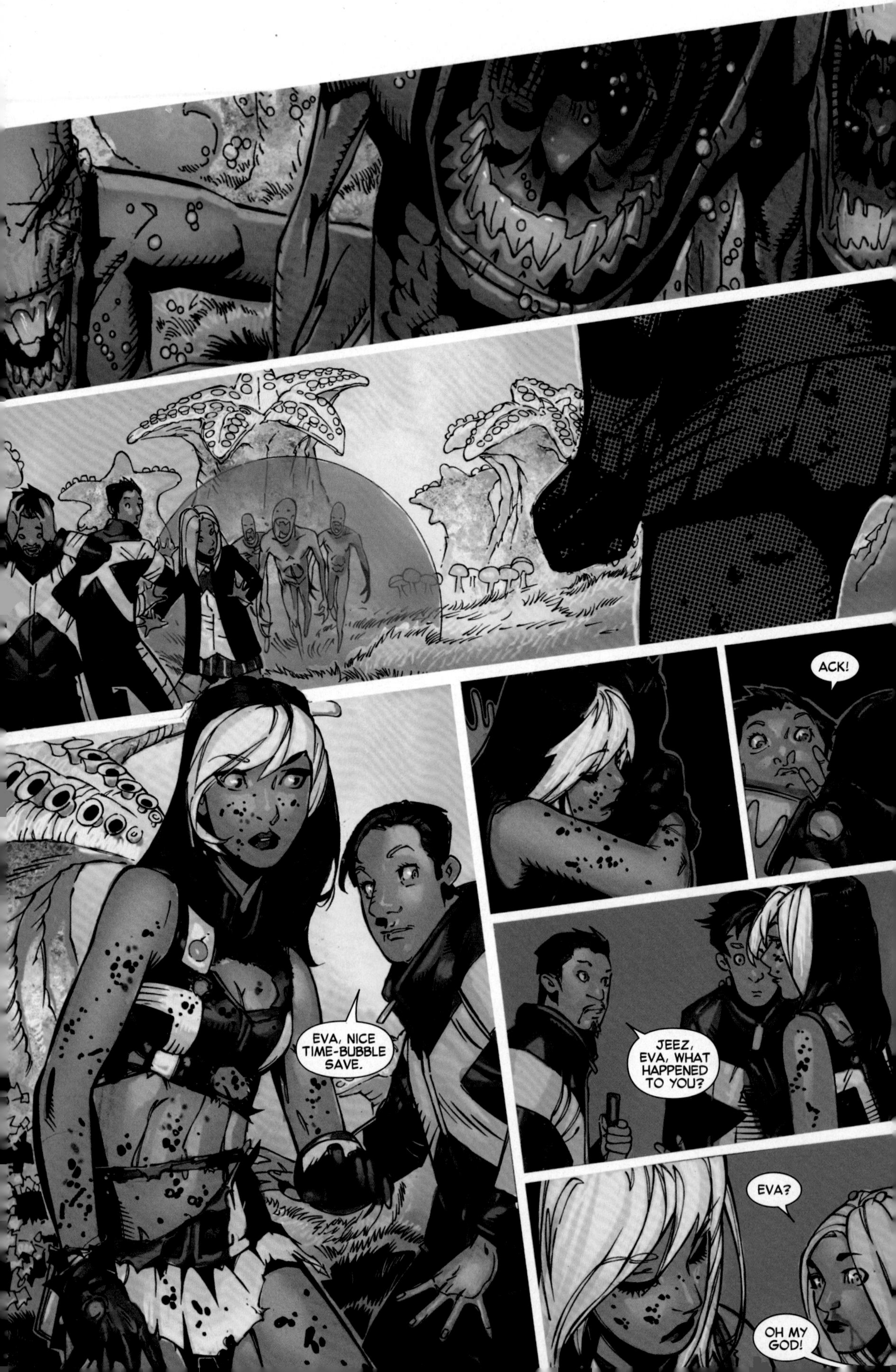
EVA, NICE TIME-BUBBLE SAVE.
ACK!
JEEZ, EVA, WHAT HAPPENED TO YOU?
EVA?
OH MY GOD!

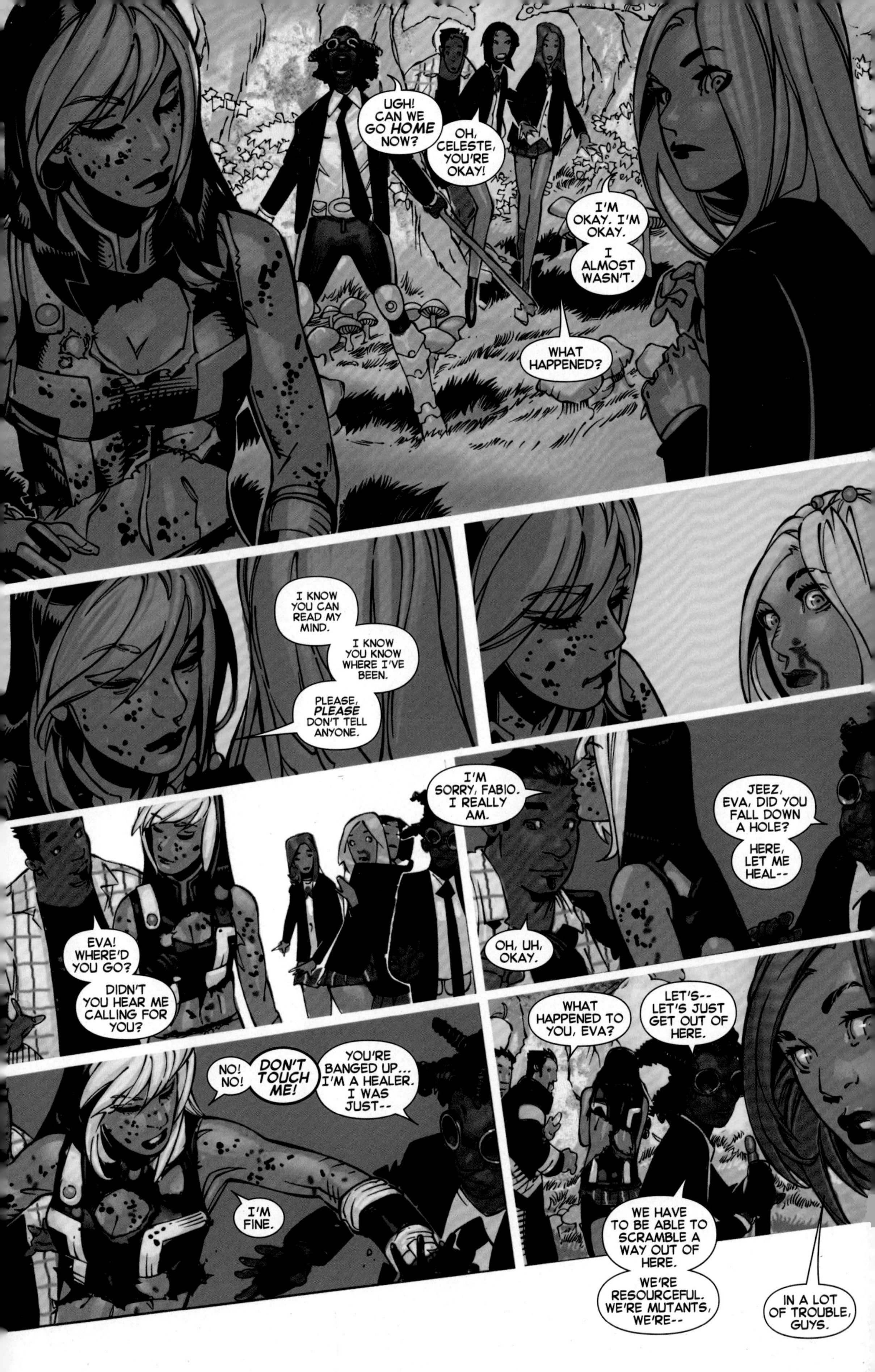
UGH! CAN WE GO *HOME* NOW?
OH, CELESTE, YOU'RE OKAY!
I'M OKAY. I'M OKAY.
I ALMOST WASN'T.
WHAT HAPPENED?
I KNOW YOU CAN READ MY MIND.
I KNOW YOU KNOW WHERE I'VE BEEN.
PLEASE, *PLEASE* DON'T TELL ANYONE.
EVA! WHERE'D YOU GO?
DIDN'T YOU HEAR ME CALLING FOR YOU?
I'M SORRY, FABIO. I REALLY AM.
OH, UH, OKAY.
JEEZ, EVA, DID YOU FALL DOWN A HOLE?
HERE, LET ME HEAL--
NO! NO!
DON'T TOUCH ME!
YOU'RE BANGED UP... I'M A HEALER. I WAS JUST--
I'M FINE.
WHAT HAPPENED TO YOU, EVA?
LET'S-- LET'S JUST GET OUT OF HERE.
WE HAVE TO BE ABLE TO SCRAMBLE A WAY OUT OF HERE.
WE'RE RESOURCEFUL. WE'RE MUTANTS, WE'RE--
IN A LOT OF TROUBLE, GUYS.

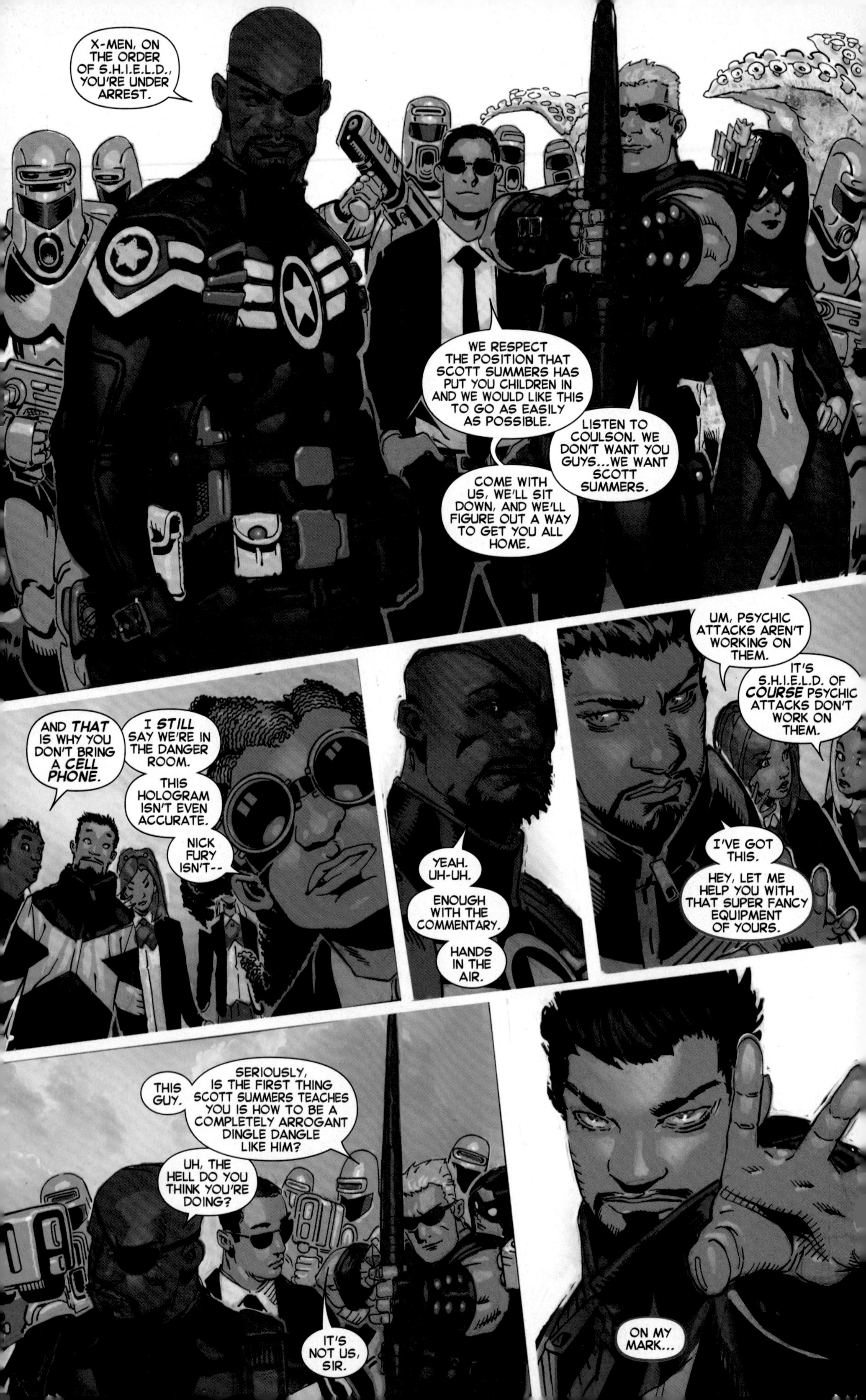
X-MEN, ON THE ORDER OF S.H.I.E.L.D., YOU'RE UNDER ARREST.
WE RESPECT THE POSITION THAT SCOTT SUMMERS HAS PUT YOU CHILDREN IN AND WE WOULD LIKE THIS TO GO AS EASILY AS POSSIBLE.
COME WITH US, WE'LL SIT DOWN, AND WE'LL FIGURE OUT A WAY TO GET YOU ALL HOME.
LISTEN TO COULSON. WE DON'T WANT YOU GUYS...WE WANT SCOTT SUMMERS.
AND *THAT* IS WHY YOU DON'T BRING A *CELL PHONE*.
I *STILL* SAY WE'RE IN THE DANGER ROOM.
THIS HOLOGRAM ISN'T EVEN ACCURATE.
NICK FURY ISN'T--
YEAH. UH-UH.
ENOUGH WITH THE COMMENTARY.
HANDS IN THE AIR.
UM, PSYCHIC ATTACKS AREN'T WORKING ON THEM.
IT'S S.H.I.E.L.D. OF *COURSE* PSYCHIC ATTACKS DON'T WORK ON THEM.
I'VE GOT THIS.
HEY, LET ME HELP YOU WITH THAT SUPER FANCY EQUIPMENT OF YOURS.
THIS GUY.
SERIOUSLY, IS THE FIRST THING SCOTT SUMMERS TEACHES YOU IS HOW TO BE A COMPLETELY ARROGANT DINGLE DANGLE LIKE HIM?
UH, THE HELL DO YOU THINK YOU'RE DOING?
IT'S NOT US, SIR.
ON MY MARK...

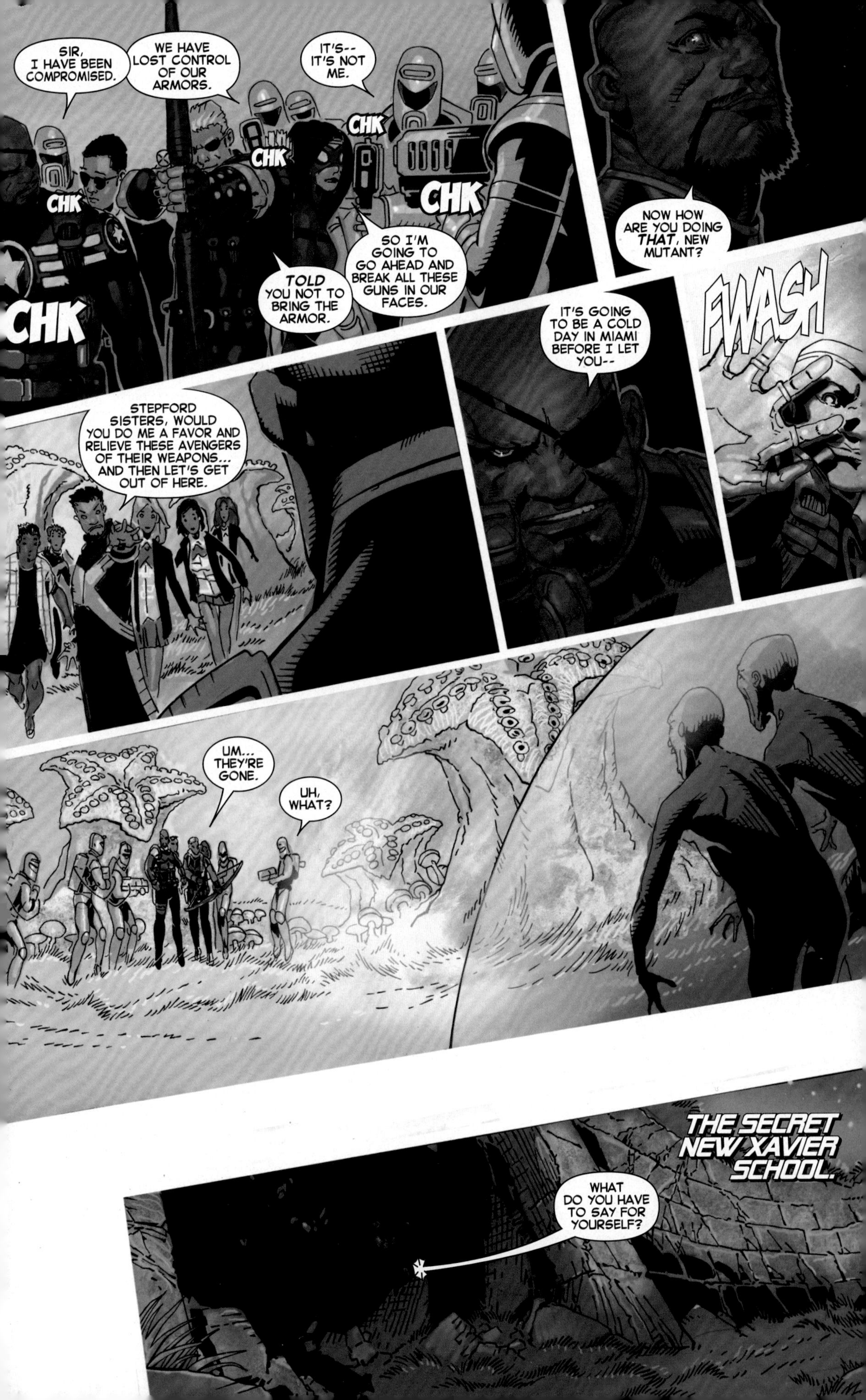
SIR, I HAVE BEEN COMPROMISED.
WE HAVE LOST CONTROL OF OUR ARMORS.
IT'S-- IT'S NOT ME.
CHK
CHK
CHK
CHK
CHK
TOLD YOU NOT TO BRING THE ARMOR.
SO I'M GOING TO GO AHEAD AND BREAK ALL THESE GUNS IN OUR FACES.
NOW HOW ARE YOU DOING THAT, NEW MUTANT?
STEPFORD SISTERS, WOULD YOU DO ME A FAVOR AND RELIEVE THESE AVENGERS OF THEIR WEAPONS... AND THEN LET'S GET OUT OF HERE.
IT'S GOING TO BE A COLD DAY IN MIAMI BEFORE I LET YOU--
FWASH
UM... THEY'RE GONE.
UH, WHAT?
THE SECRET NEW XAVIER SCHOOL.
WHAT DO YOU HAVE TO SAY FOR YOURSELF?

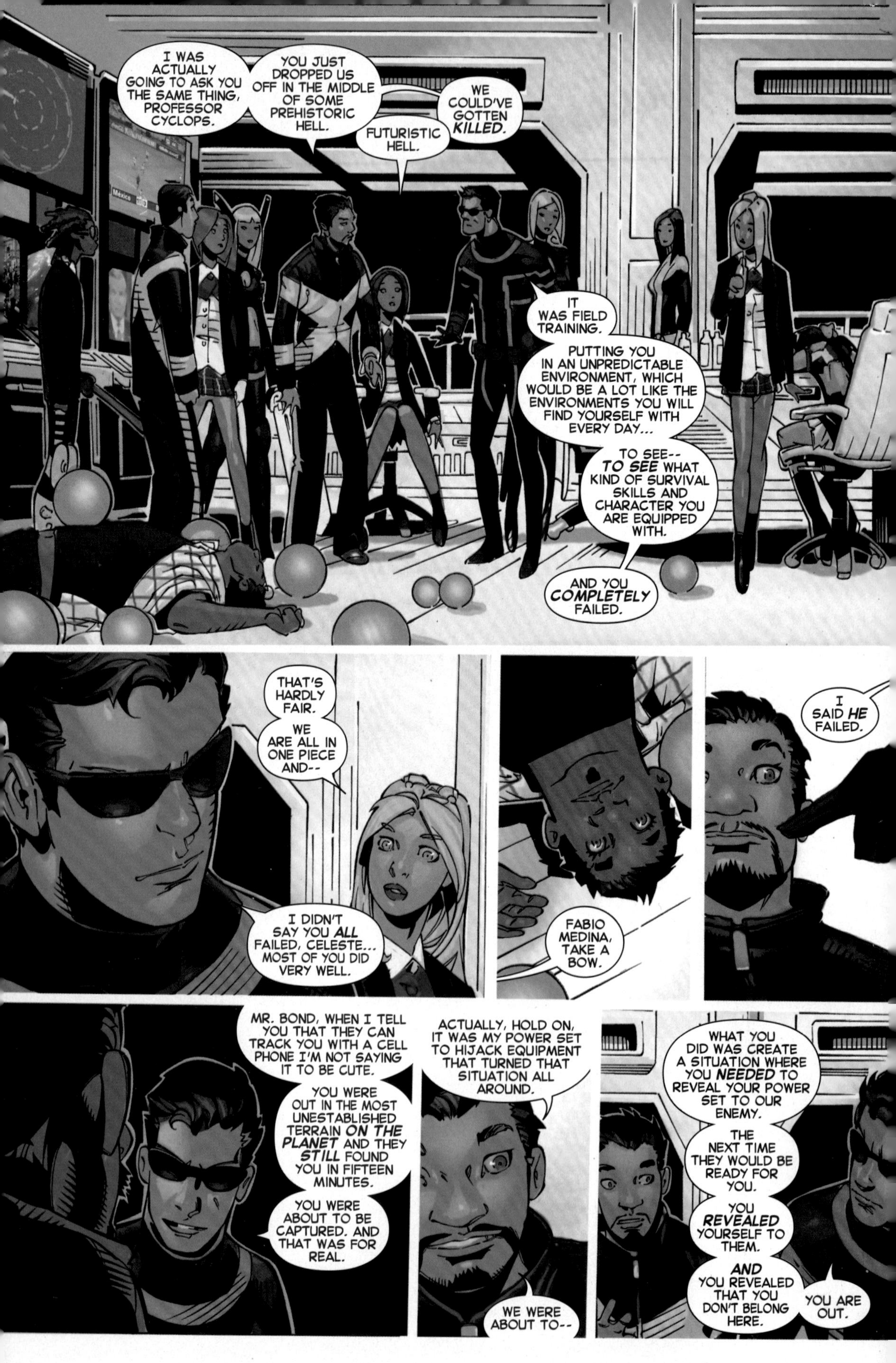
I WAS ACTUALLY GOING TO ASK YOU THE SAME THING, PROFESSOR CYCLOPS.
YOU JUST DROPPED US OFF IN THE MIDDLE OF SOME PREHISTORIC HELL.
WE COULD'VE GOTTEN KILLED.
FUTURISTIC HELL.
IT WAS FIELD TRAINING.
PUTTING YOU IN AN UNPREDICTABLE ENVIRONMENT, WHICH WOULD BE A LOT LIKE THE ENVIRONMENTS YOU WILL FIND YOURSELF WITH EVERY DAY...
TO SEE-- TO SEE WHAT KIND OF SURVIVAL SKILLS AND CHARACTER YOU ARE EQUIPPED WITH.
AND YOU COMPLETELY FAILED.
THAT'S HARDLY FAIR.
WE ARE ALL IN ONE PIECE AND--
I DIDN'T SAY YOU ALL FAILED, CELESTE... MOST OF YOU DID VERY WELL.
FABIO MEDINA, TAKE A BOW.
I SAID HE FAILED.
MR. BOND, WHEN I TELL YOU THAT THEY CAN TRACK YOU WITH A CELL PHONE I'M NOT SAYING IT TO BE CUTE.
YOU WERE OUT IN THE MOST UNESTABLISHED TERRAIN ON THE PLANET AND THEY STILL FOUND YOU IN FIFTEEN MINUTES.
YOU WERE ABOUT TO BE CAPTURED. AND THAT WAS FOR REAL.
ACTUALLY, HOLD ON, IT WAS MY POWER SET TO HIJACK EQUIPMENT THAT TURNED THAT SITUATION ALL AROUND.
WE WERE ABOUT TO--
WHAT YOU DID WAS CREATE A SITUATION WHERE YOU NEEDED TO REVEAL YOUR POWER SET TO OUR ENEMY.
THE NEXT TIME THEY WOULD BE READY FOR YOU.
YOU REVEALED YOURSELF TO THEM.
AND YOU REVEALED THAT YOU DON'T BELONG HERE.
YOU ARE OUT.

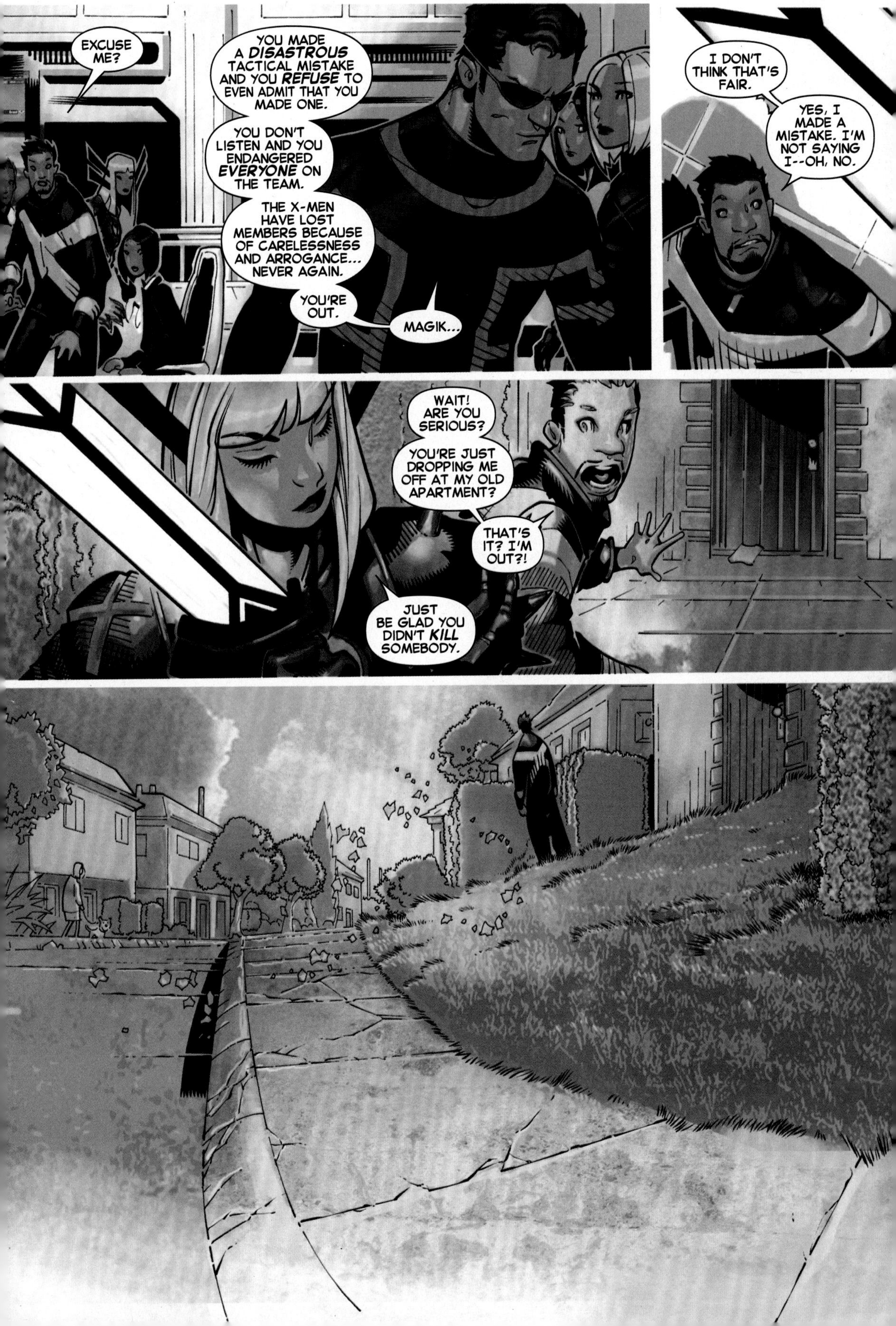
EXCUSE ME?
YOU MADE A DISASTROUS TACTICAL MISTAKE AND YOU REFUSE TO EVEN ADMIT THAT YOU MADE ONE.
YOU DON'T LISTEN AND YOU ENDANGERED EVERYONE ON THE TEAM.
THE X-MEN HAVE LOST MEMBERS BECAUSE OF CARELESSNESS AND ARROGANCE... NEVER AGAIN.
YOU'RE OUT.
MAGIK...
I DON'T THINK THAT'S FAIR.
YES, I MADE A MISTAKE. I'M NOT SAYING I--OH, NO.
WAIT! ARE YOU SERIOUS?
YOU'RE JUST DROPPING ME OFF AT MY OLD APARTMENT?
THAT'S IT? I'M OUT?!
JUST BE GLAD YOU DIDN'T KILL SOMEBODY.

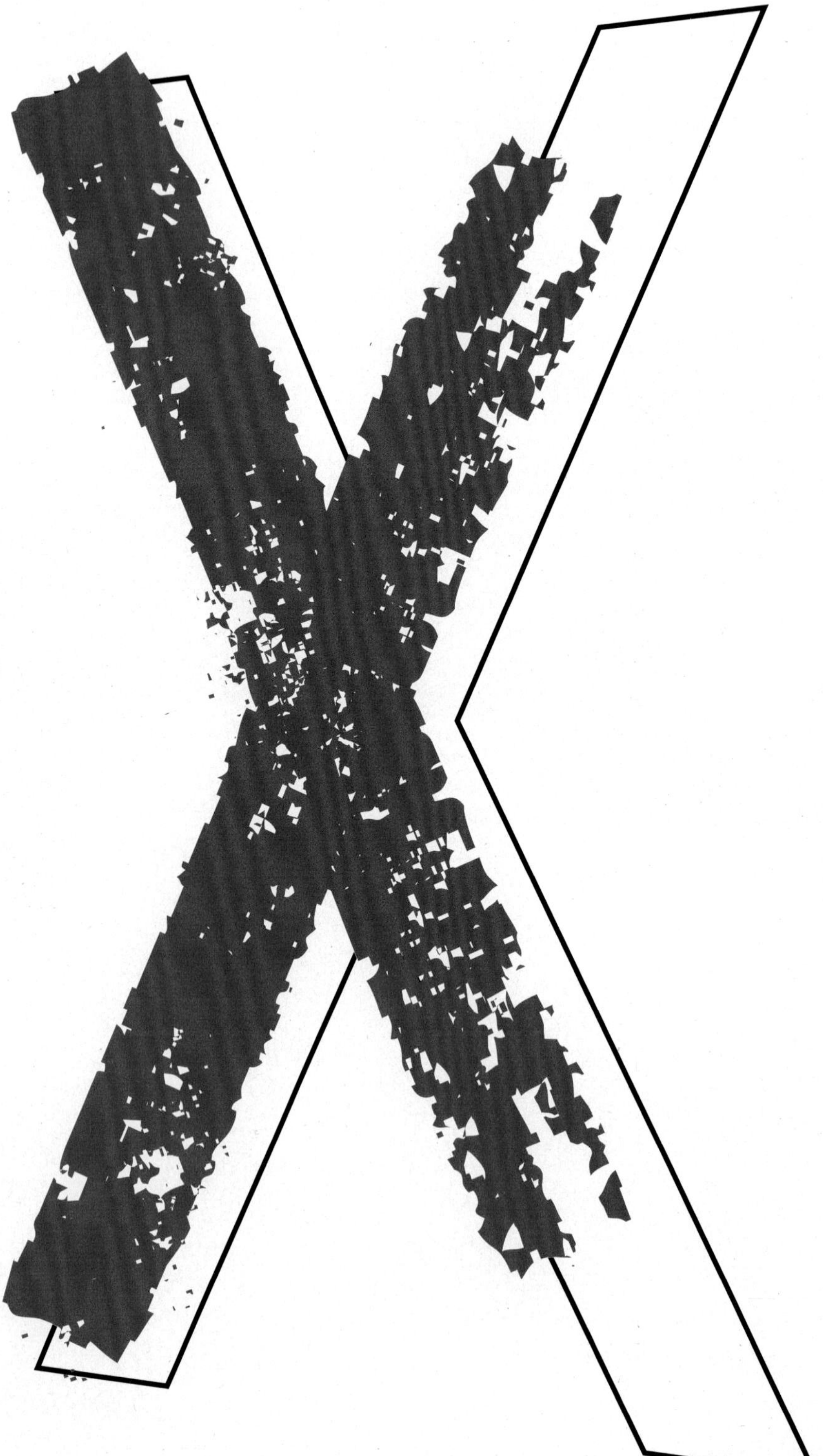

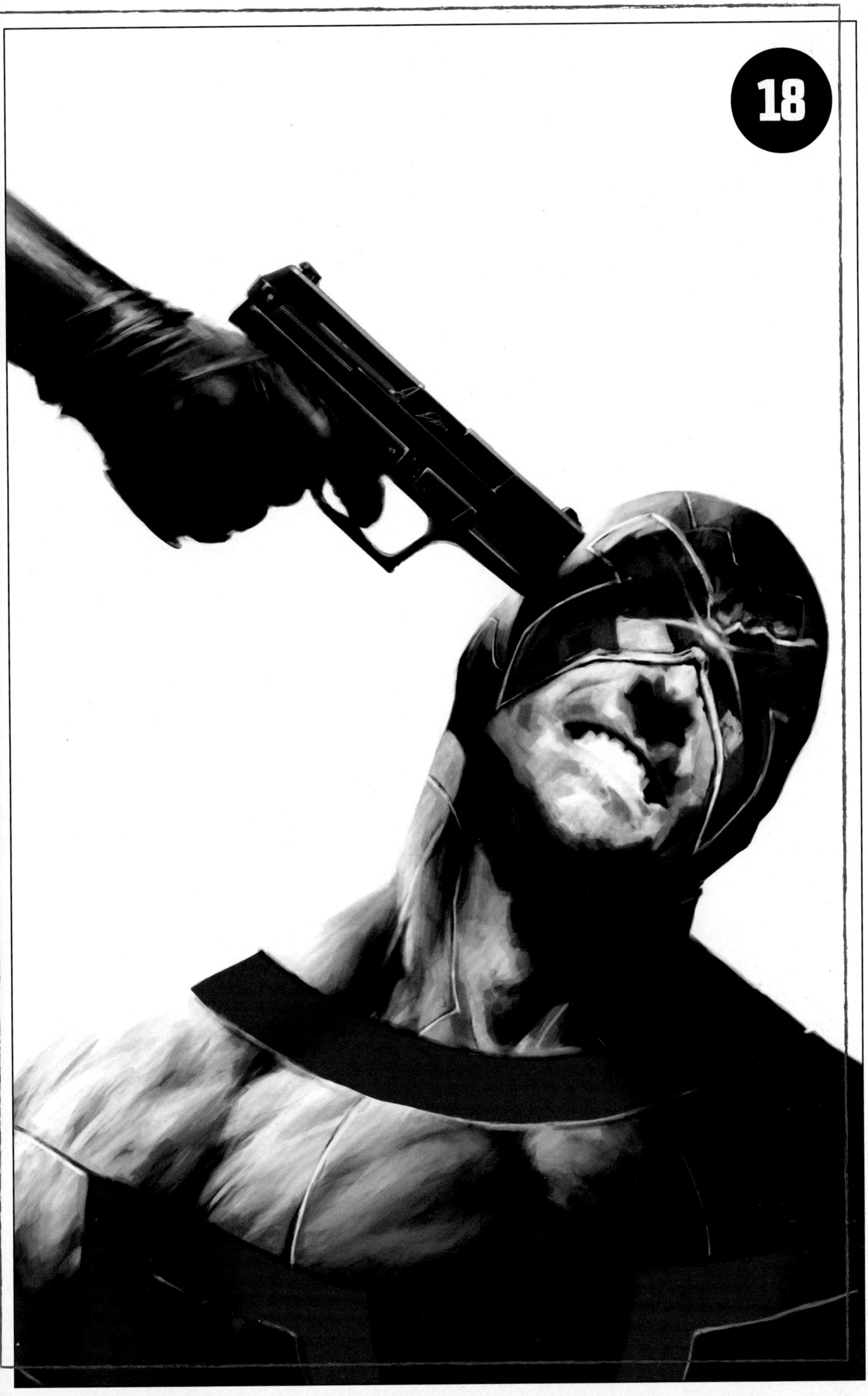
18

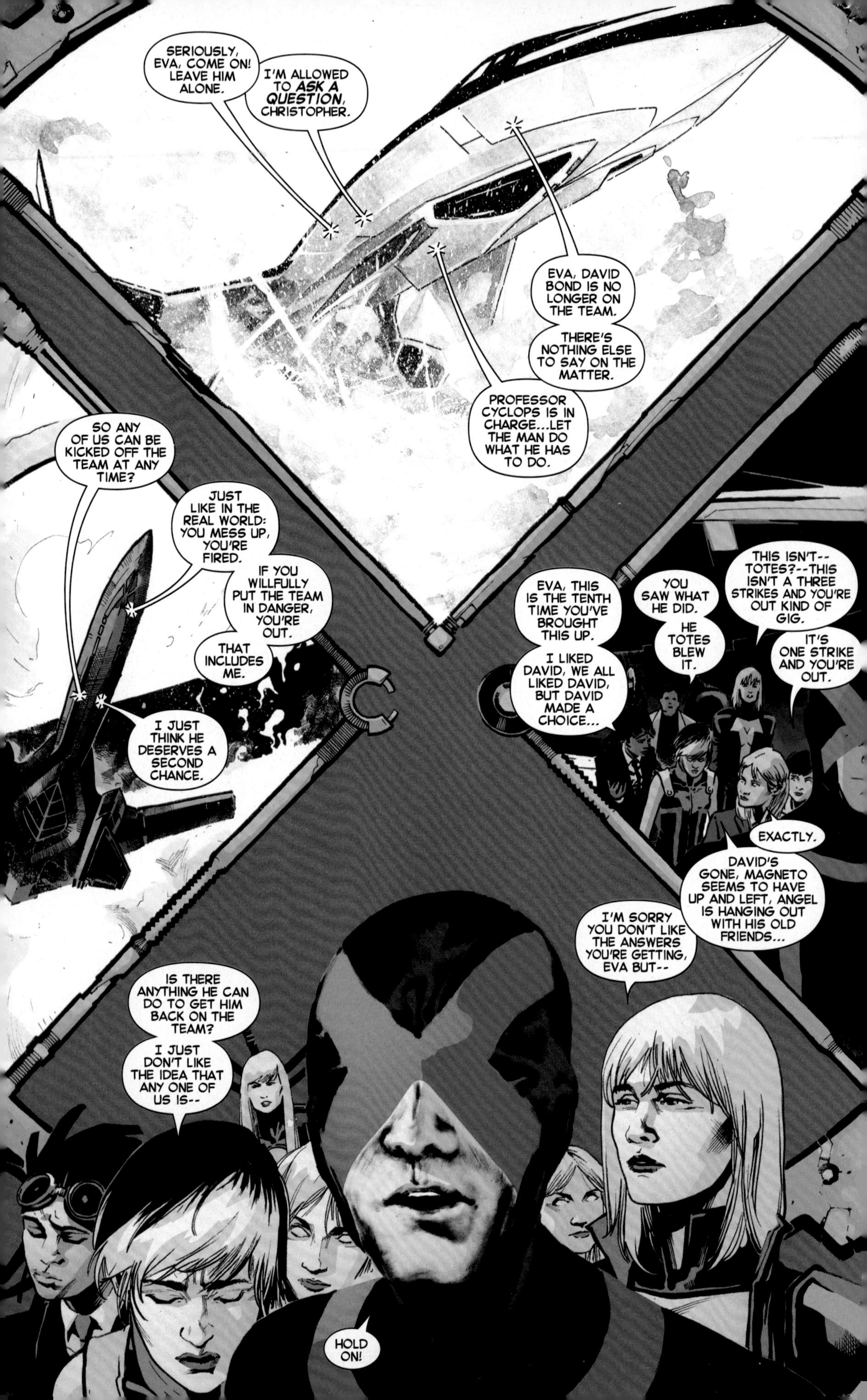
SERIOUSLY, EVA, COME ON! LEAVE HIM ALONE.
I'M ALLOWED TO ASK A QUESTION, CHRISTOPHER.
EVA, DAVID BOND IS NO LONGER ON THE TEAM.
THERE'S NOTHING ELSE TO SAY ON THE MATTER.
PROFESSOR CYCLOPS IS IN CHARGE...LET THE MAN DO WHAT HE HAS TO DO.
SO ANY OF US CAN BE KICKED OFF THE TEAM AT ANY TIME?
JUST LIKE IN THE REAL WORLD: YOU MESS UP, YOU'RE FIRED.
IF YOU WILLFULLY PUT THE TEAM IN DANGER, YOU'RE OUT.
THAT INCLUDES ME.
I JUST THINK HE DESERVES A SECOND CHANCE.
EVA, THIS IS THE TENTH TIME YOU'VE BROUGHT THIS UP.
I LIKED DAVID, WE ALL LIKED DAVID, BUT DAVID MADE A CHOICE...
YOU SAW WHAT HE DID.
HE TOTES BLEW IT.
THIS ISN'T--TOTES?--THIS ISN'T A THREE STRIKES AND YOU'RE OUT KIND OF GIG.
IT'S ONE STRIKE AND YOU'RE OUT.
EXACTLY.
DAVID'S GONE, MAGNETO SEEMS TO HAVE UP AND LEFT, ANGEL IS HANGING OUT WITH HIS OLD FRIENDS...
I'M SORRY YOU DON'T LIKE THE ANSWERS YOU'RE GETTING, EVA BUT--
IS THERE ANYTHING HE CAN DO TO GET HIM BACK ON THE TEAM?
I JUST DON'T LIKE THE IDEA THAT ANY ONE OF US IS--
HOLD ON!

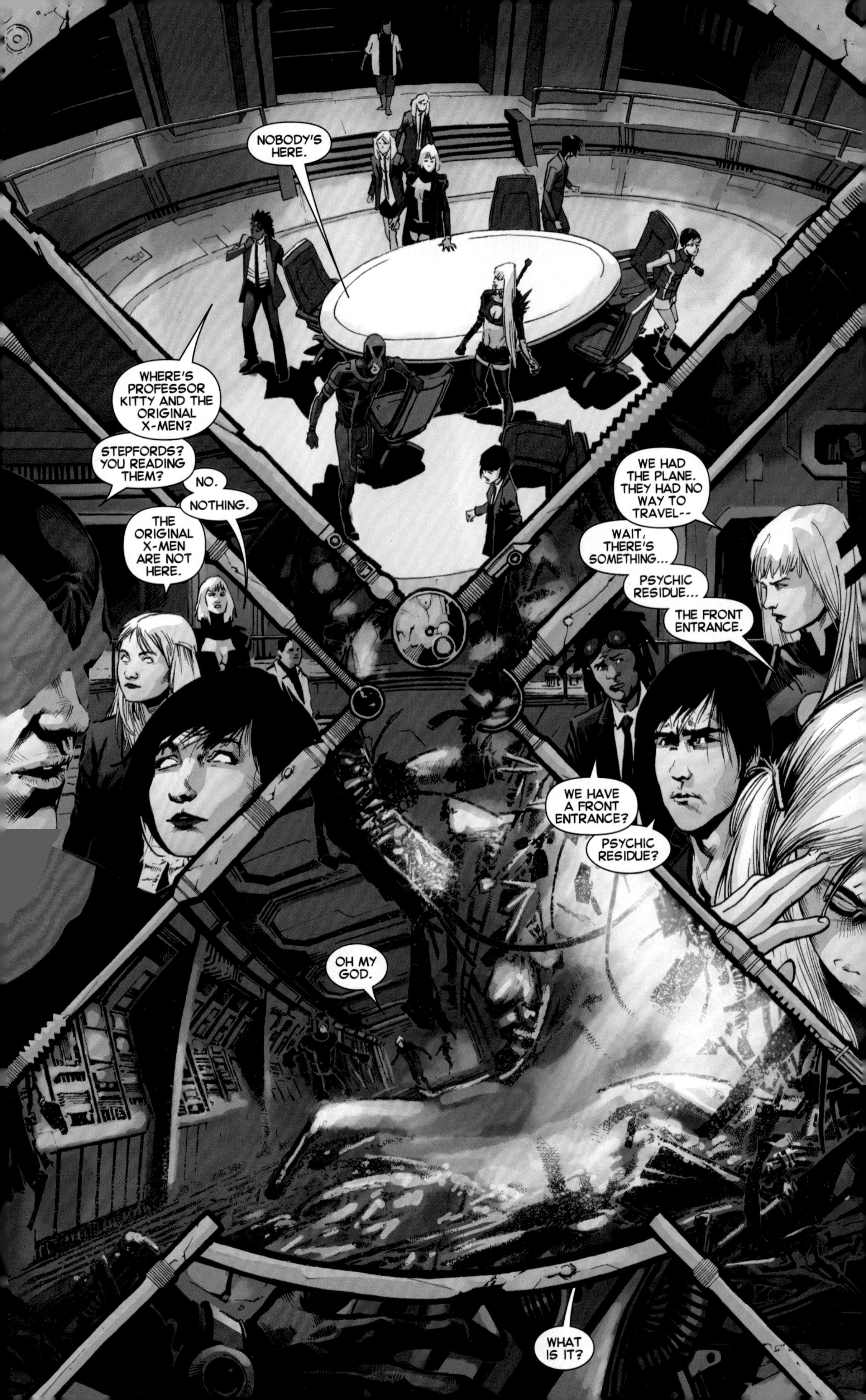
NOBODY'S HERE.
WHERE'S PROFESSOR KITTY AND THE ORIGINAL X-MEN?
STEPFORDS? YOU READING THEM?
NO.
NOTHING.
THE ORIGINAL X-MEN ARE NOT HERE.
WE HAD THE PLANE. THEY HAD NO WAY TO TRAVEL--
WAIT, THERE'S SOMETHING...
PSYCHIC RESIDUE...
THE FRONT ENTRANCE.
WE HAVE A FRONT ENTRANCE?
PSYCHIC RESIDUE?
OH MY GOD.
WHAT IS IT?

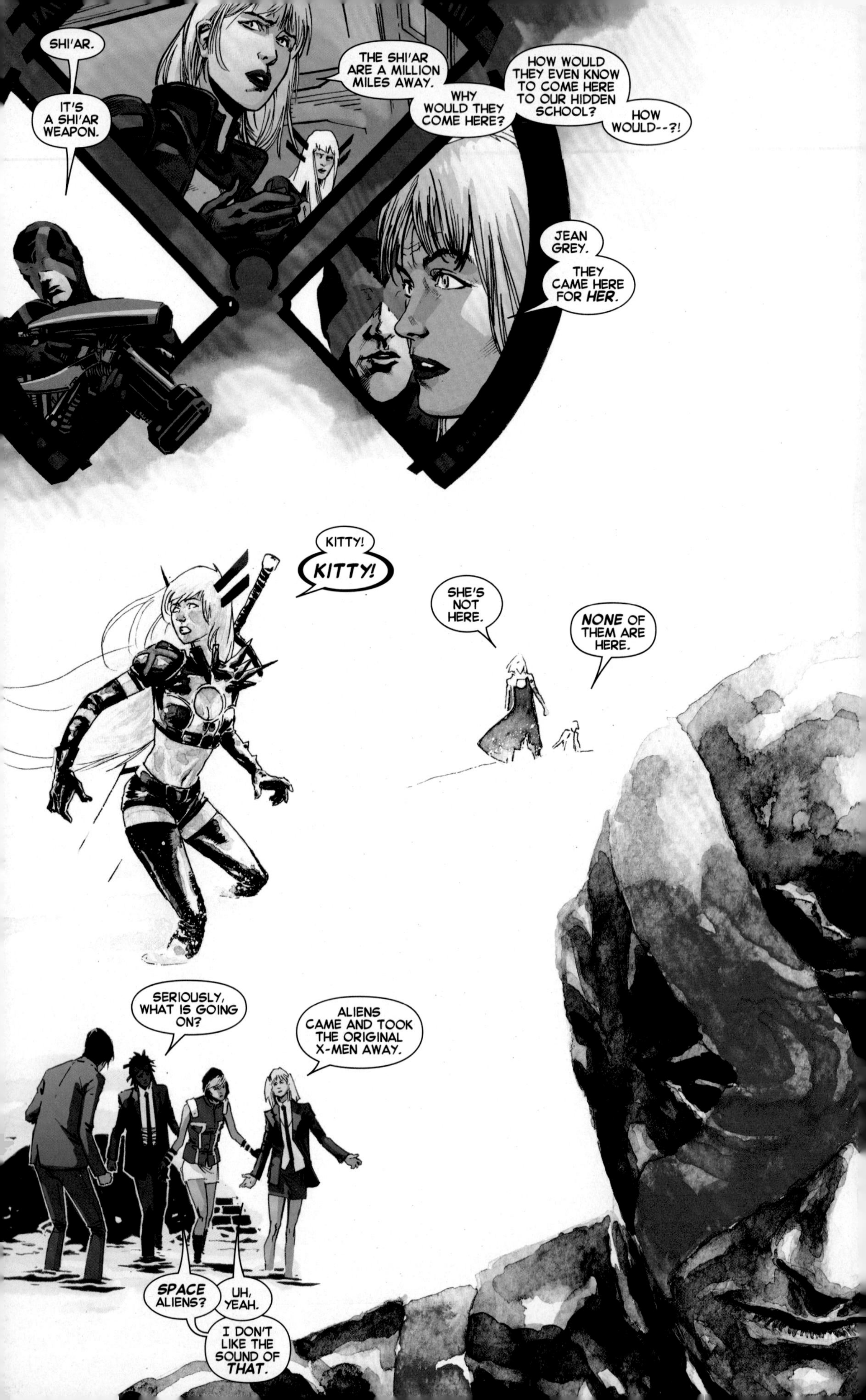
SHI'AR.
IT'S A SHI'AR WEAPON.
THE SHI'AR ARE A MILLION MILES AWAY.
WHY WOULD THEY COME HERE?
HOW WOULD THEY EVEN KNOW TO COME HERE TO OUR HIDDEN SCHOOL?
HOW WOULD--?!
JEAN GREY.
THEY CAME HERE FOR HER.
KITTY!
KITTY!
SHE'S NOT HERE.
NONE OF THEM ARE HERE.
SERIOUSLY, WHAT IS GOING ON?
ALIENS CAME AND TOOK THE ORIGINAL X-MEN AWAY.
SPACE ALIENS?
UH, YEAH.
I DON'T LIKE THE SOUND OF THAT.

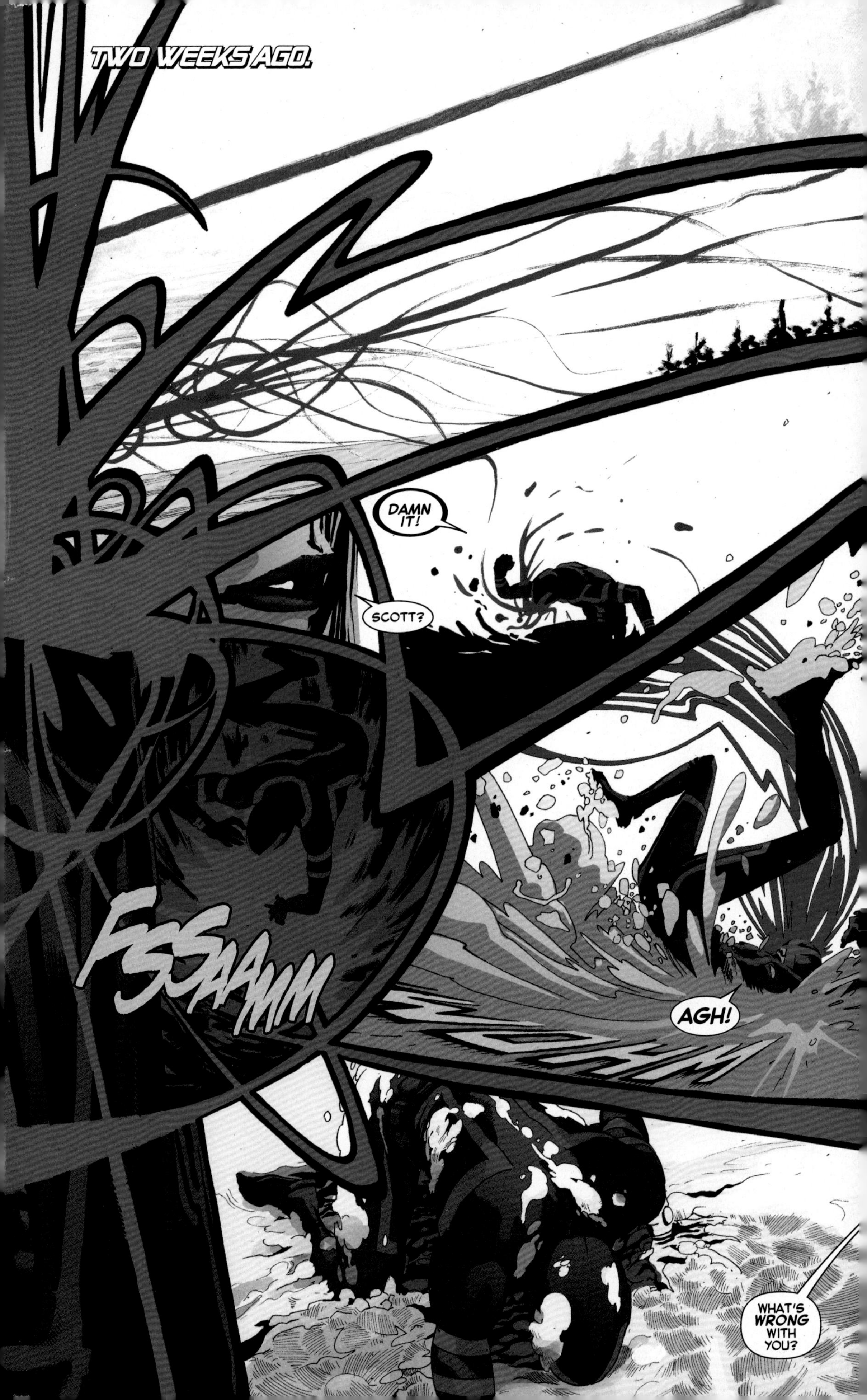
TWO WEEKS AGO.
DAMN IT!
SCOTT?
FSSAAMM
AGH!
WHAT'S WRONG WITH YOU?

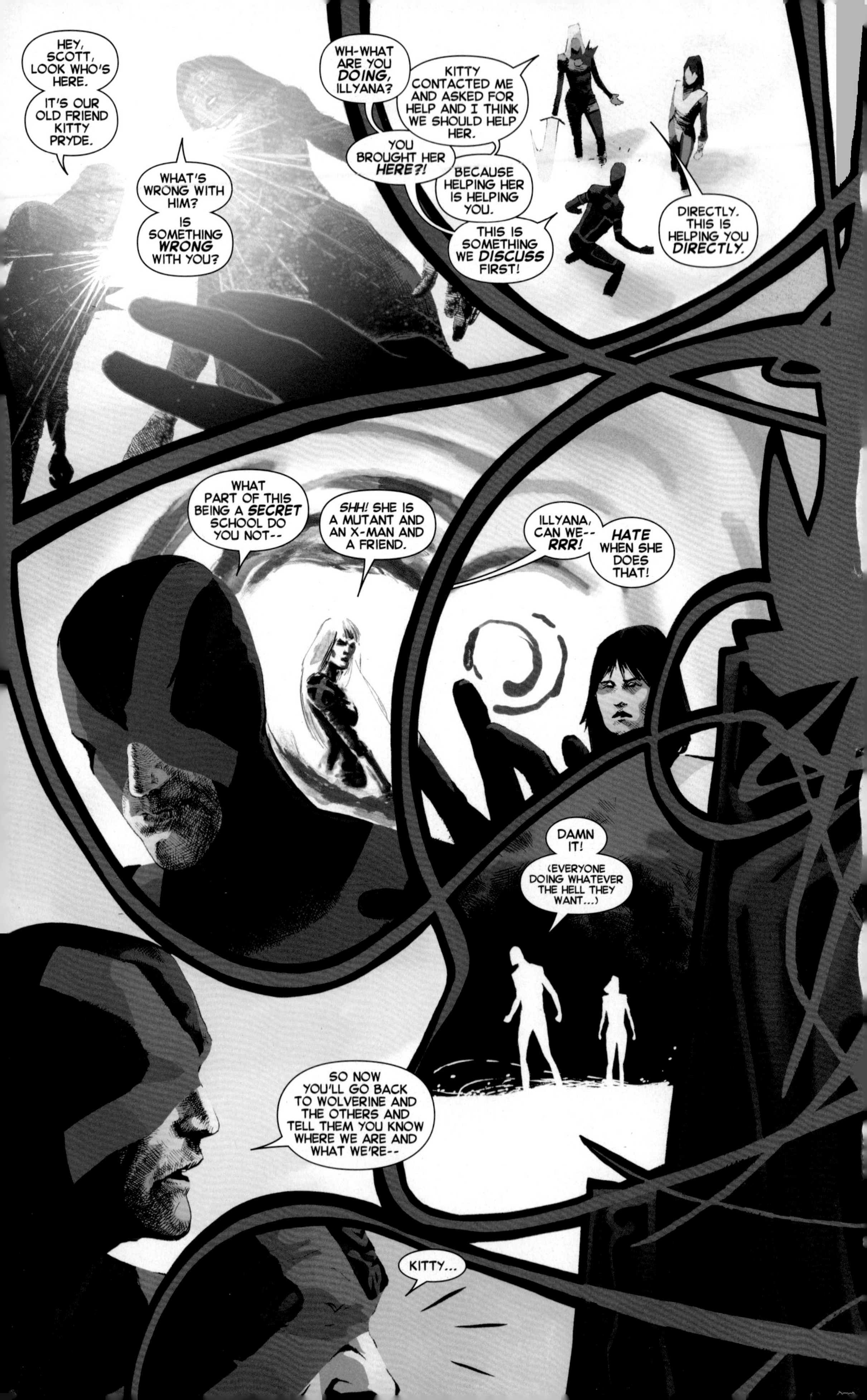
HEY, SCOTT, LOOK WHO'S HERE.
IT'S OUR OLD FRIEND KITTY PRYDE.
WHAT'S WRONG WITH HIM?
IS SOMETHING WRONG WITH YOU?
WH-WHAT ARE YOU DOING, ILLYANA?
KITTY CONTACTED ME AND ASKED FOR HELP AND I THINK WE SHOULD HELP HER.
YOU BROUGHT HER HERE?!
BECAUSE HELPING HER IS HELPING YOU.
THIS IS SOMETHING WE DISCUSS FIRST!
DIRECTLY. THIS IS HELPING YOU DIRECTLY.
WHAT PART OF THIS BEING A SECRET SCHOOL DO YOU NOT--
SHH! SHE IS A MUTANT AND AN X-MAN AND A FRIEND.
ILLYANA, CAN WE-- RRR!
HATE WHEN SHE DOES THAT!
DAMN IT!
(EVERYONE DOING WHATEVER THE HELL THEY WANT...)
SO NOW YOU'LL GO BACK TO WOLVERINE AND THE OTHERS AND TELL THEM YOU KNOW WHERE WE ARE AND WHAT WE'RE--
KITTY...

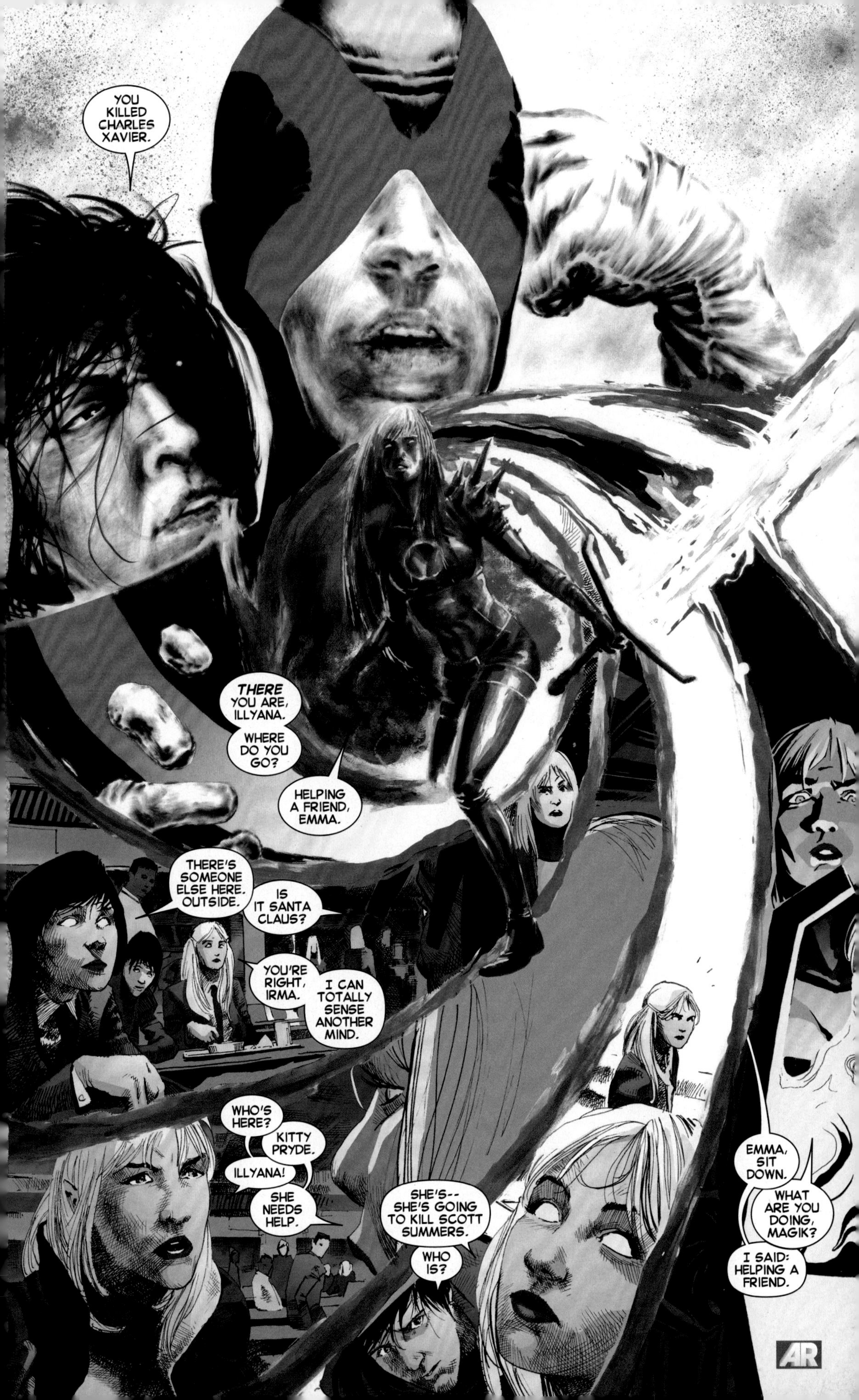
YOU KILLED CHARLES XAVIER.
THERE YOU ARE, ILLYANA.
WHERE DO YOU GO?
HELPING A FRIEND, EMMA.
THERE'S SOMEONE ELSE HERE. OUTSIDE.
IS IT SANTA CLAUS?
YOU'RE RIGHT, IRMA.
I CAN TOTALLY SENSE ANOTHER MIND.
WHO'S HERE?
KITTY PRYDE.
ILLYANA!
SHE NEEDS HELP.
SHE'S-- SHE'S GOING TO KILL SCOTT SUMMERS.
WHO IS?
EMMA, SIT DOWN.
WHAT ARE YOU DOING, MAGIK?
I SAID: HELPING A FRIEND.

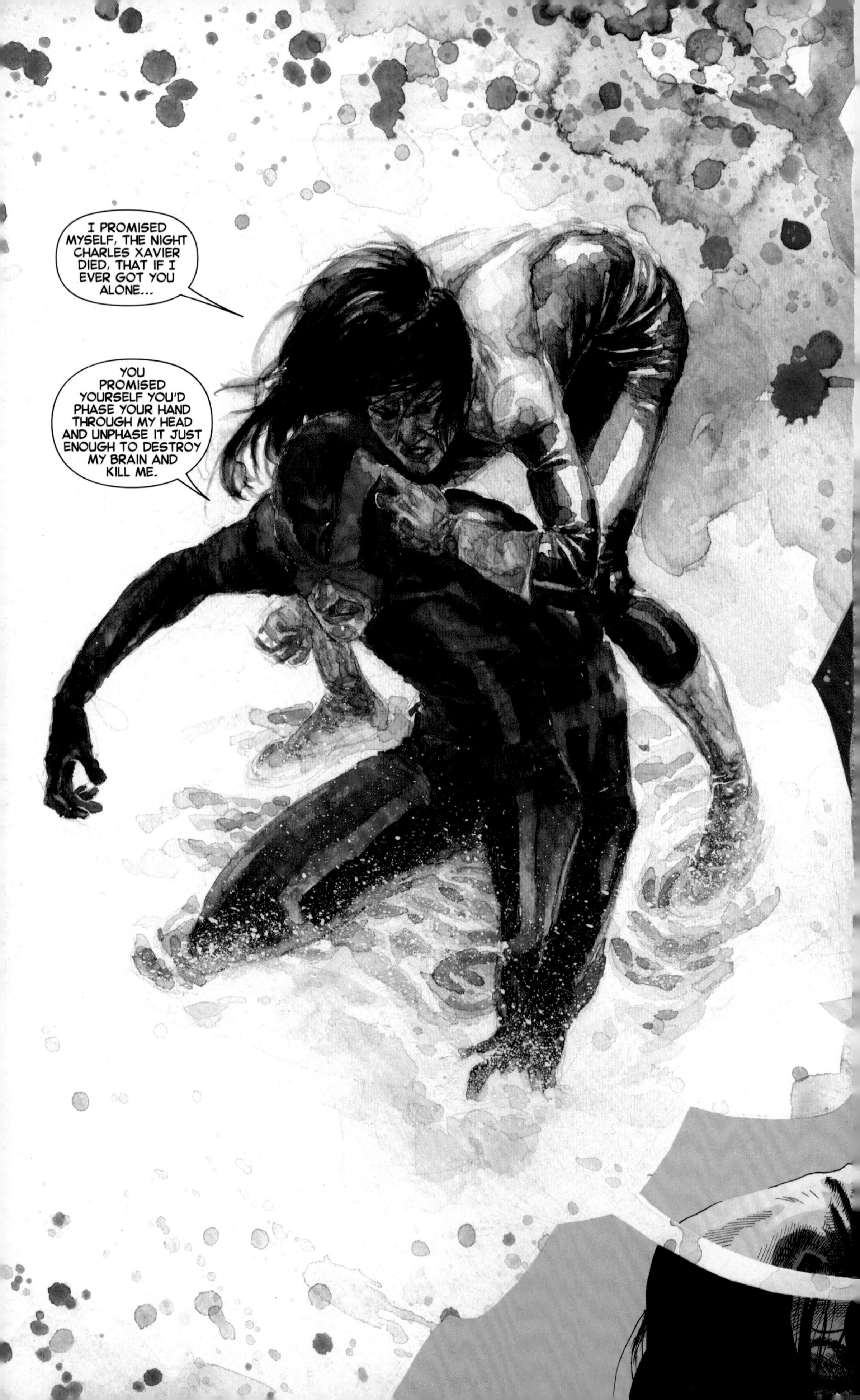
I PROMISED MYSELF, THE NIGHT CHARLES XAVIER DIED, THAT IF I EVER GOT YOU ALONE...
YOU PROMISED YOURSELF YOU'D PHASE YOUR HAND THROUGH MY HEAD AND UNPHASE IT JUST ENOUGH TO DESTROY MY BRAIN AND KILL ME.

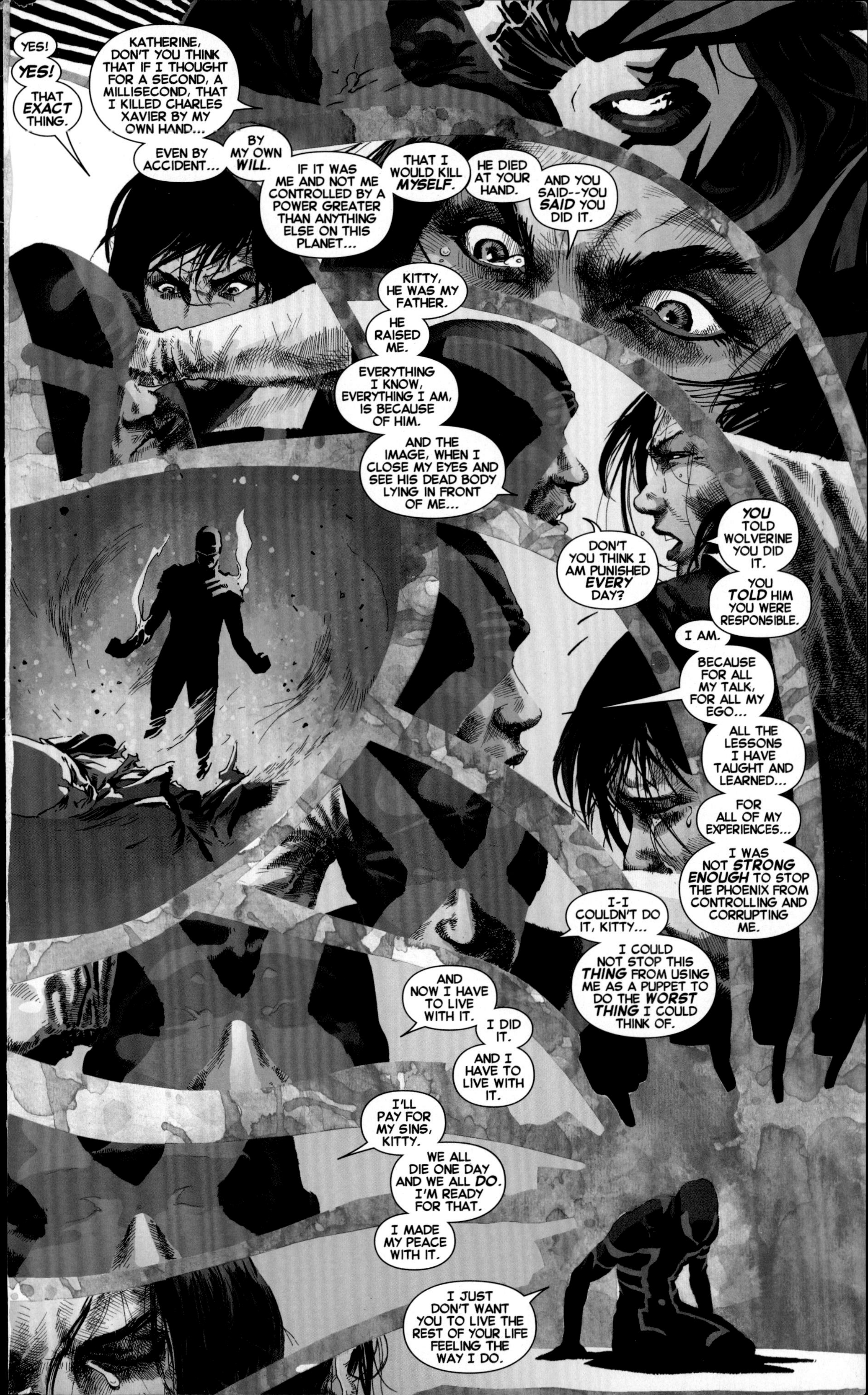
YES! YES! THAT EXACT THING.
KATHERINE, DON'T YOU THINK THAT IF I THOUGHT FOR A SECOND, A MILLISECOND, THAT I KILLED CHARLES XAVIER BY MY OWN HAND...
EVEN BY ACCIDENT...
BY MY OWN WILL.
IF IT WAS ME AND NOT ME CONTROLLED BY A POWER GREATER THAN ANYTHING ELSE ON THIS PLANET...
THAT I WOULD KILL MYSELF.
HE DIED AT YOUR HAND.
AND YOU SAID--YOU SAID YOU DID IT.
KITTY, HE WAS MY FATHER.
HE RAISED ME.
EVERYTHING I KNOW, EVERYTHING I AM, IS BECAUSE OF HIM.
AND THE IMAGE, WHEN I CLOSE MY EYES AND SEE HIS DEAD BODY LYING IN FRONT OF ME...
DON'T YOU THINK I AM PUNISHED EVERY DAY?
YOU TOLD WOLVERINE YOU DID IT.
YOU TOLD HIM YOU WERE RESPONSIBLE.
I AM.
BECAUSE FOR ALL MY TALK, FOR ALL MY EGO...
ALL THE LESSONS I HAVE TAUGHT AND LEARNED...
FOR ALL OF MY EXPERIENCES...
I WAS NOT STRONG ENOUGH TO STOP THE PHOENIX FROM CONTROLLING AND CORRUPTING ME.
I-I COULDN'T DO IT, KITTY...
I COULD NOT STOP THIS THING FROM USING ME AS A PUPPET TO DO THE WORST THING I COULD THINK OF.
AND NOW I HAVE TO LIVE WITH IT.
I DID IT.
AND I HAVE TO LIVE WITH IT.
I'LL PAY FOR MY SINS, KITTY.
WE ALL DIE ONE DAY AND WE ALL DO. I'M READY FOR THAT.
I MADE MY PEACE WITH IT.
I JUST DON'T WANT YOU TO LIVE THE REST OF YOUR LIFE FEELING THE WAY I DO.

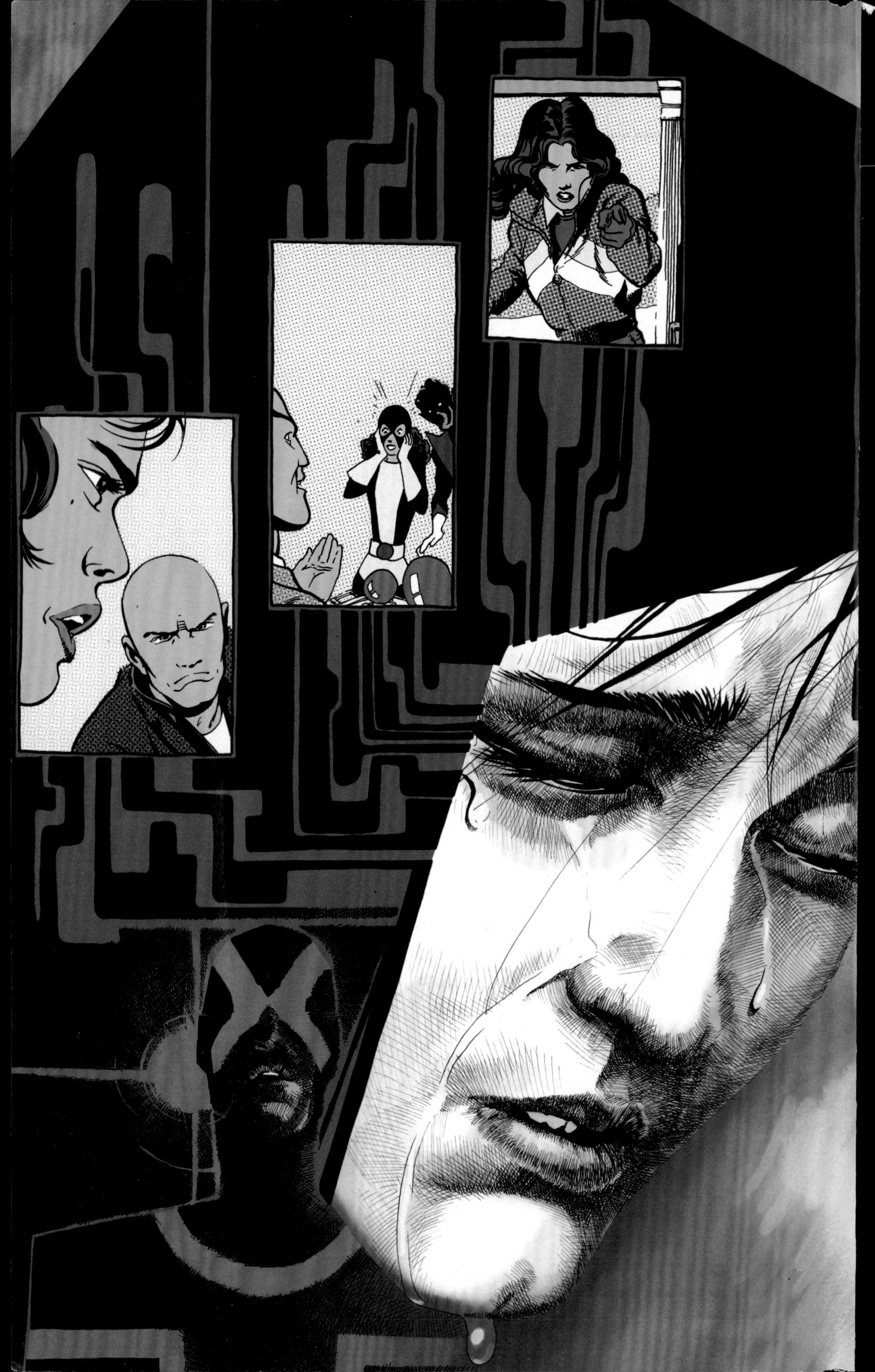

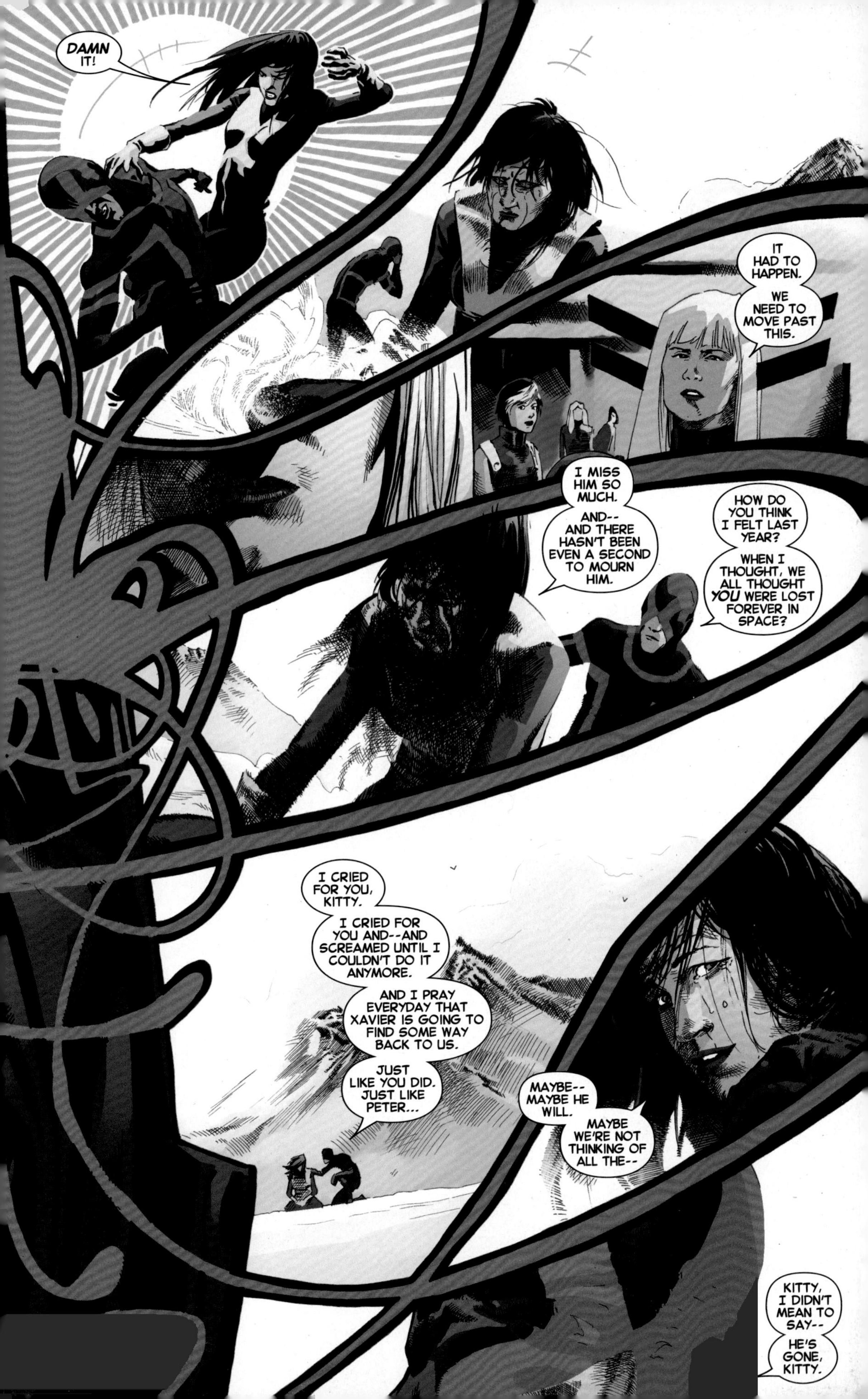
DAMN IT!
IT HAD TO HAPPEN.
WE NEED TO MOVE PAST THIS.
I MISS HIM SO MUCH.
AND-- AND THERE HASN'T BEEN EVEN A SECOND TO MOURN HIM.
HOW DO YOU THINK I FELT LAST YEAR?
WHEN I THOUGHT, WE ALL THOUGHT *YOU* WERE LOST FOREVER IN SPACE?
I CRIED FOR YOU, KITTY.
I CRIED FOR YOU AND--AND SCREAMED UNTIL I COULDN'T DO IT ANYMORE.
AND I PRAY EVERYDAY THAT XAVIER IS GOING TO FIND SOME WAY BACK TO US.
JUST LIKE YOU DID. JUST LIKE PETER...
MAYBE-- MAYBE HE WILL.
MAYBE WE'RE NOT THINKING OF ALL THE--
KITTY, I DIDN'T MEAN TO SAY--
HE'S GONE, KITTY.

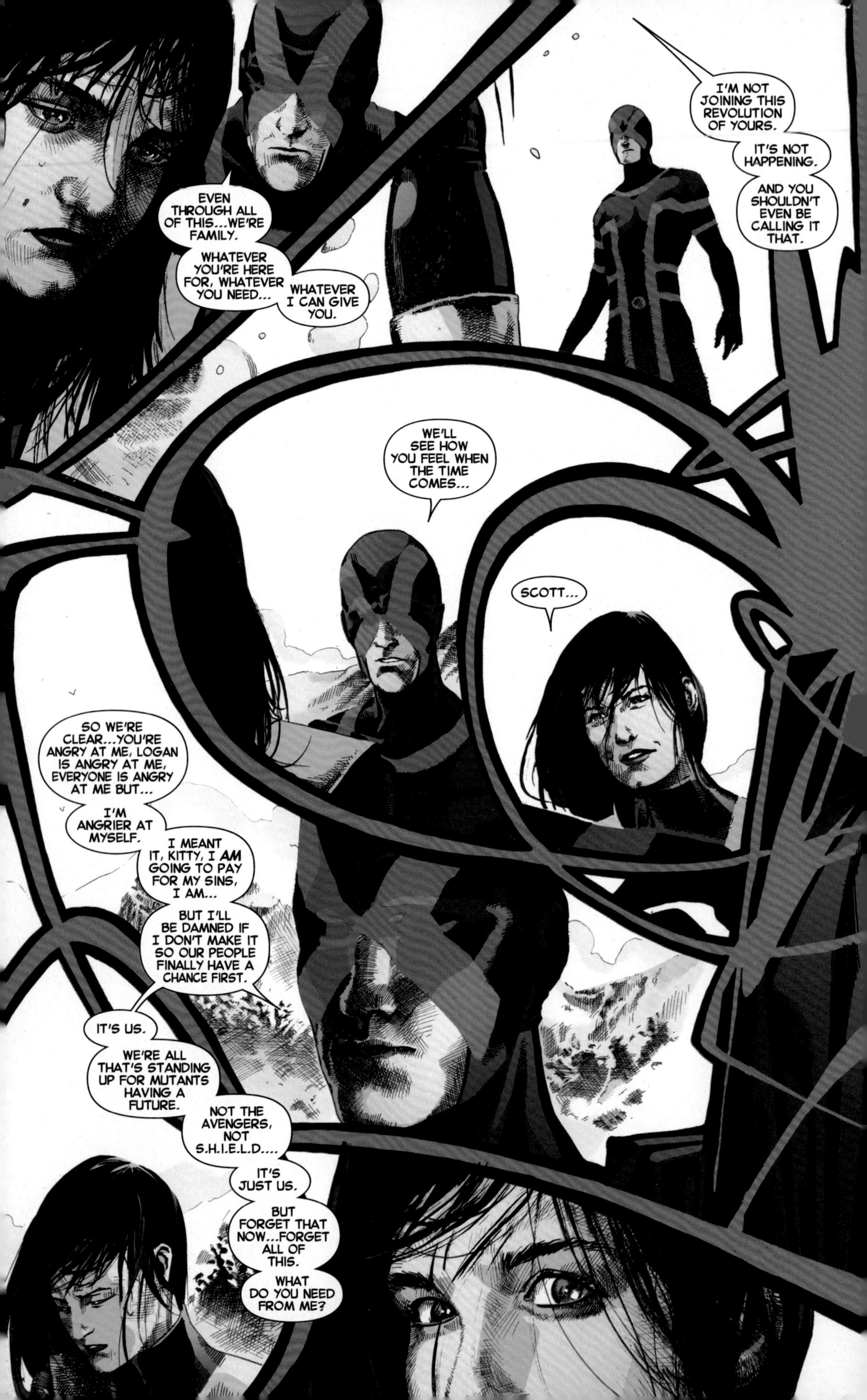
EVEN THROUGH ALL OF THIS...WE'RE FAMILY.
WHATEVER YOU'RE HERE FOR, WHATEVER YOU NEED...
WHATEVER I CAN GIVE YOU.
I'M NOT JOINING THIS REVOLUTION OF YOURS.
IT'S NOT HAPPENING.
AND YOU SHOULDN'T EVEN BE CALLING IT THAT.
WE'LL SEE HOW YOU FEEL WHEN THE TIME COMES...
SCOTT...
SO WE'RE CLEAR...YOU'RE ANGRY AT ME, LOGAN IS ANGRY AT ME, EVERYONE IS ANGRY AT ME BUT...
I'M ANGRIER AT MYSELF.
I MEANT IT, KITTY, I **AM** GOING TO PAY FOR MY SINS, I AM...
BUT I'LL BE DAMNED IF I DON'T MAKE IT SO OUR PEOPLE FINALLY HAVE A CHANCE FIRST.
IT'S US.
WE'RE ALL THAT'S STANDING UP FOR MUTANTS HAVING A FUTURE.
NOT THE AVENGERS, NOT S.H.I.E.L.D....
IT'S JUST US.
BUT FORGET THAT NOW...FORGET ALL OF THIS.
WHAT DO YOU NEED FROM ME?

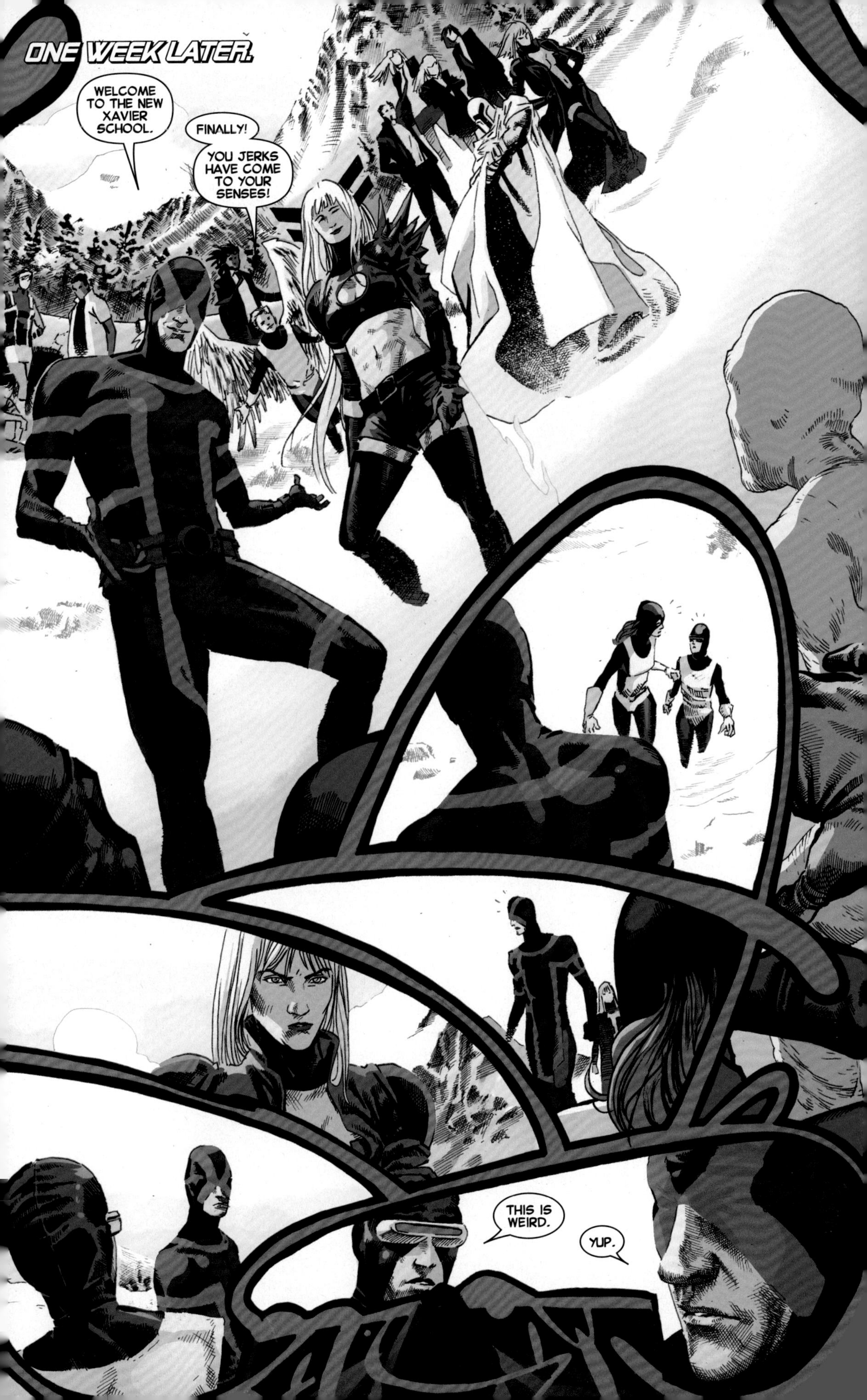
ONE WEEK LATER.
WELCOME TO THE NEW XAVIER SCHOOL.
FINALLY!
YOU JERKS HAVE COME TO YOUR SENSES!
THIS IS WEIRD.
YUP.

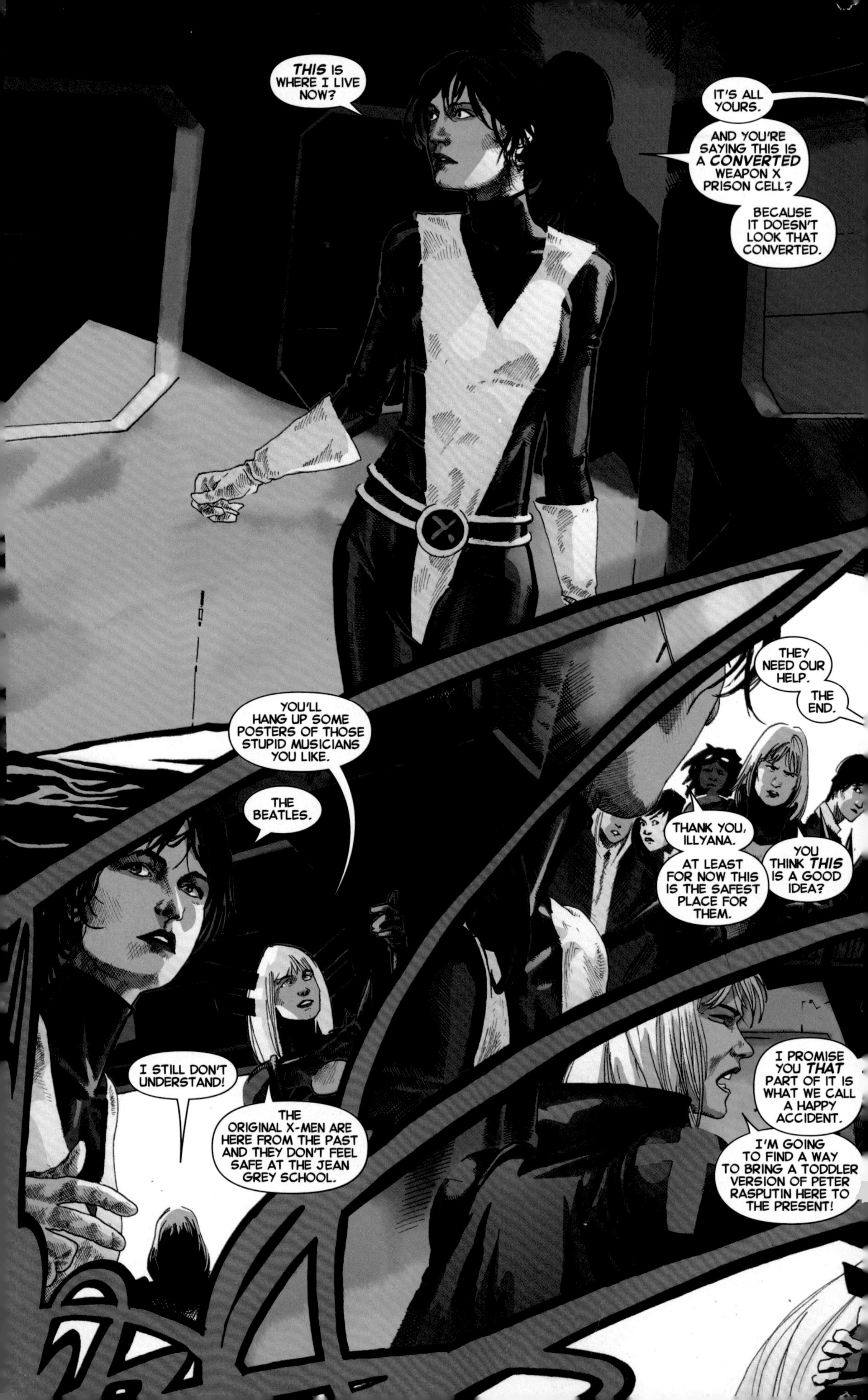
THIS IS WHERE I LIVE NOW?
IT'S ALL YOURS.
AND YOU'RE SAYING THIS IS A CONVERTED WEAPON X PRISON CELL?
BECAUSE IT DOESN'T LOOK THAT CONVERTED.
YOU'LL HANG UP SOME POSTERS OF THOSE STUPID MUSICIANS YOU LIKE.
THE BEATLES.
THEY NEED OUR HELP.
THE END.
THANK YOU, ILLYANA.
AT LEAST FOR NOW THIS IS THE SAFEST PLACE FOR THEM.
YOU THINK THIS IS A GOOD IDEA?
I STILL DON'T UNDERSTAND!
THE ORIGINAL X-MEN ARE HERE FROM THE PAST AND THEY DON'T FEEL SAFE AT THE JEAN GREY SCHOOL.
I PROMISE YOU THAT PART OF IT IS WHAT WE CALL A HAPPY ACCIDENT.
I'M GOING TO FIND A WAY TO BRING A TODDLER VERSION OF PETER RASPUTIN HERE TO THE PRESENT!

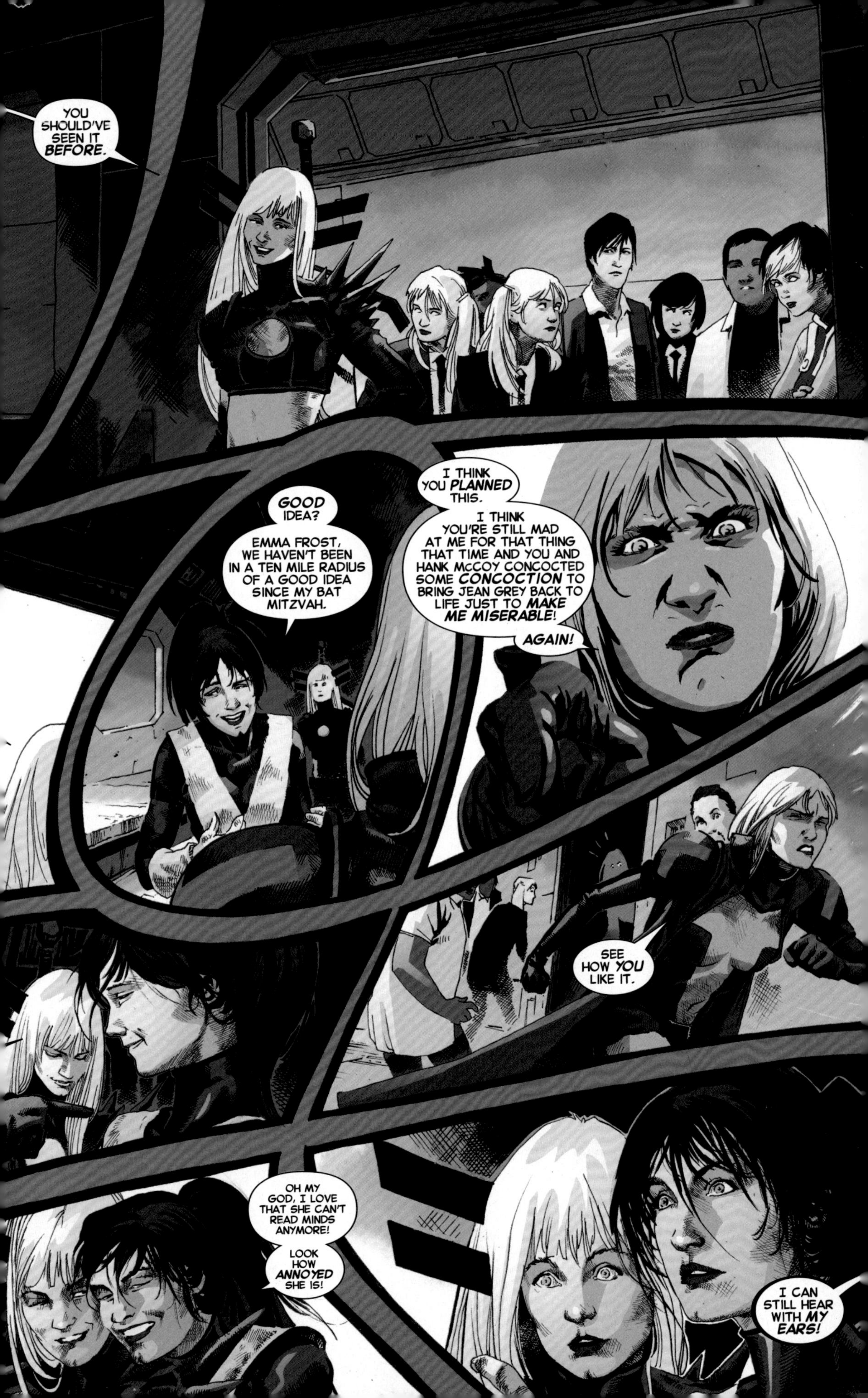
YOU SHOULD'VE SEEN IT BEFORE.
GOOD IDEA?
EMMA FROST, WE HAVEN'T BEEN IN A TEN MILE RADIUS OF A GOOD IDEA SINCE MY BAT MITZVAH.
I THINK YOU PLANNED THIS.
I THINK YOU'RE STILL MAD AT ME FOR THAT THING THAT TIME AND YOU AND HANK McCOY CONCOCTED SOME CONCOCTION TO BRING JEAN GREY BACK TO LIFE JUST TO MAKE ME MISERABLE!
AGAIN!
SEE HOW YOU LIKE IT.
OH MY GOD, I LOVE THAT SHE CAN'T READ MINDS ANYMORE!
LOOK HOW ANNOYED SHE IS!
I CAN STILL HEAR WITH MY EARS!

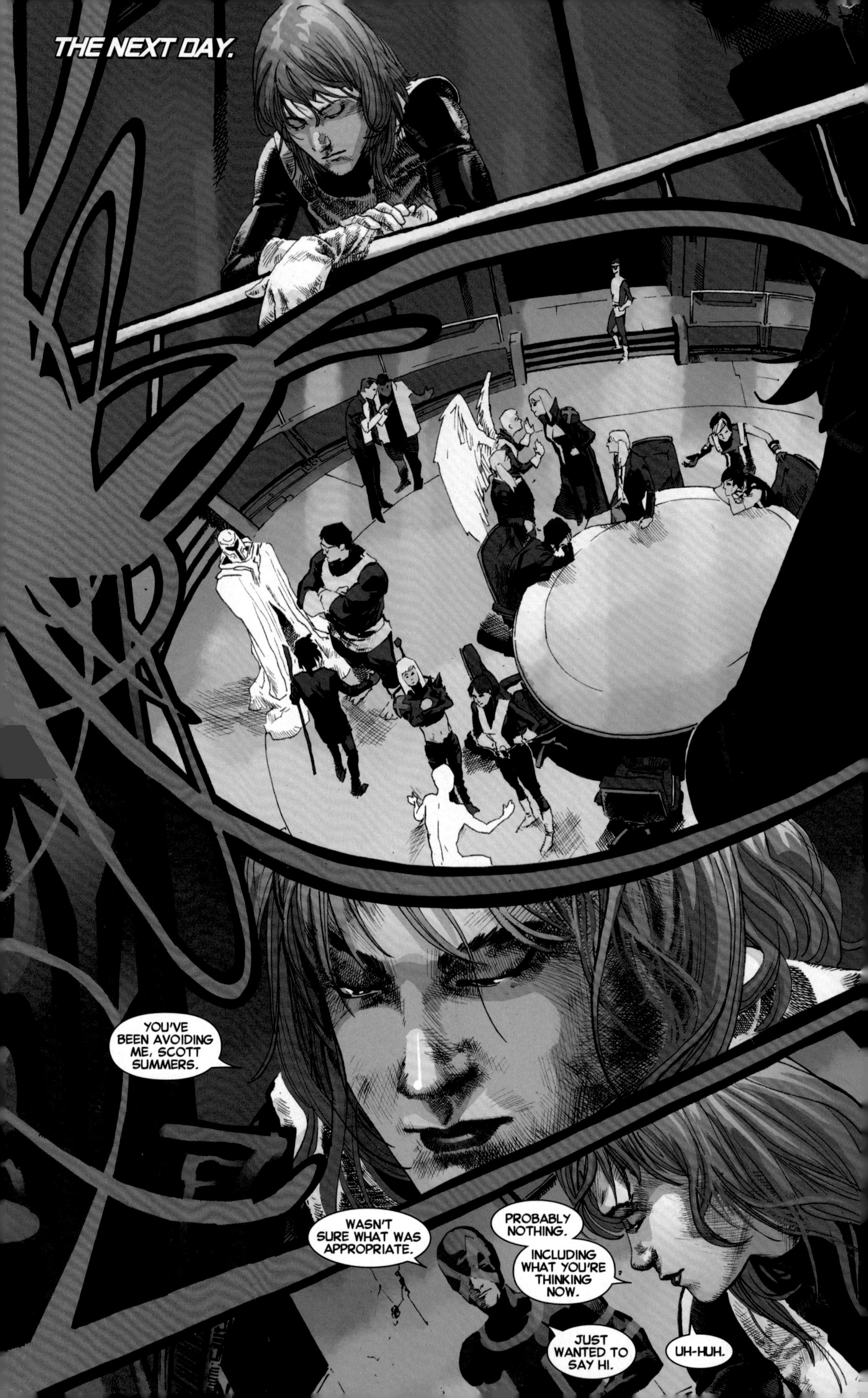
THE NEXT DAY.
YOU'VE BEEN AVOIDING ME, SCOTT SUMMERS.
WASN'T SURE WHAT WAS APPROPRIATE.
PROBABLY NOTHING.
INCLUDING WHAT YOU'RE THINKING NOW.
JUST WANTED TO SAY HI.
UH-HUH.

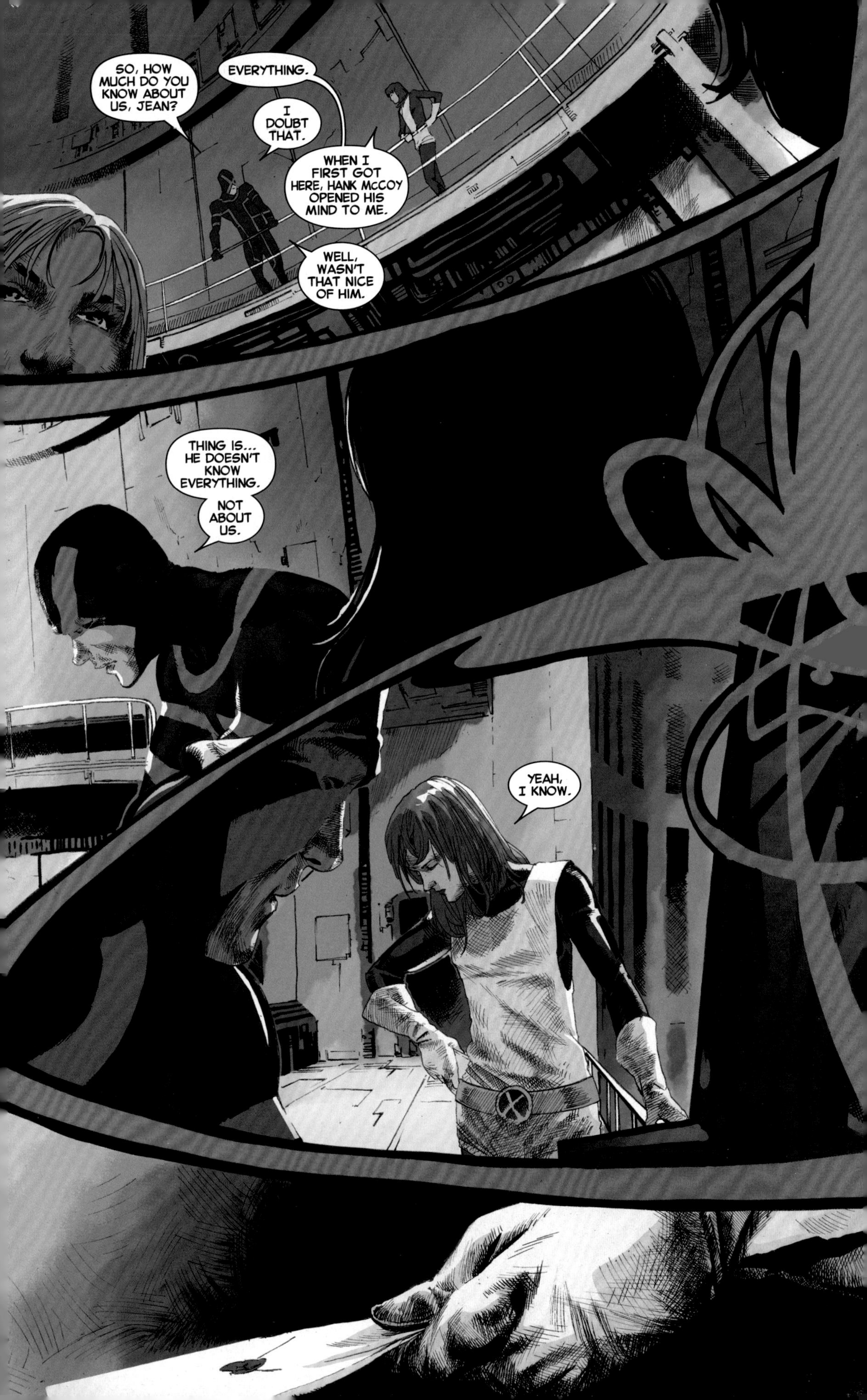
SO, HOW MUCH DO YOU KNOW ABOUT US, JEAN?
EVERYTHING.
I DOUBT THAT.
WHEN I FIRST GOT HERE, HANK McCOY OPENED HIS MIND TO ME.
WELL, WASN'T THAT NICE OF HIM.
THING IS... HE DOESN'T KNOW EVERYTHING.
NOT ABOUT US.
YEAH, I KNOW.

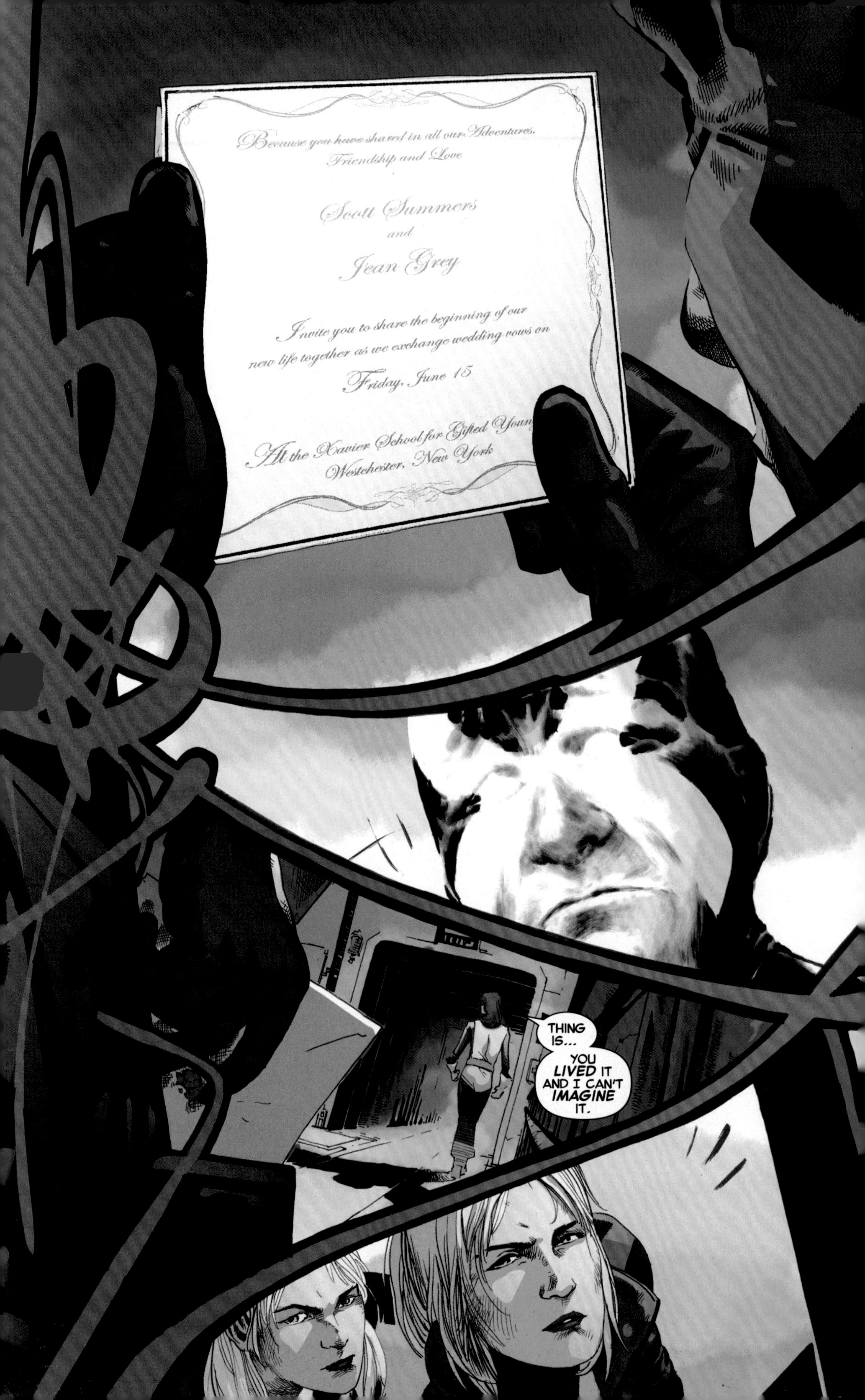

Because you have shared in all our Adventures, Friendship and Love
Scott Summers
and
Jean Grey
Invite you to share the beginning of our new life together as we exchange wedding vows on
Friday, June 15
At the Xavier School for Gifted Young
Westchester, New York
THING IS... YOU LIVED IT AND I CAN'T IMAGINE IT.

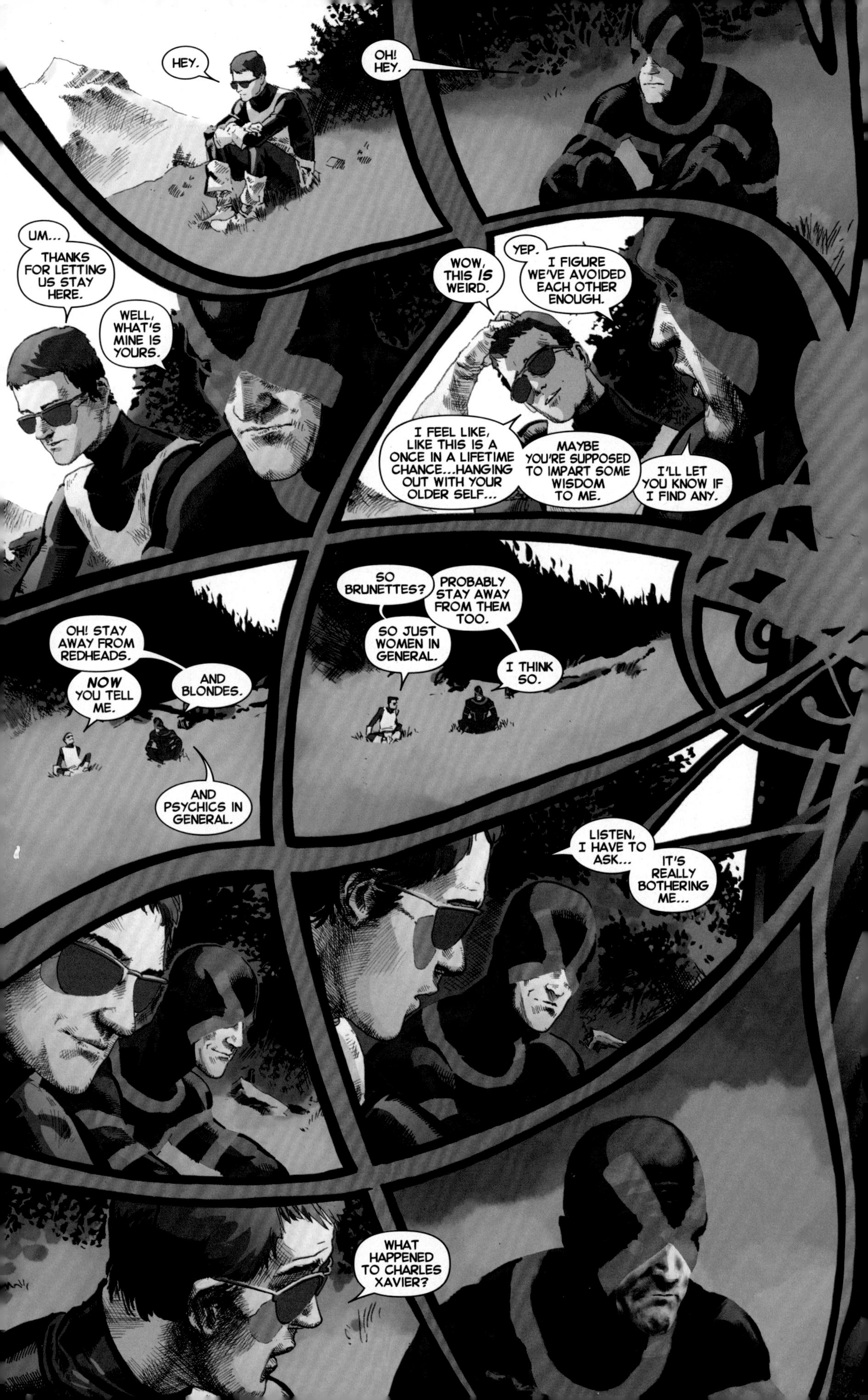
HEY.
OH! HEY.
UM...
THANKS FOR LETTING US STAY HERE.
WELL, WHAT'S MINE IS YOURS.
WOW, THIS *IS* WEIRD.
YEP.
I FIGURE WE'VE AVOIDED EACH OTHER ENOUGH.
I FEEL LIKE, LIKE THIS IS A ONCE IN A LIFETIME CHANCE...HANGING OUT WITH YOUR OLDER SELF...
MAYBE YOU'RE SUPPOSED TO IMPART SOME WISDOM TO ME.
I'LL LET YOU KNOW IF I FIND ANY.
OH! STAY AWAY FROM REDHEADS.
NOW YOU TELL ME.
AND BLONDES.
AND PSYCHICS IN GENERAL.
SO BRUNETTES?
PROBABLY STAY AWAY FROM THEM TOO.
SO JUST WOMEN IN GENERAL.
I THINK SO.
LISTEN, I HAVE TO ASK...
IT'S REALLY BOTHERING ME...
WHAT HAPPENED TO CHARLES XAVIER?

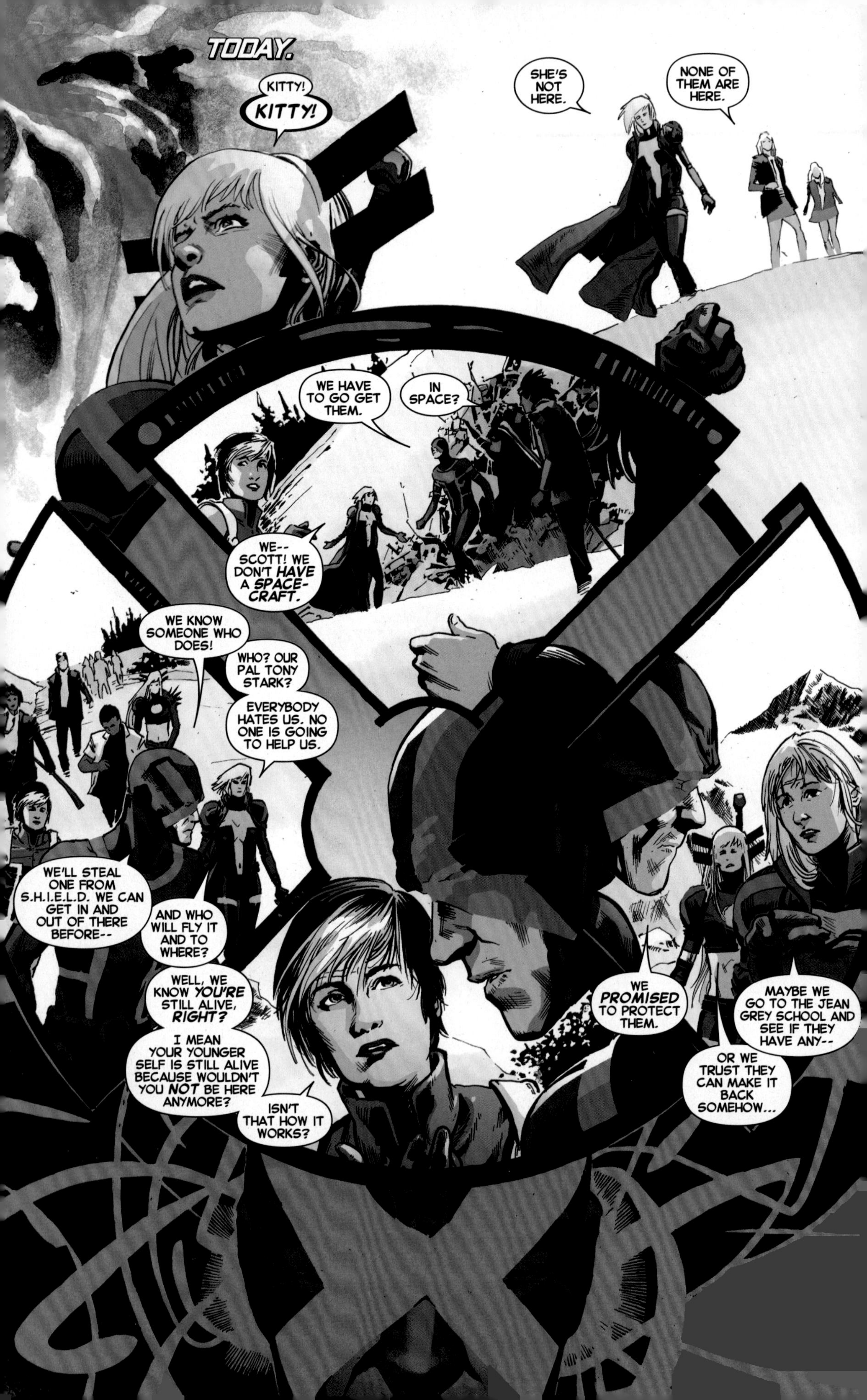
TODAY.
KITTY! KITTY!
SHE'S NOT HERE.
NONE OF THEM ARE HERE.
WE HAVE TO GO GET THEM.
IN SPACE?
WE-- SCOTT! WE DON'T HAVE A SPACE-CRAFT.
WE KNOW SOMEONE WHO DOES!
WHO? OUR PAL TONY STARK?
EVERYBODY HATES US. NO ONE IS GOING TO HELP US.
WE'LL STEAL ONE FROM S.H.I.E.L.D. WE CAN GET IN AND OUT OF THERE BEFORE--
AND WHO WILL FLY IT AND TO WHERE?
WELL, WE KNOW YOU'RE STILL ALIVE, RIGHT?
I MEAN YOUR YOUNGER SELF IS STILL ALIVE BECAUSE WOULDN'T YOU NOT BE HERE ANYMORE?
ISN'T THAT HOW IT WORKS?
WE PROMISED TO PROTECT THEM.
MAYBE WE GO TO THE JEAN GREY SCHOOL AND SEE IF THEY HAVE ANY--
OR WE TRUST THEY CAN MAKE IT BACK SOMEHOW...

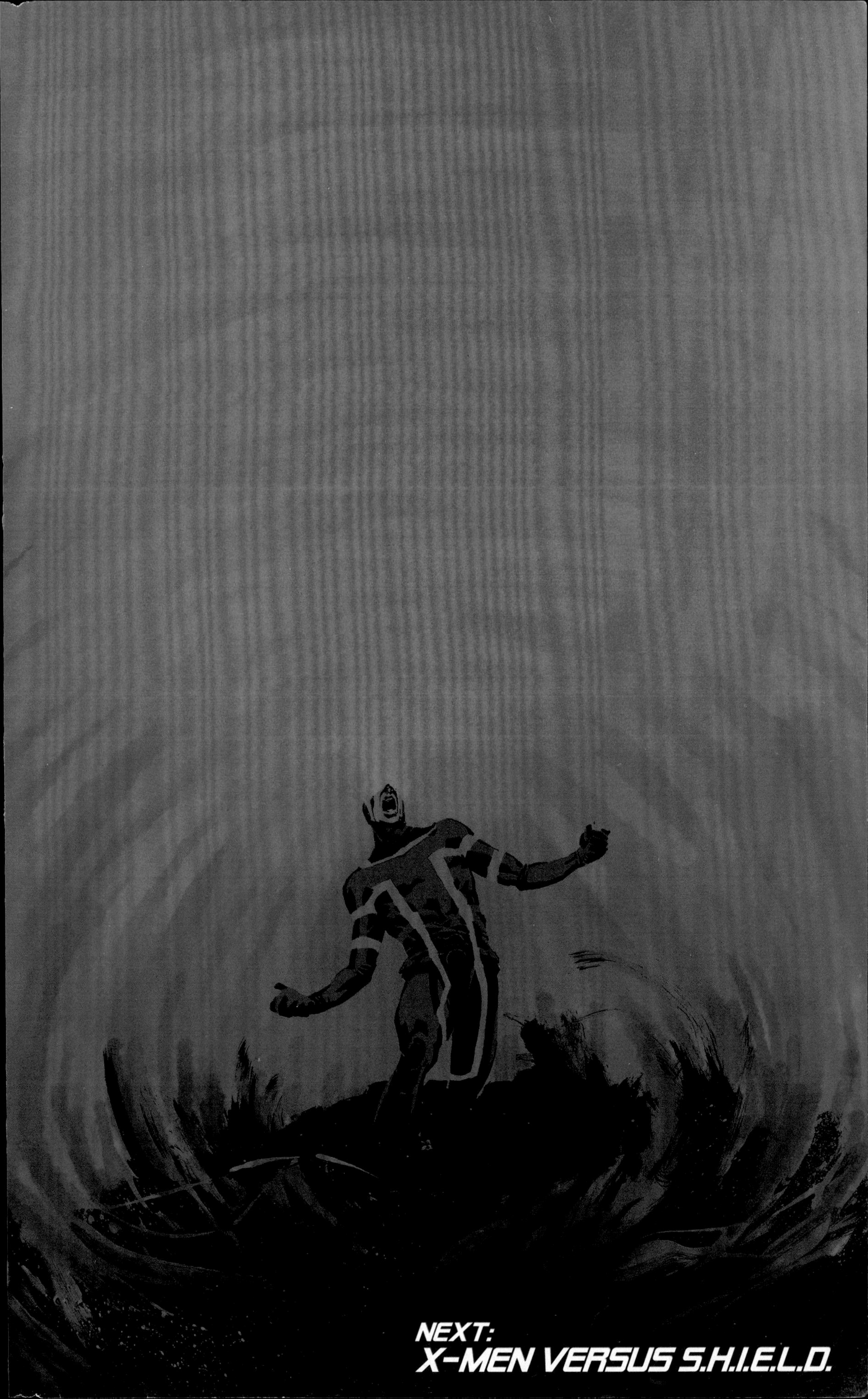
NEXT:
X-MEN VERSUS S.H.I.E.L.D.

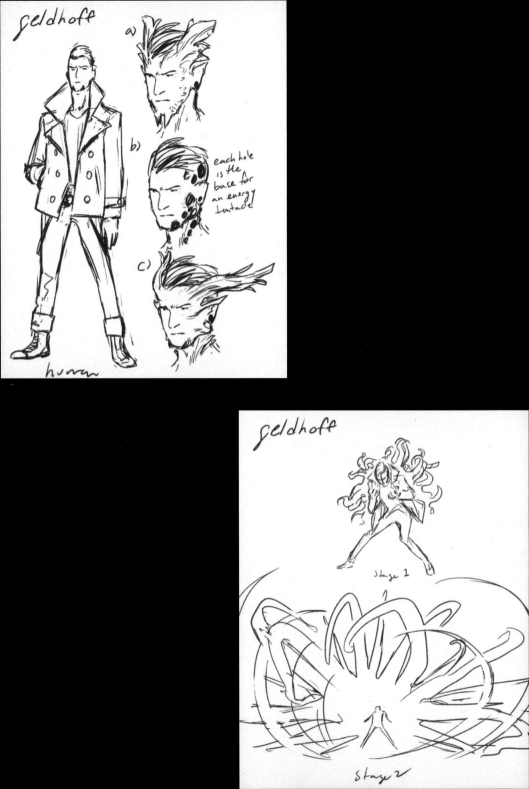

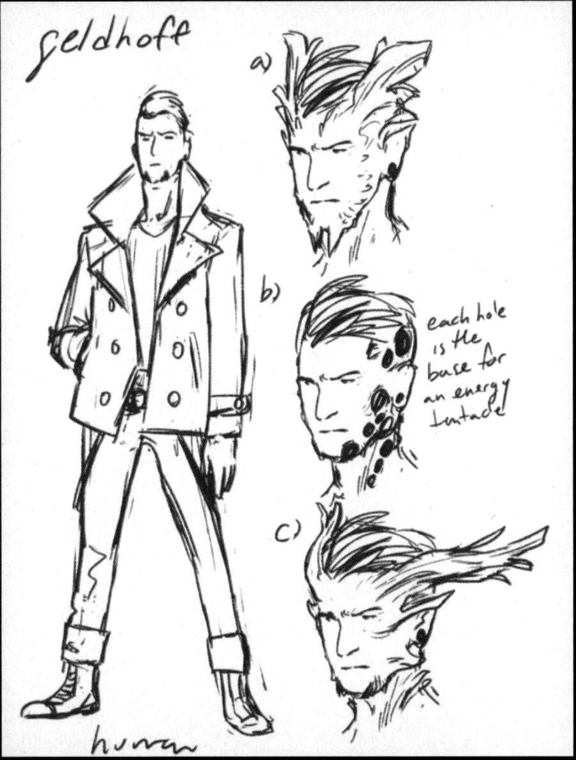
geldhoff
a)
b)
each hole is the base for an energy tentacle
c)
human

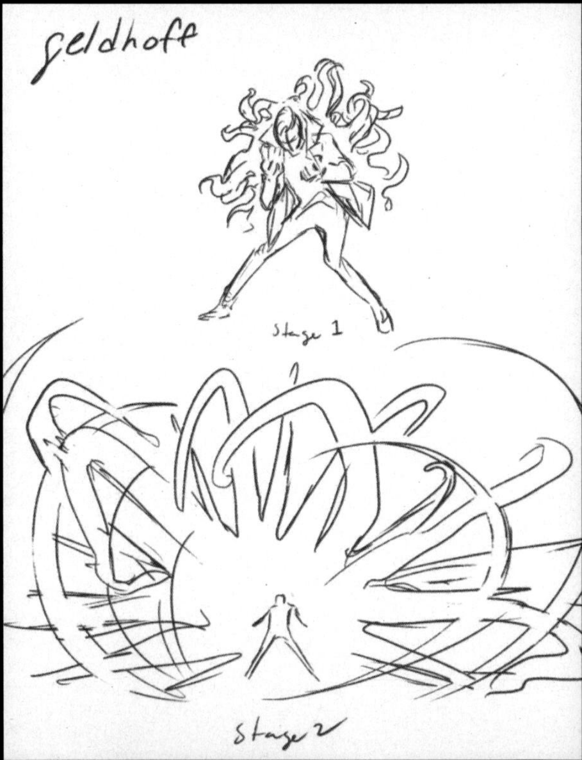
geldhoff
Stage 1
Stage 2

#14 COVER PROCESS BY

CHRIS BACHALO & TIM TOWNSEND

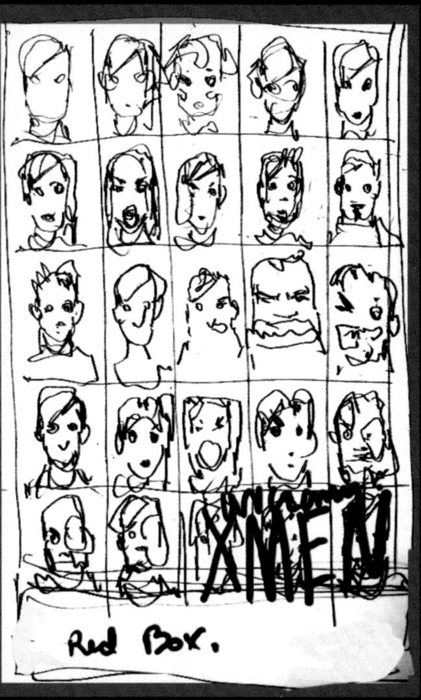
X-MEN
Red Box.

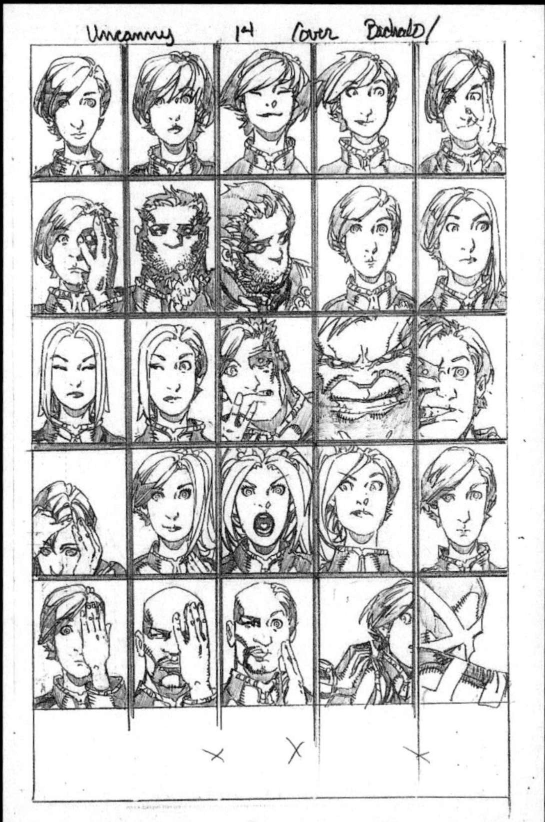
Uncanny 14 Cover Bachalo!

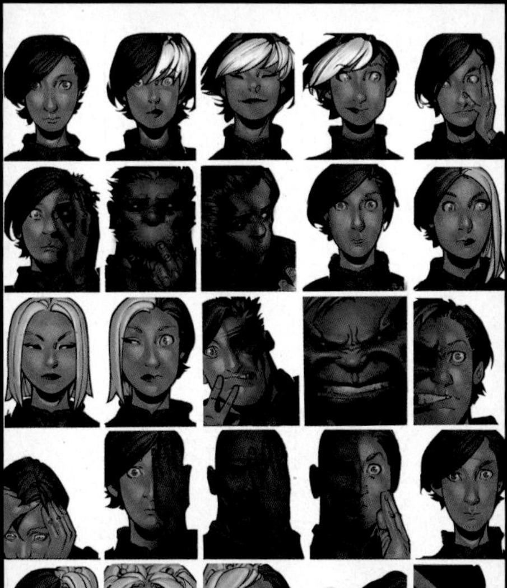

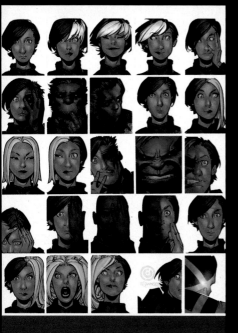

#16 COVER PROCESS BY

CHRIS BACHALO & TIM TOWNSEND

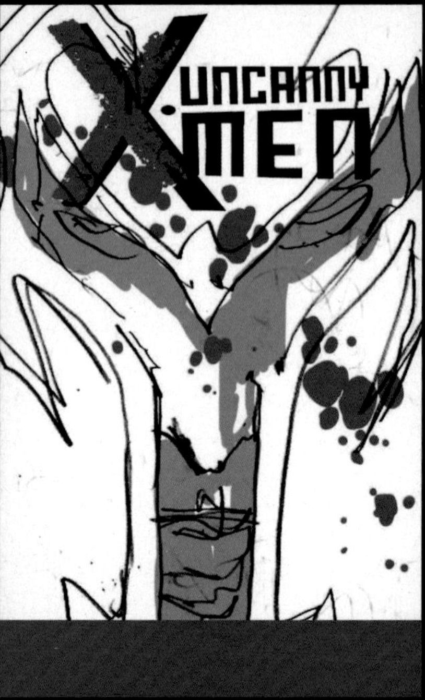
UNCANNY
X-MEN

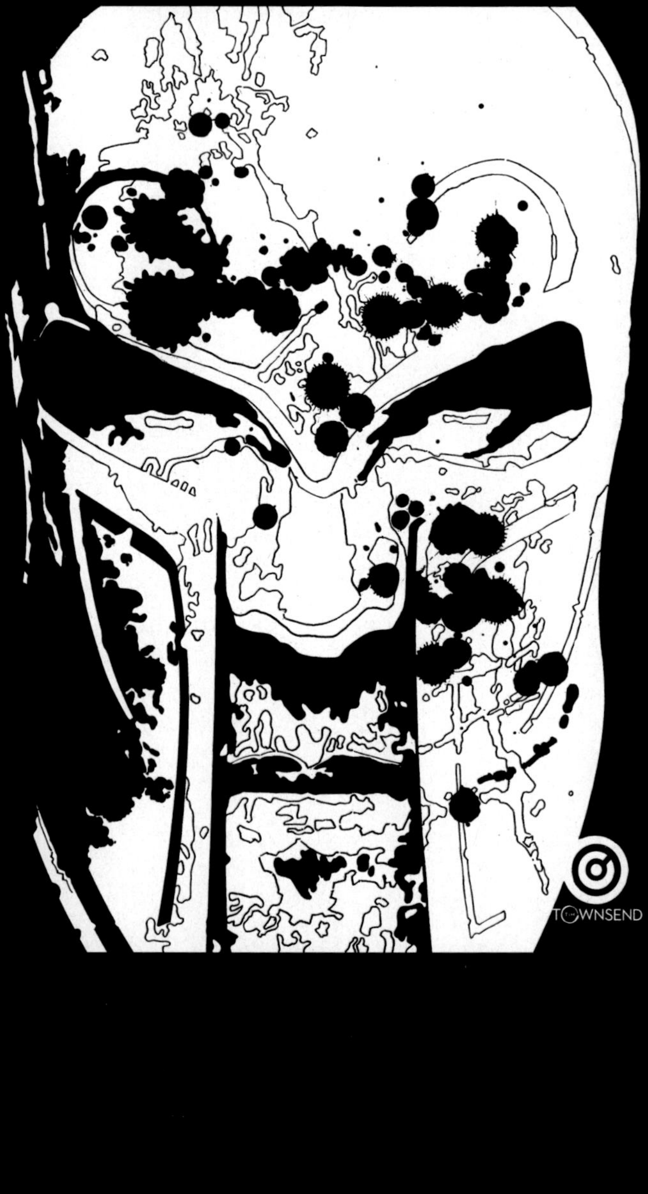
TOWNSEND

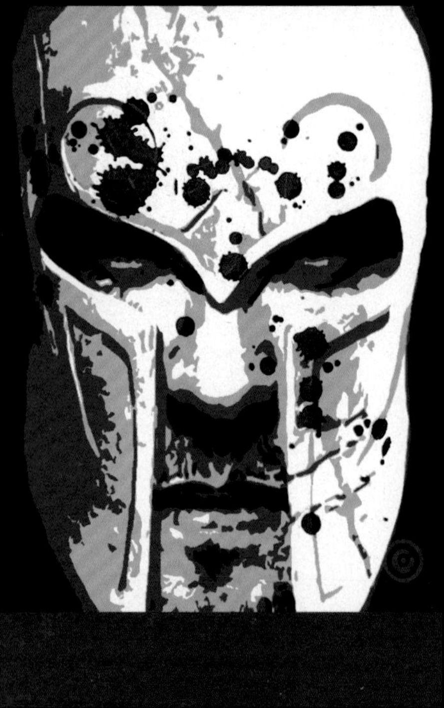

#17 COVER SKETCHES BY

CHRIS BACHALO

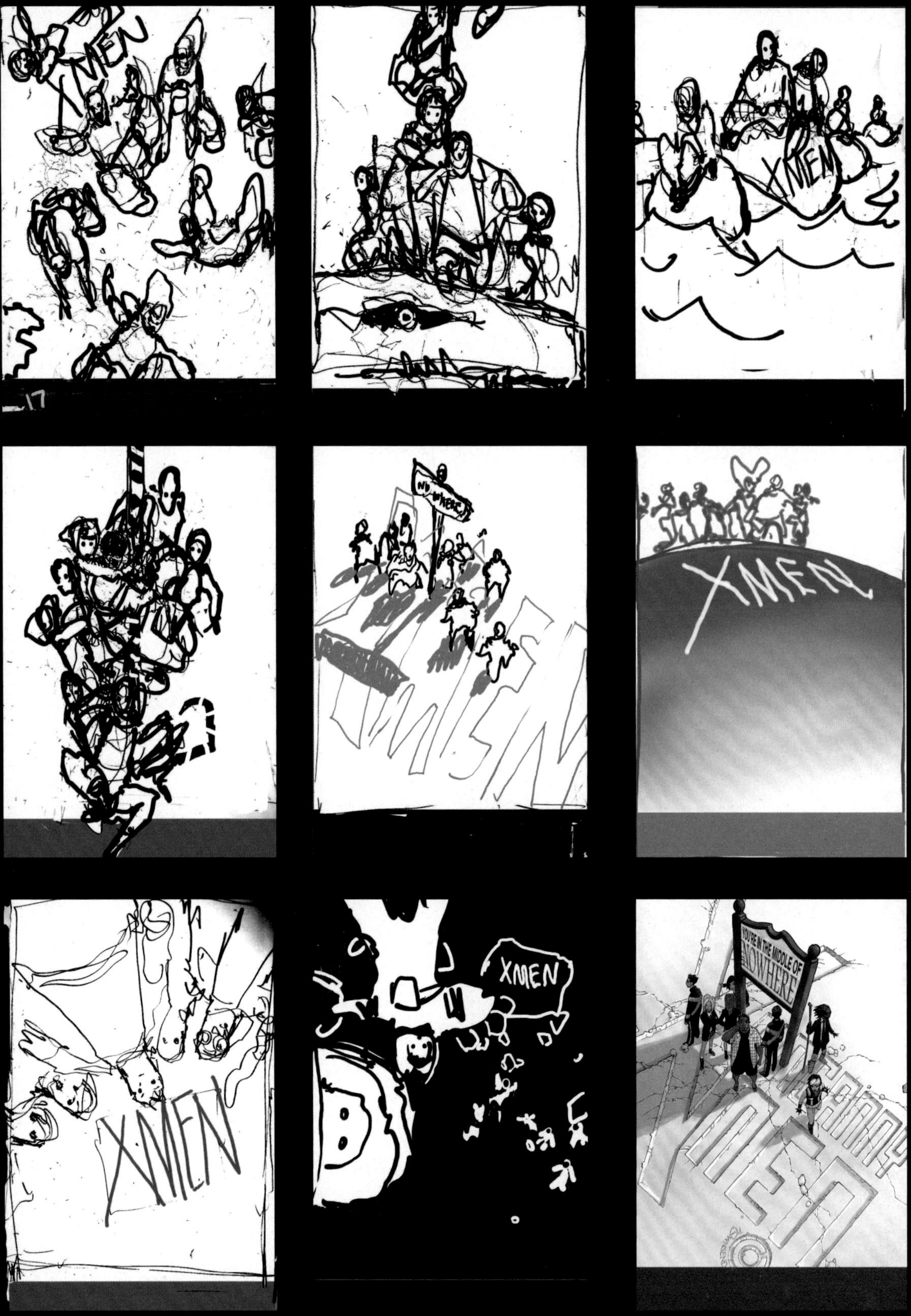
XMEN
XMEN
XMEN
XMEN
XMEN
YOU'RE IN THE MIDDLE OF
NOWHERE

FINAL COVER

#18 COVER SKETCHES BY
ALEXANDER LOZANO

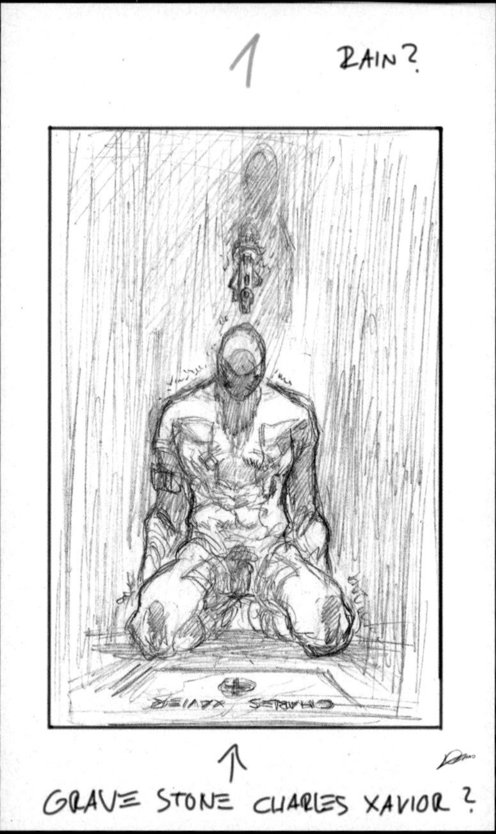
1
RAIN?
GRAVE STONE CHARLES XAVIOR?

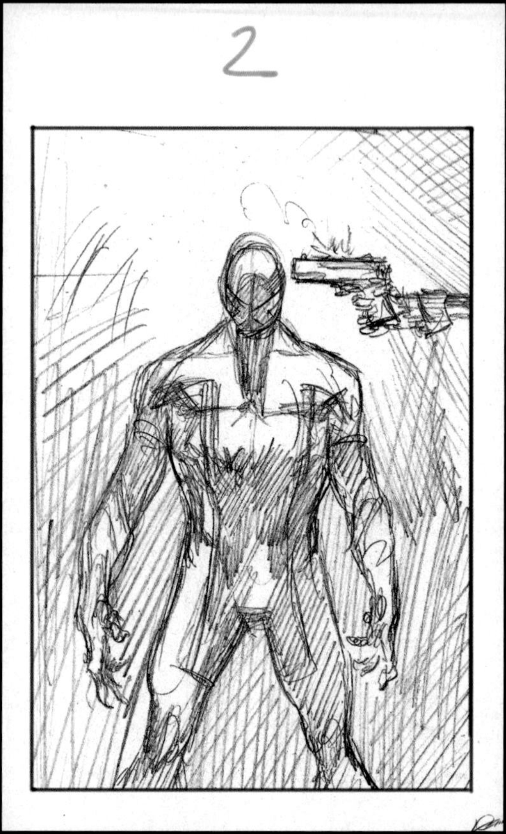
2

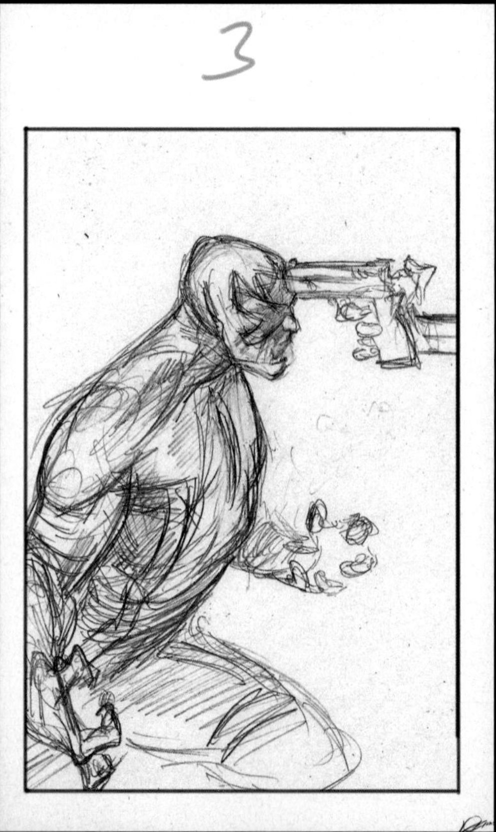
3

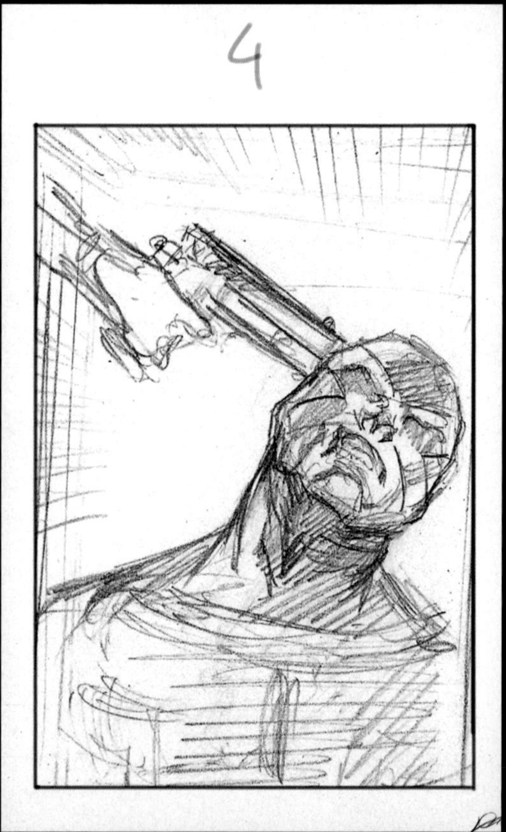
4

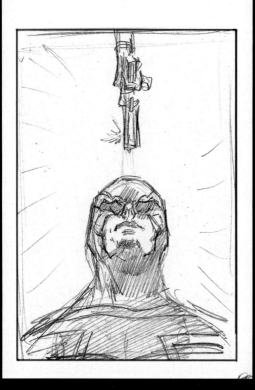

5

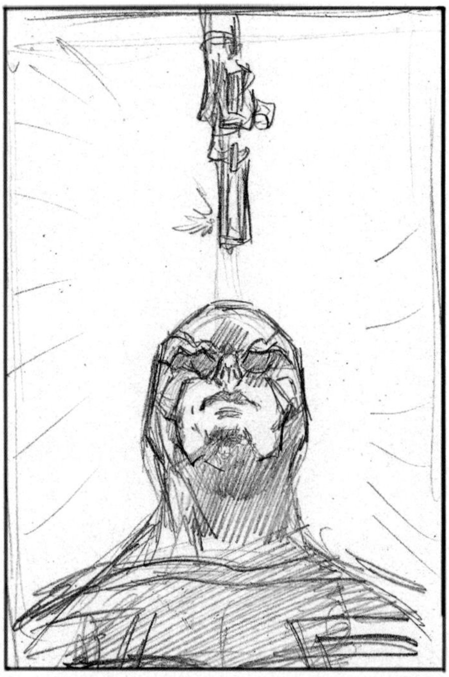

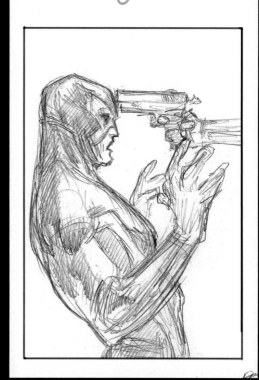

6

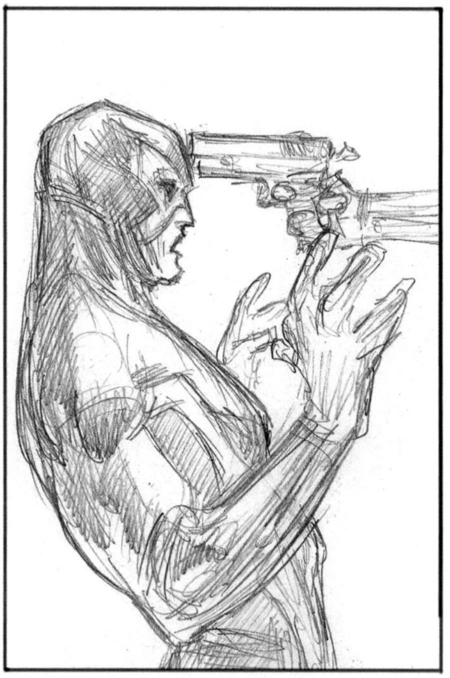

7

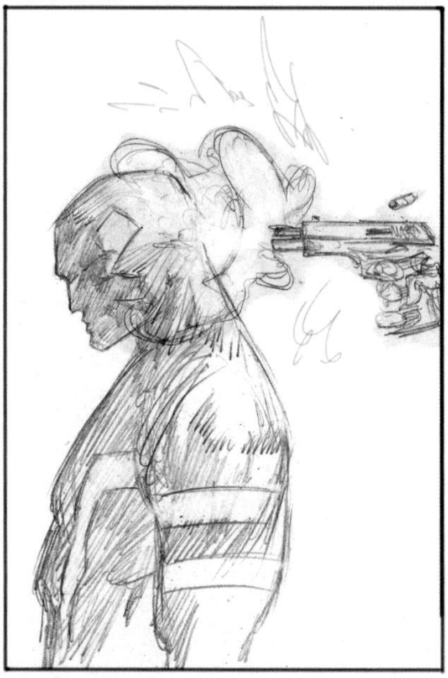

IF KITTY FIRES A GUN WHILE SHE'S UNTANGIBLE → DOES THAT MEAN THE BULLET WOULD ALSO GO THROUGH CYCLOP'S HEAD WITHOUT CAUSING DAMAGE?

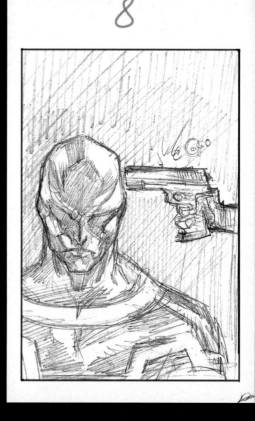

8

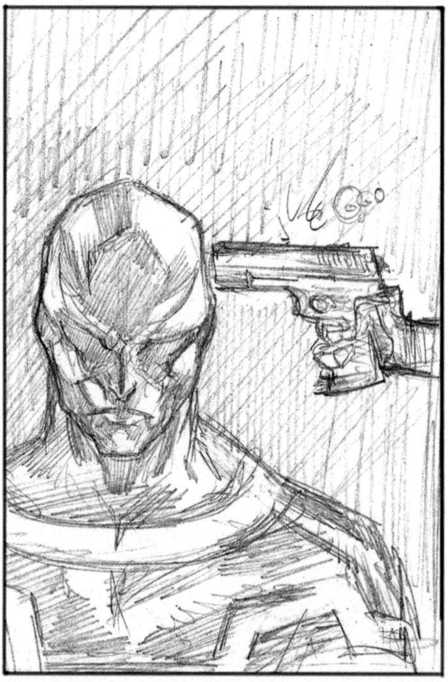

g

FINAL COVER

#15 ART BY
KRIS ANKA

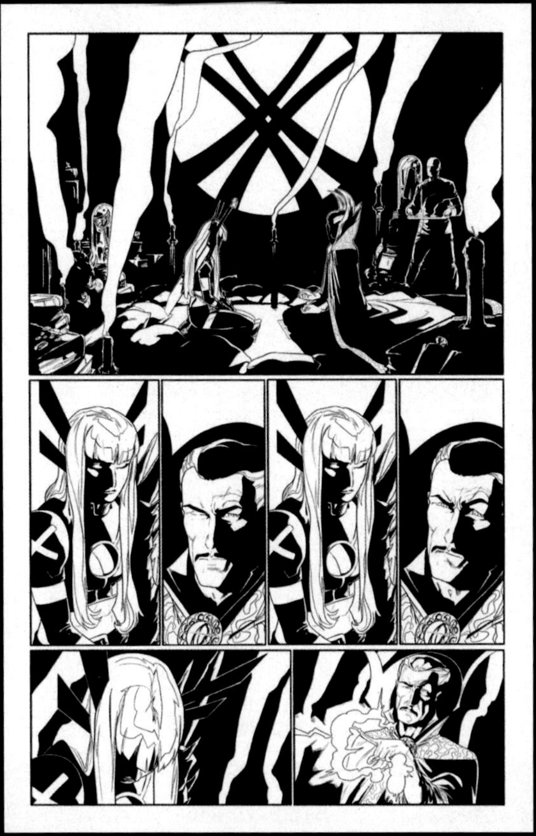

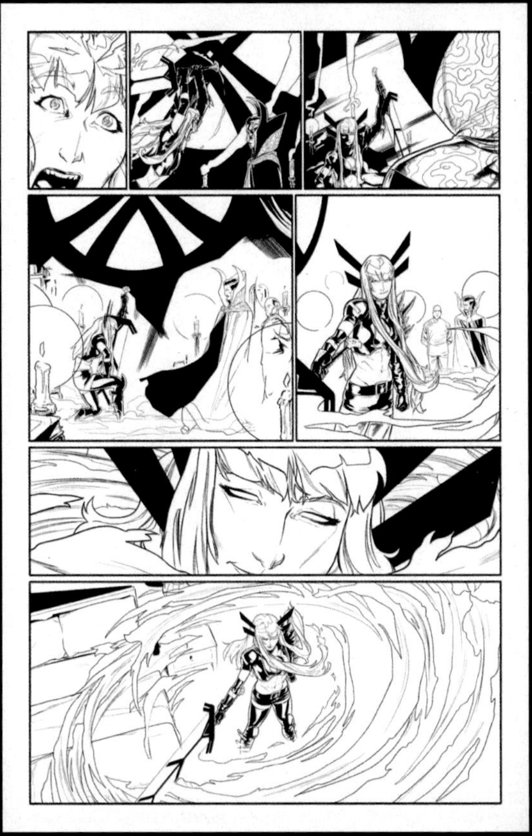

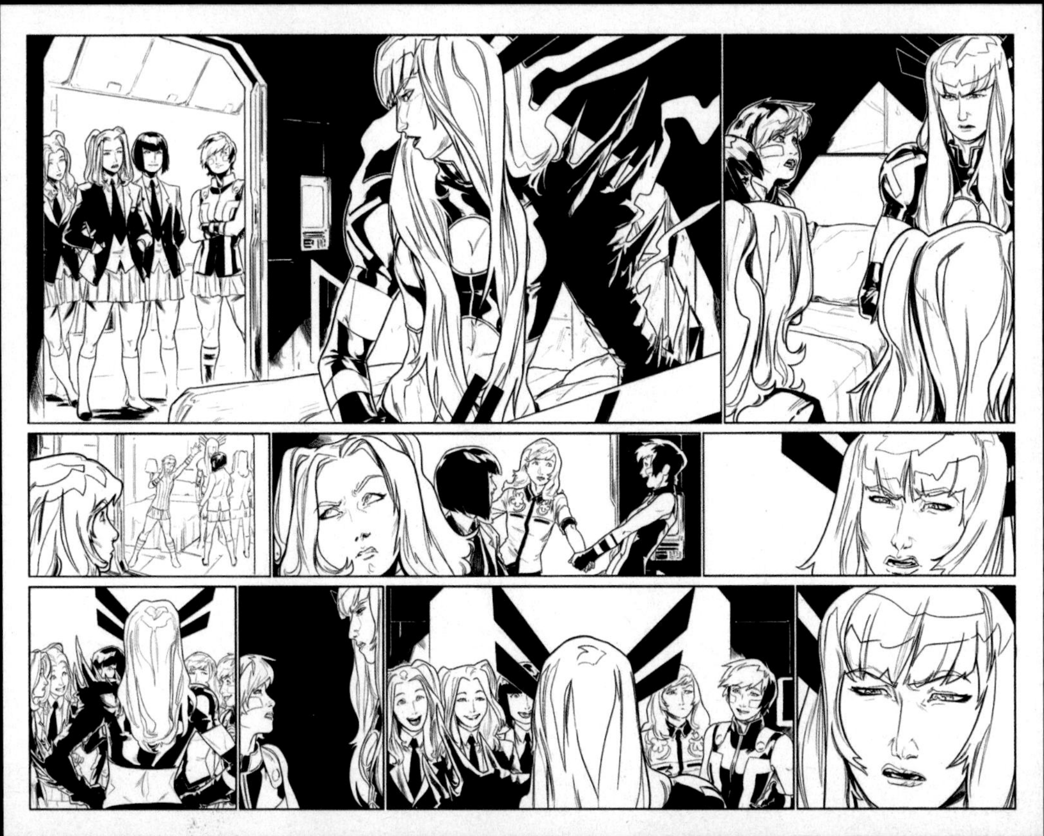

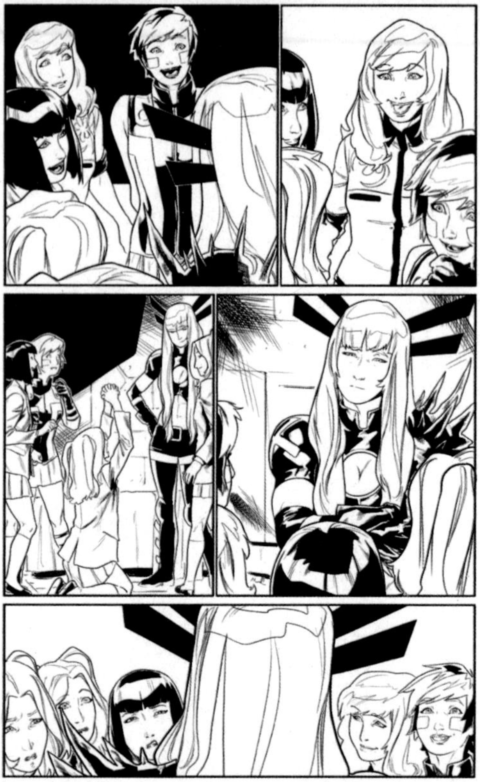

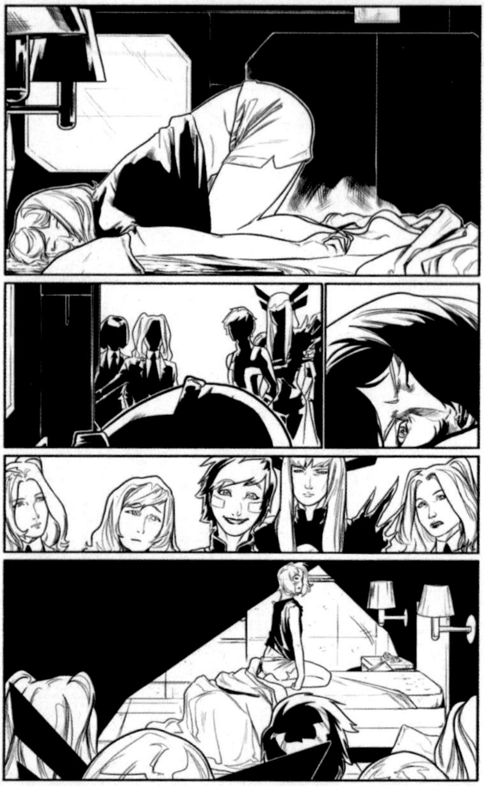

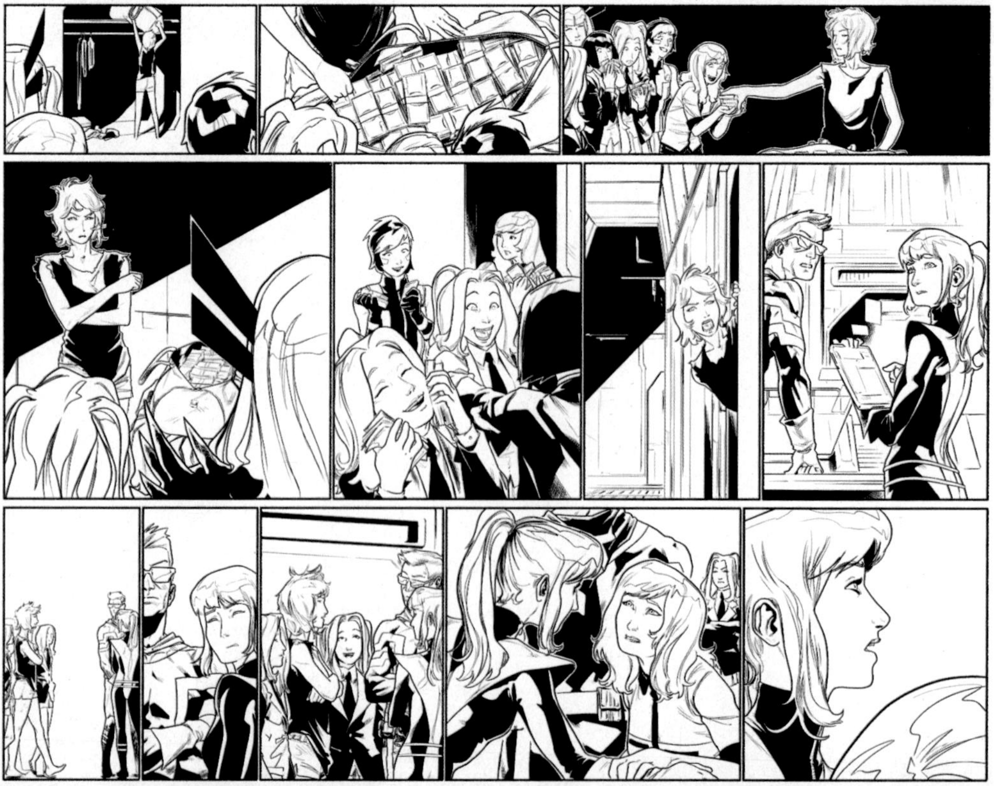

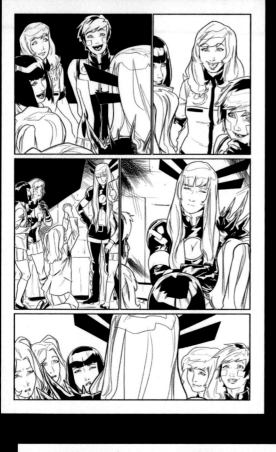

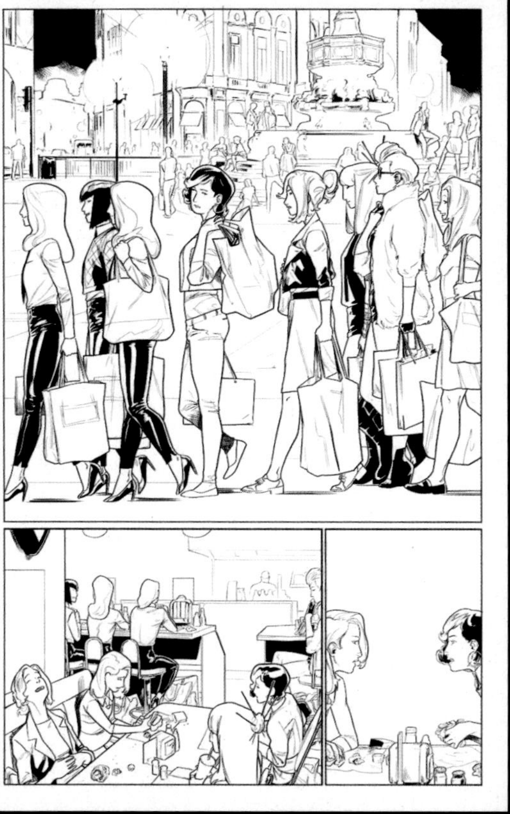

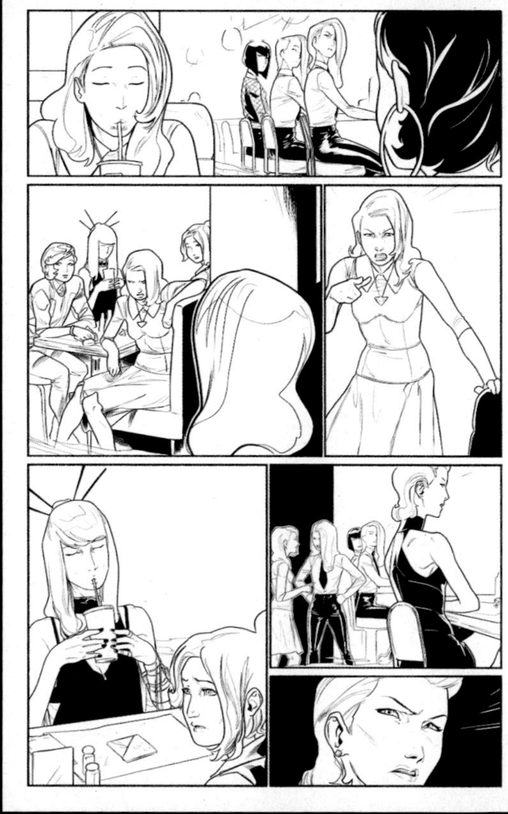

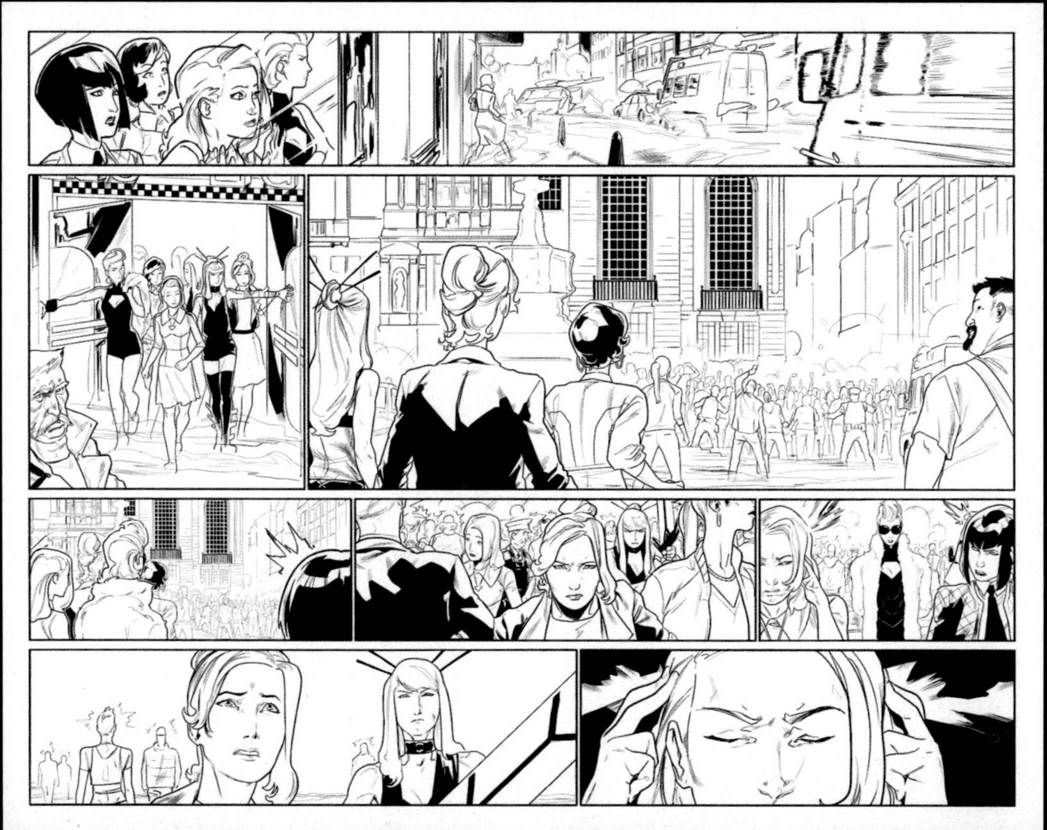

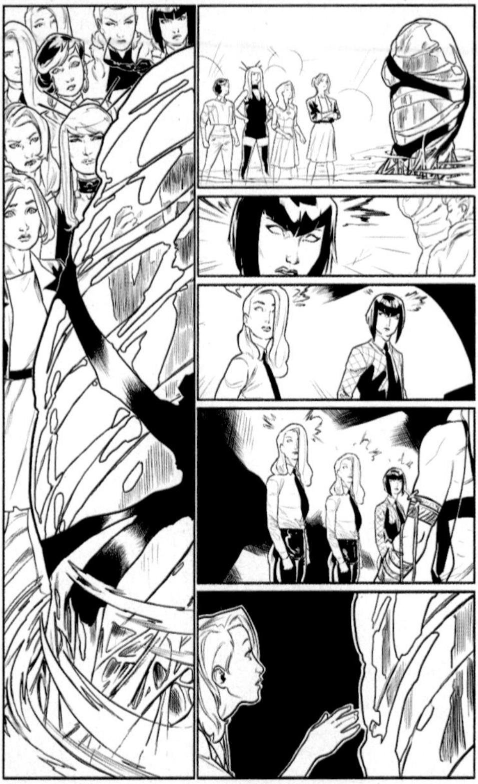

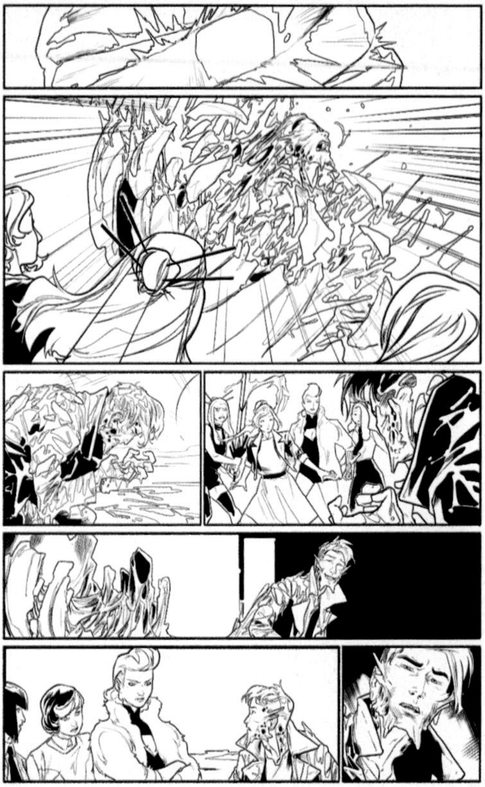

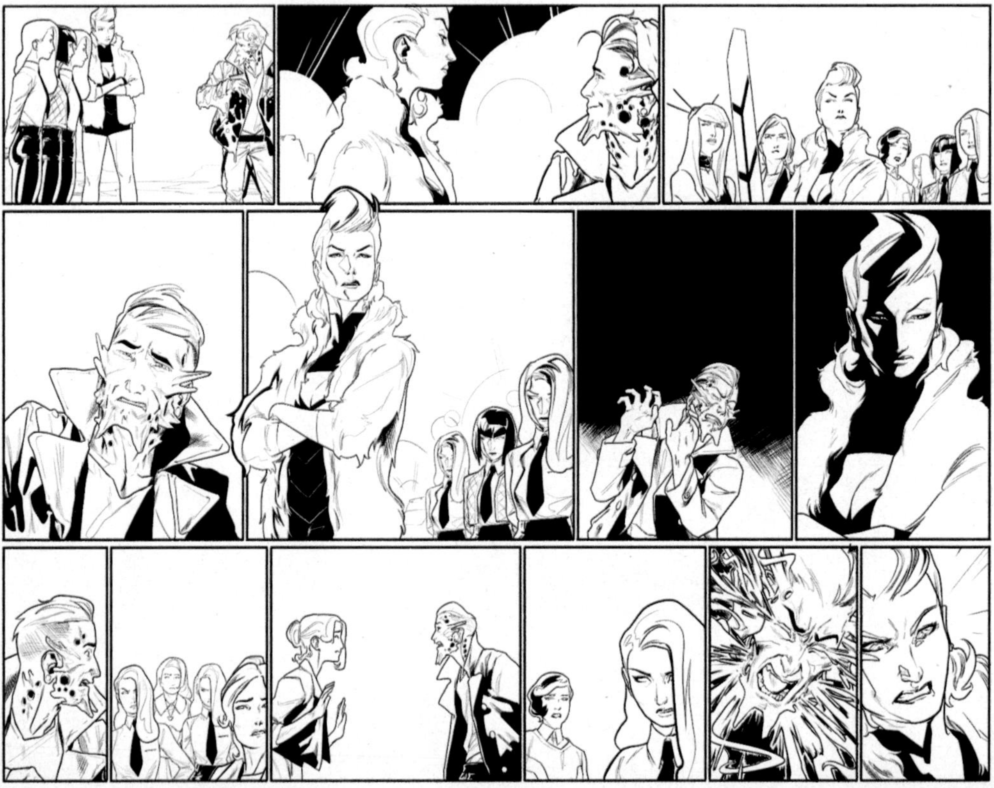

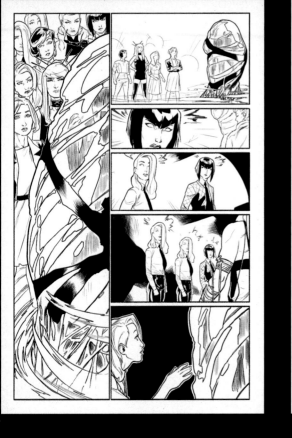

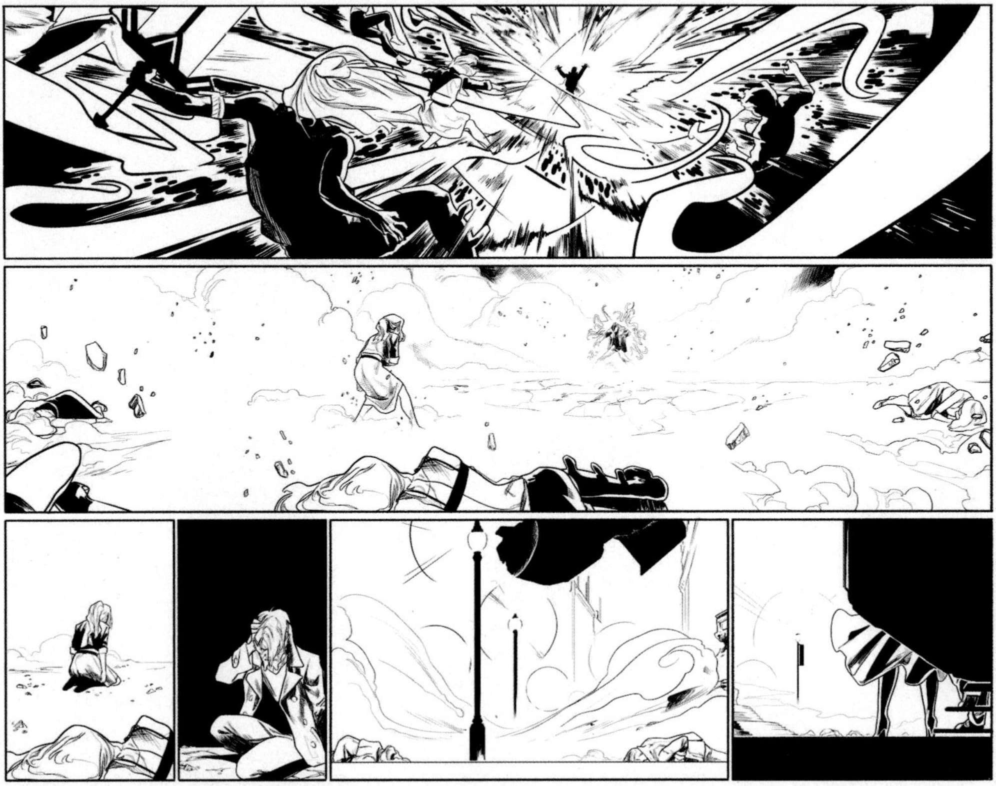

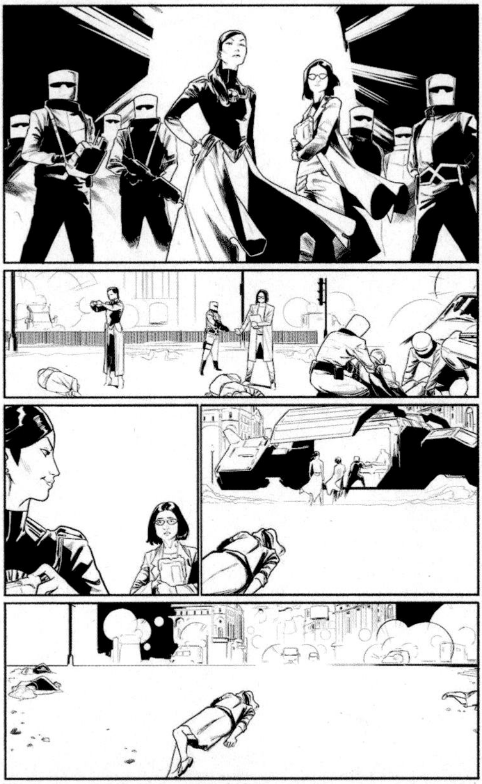

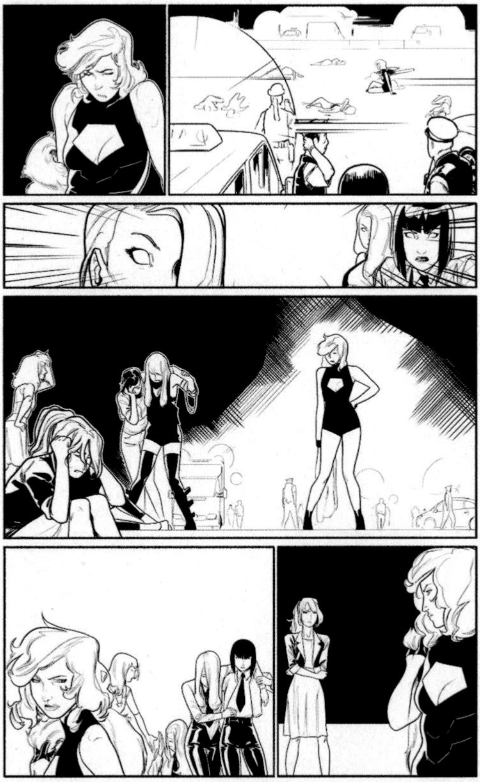

#18 ART BY

MARCO RUDY

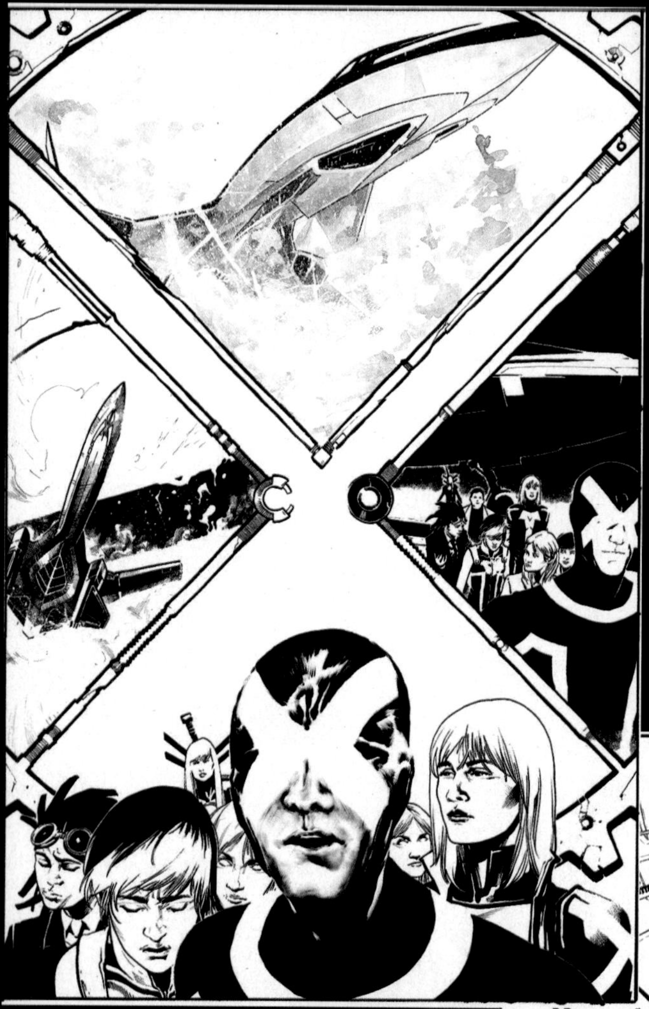

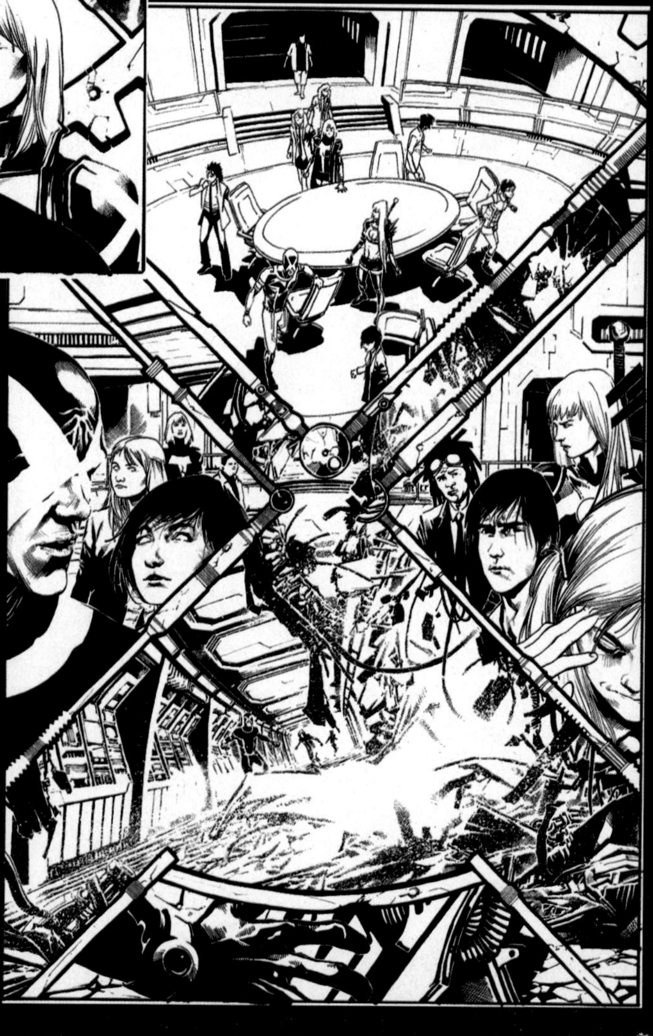

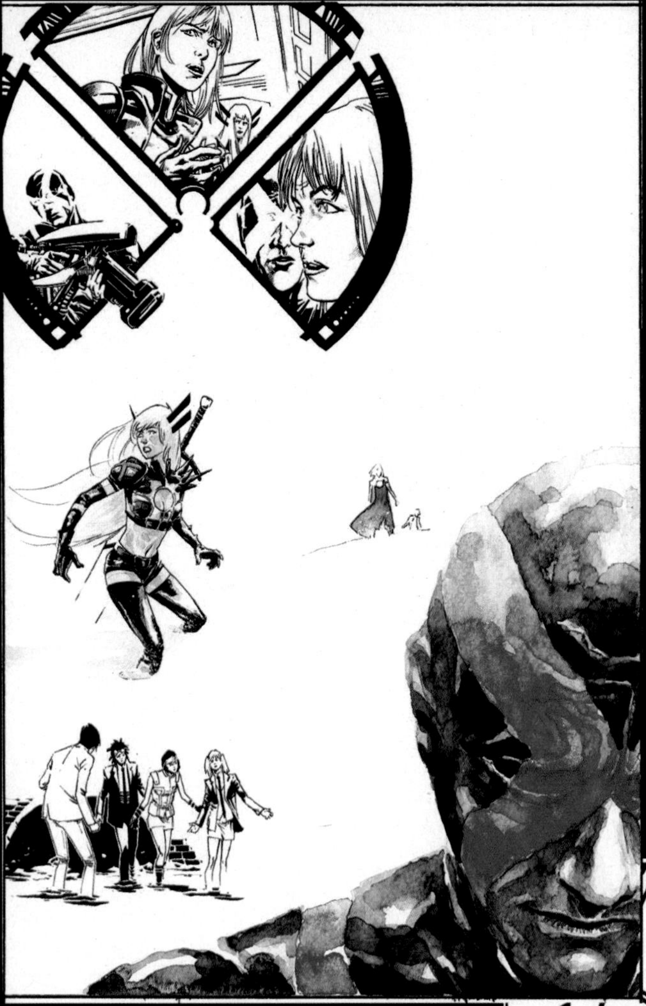

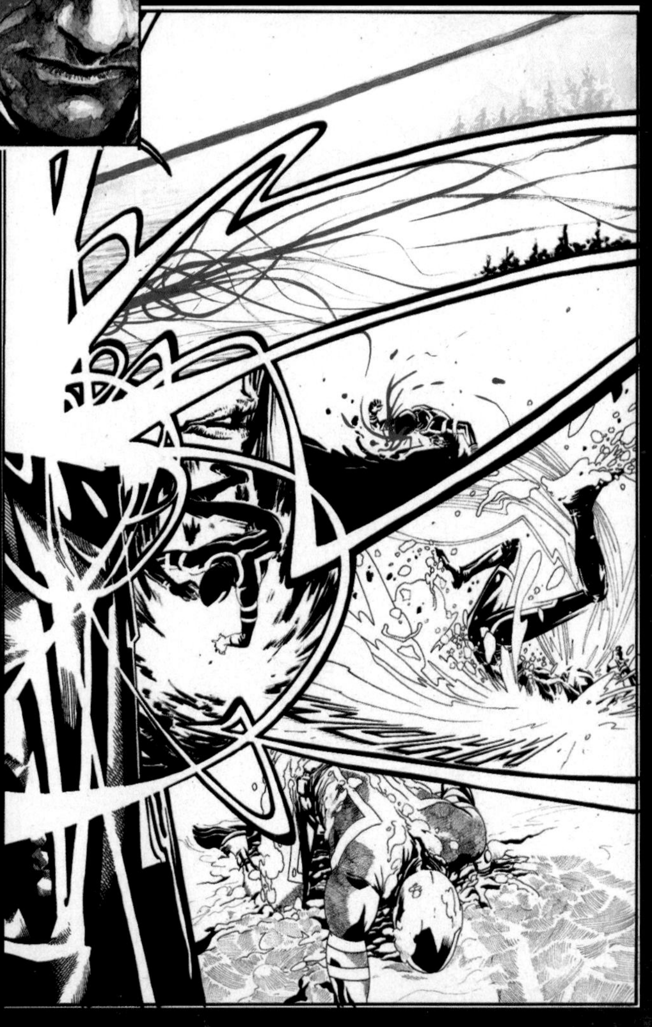

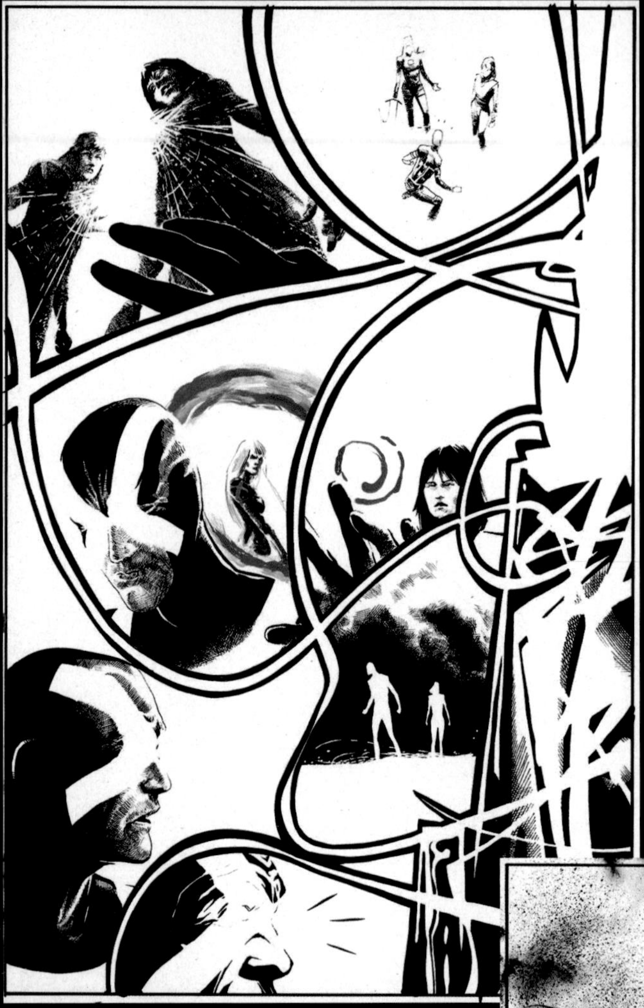
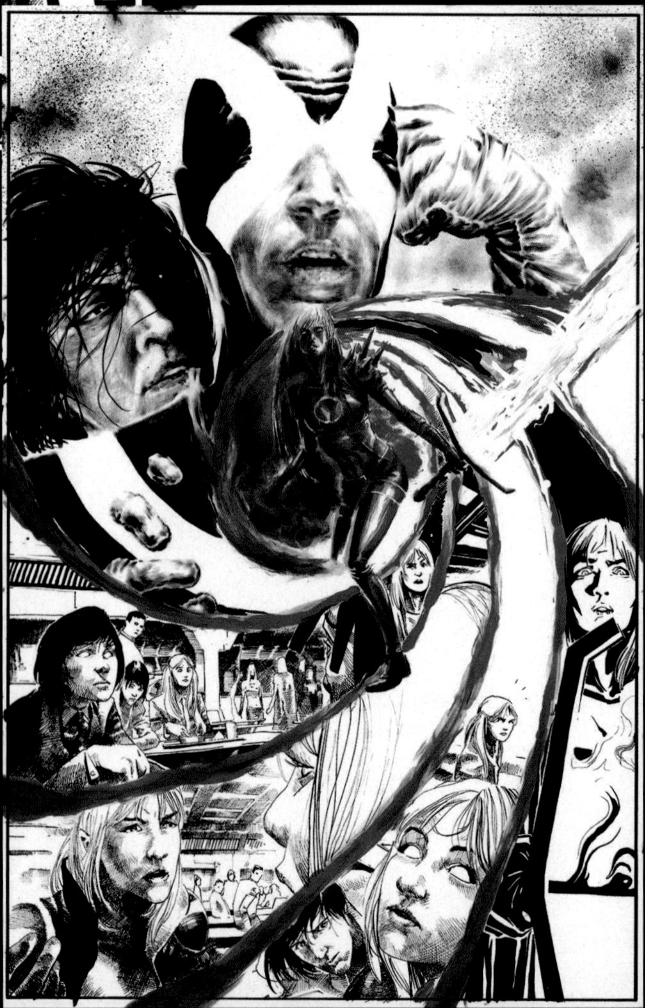

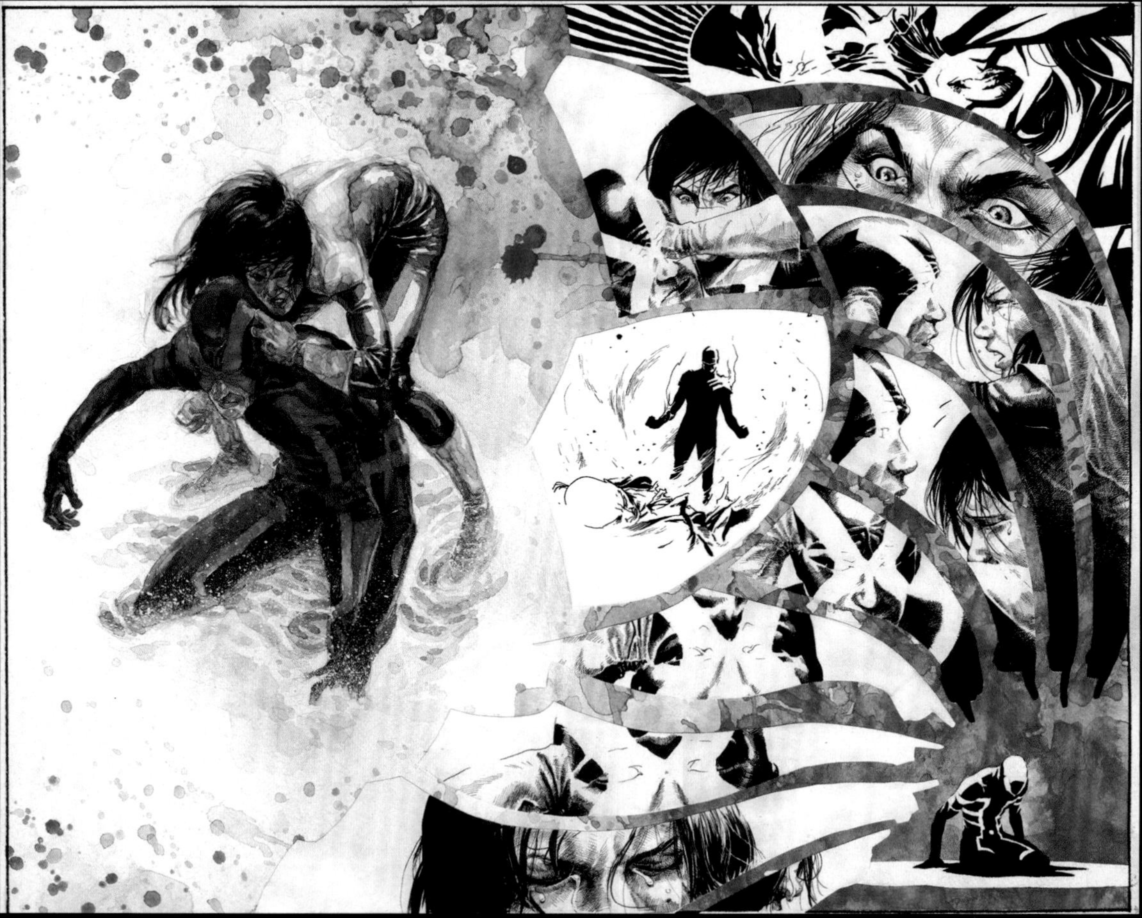

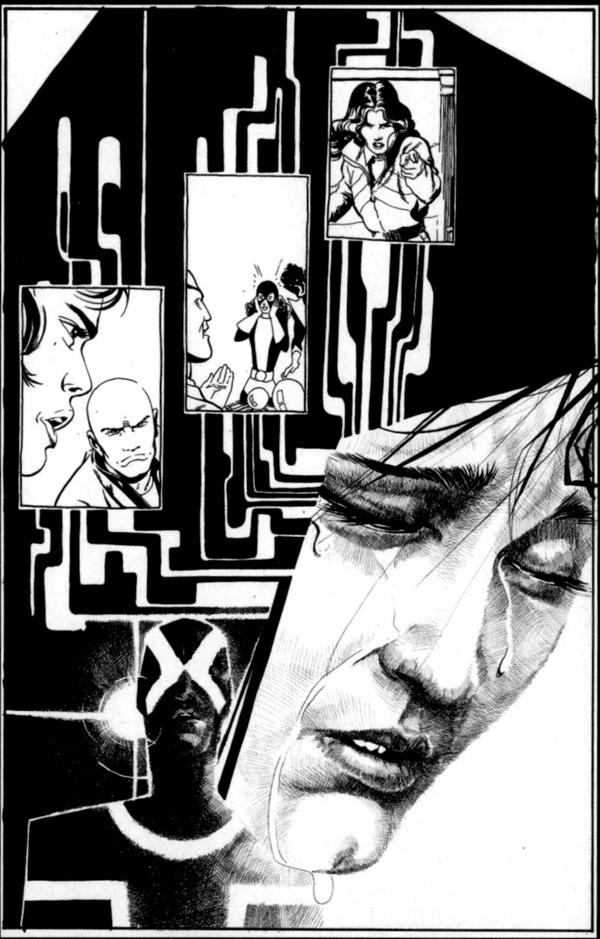

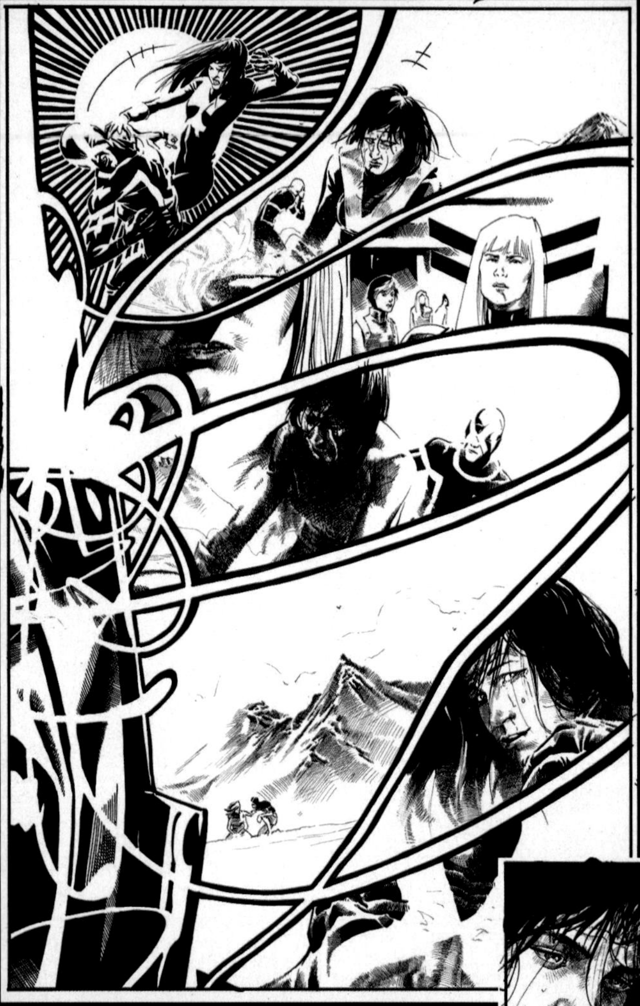

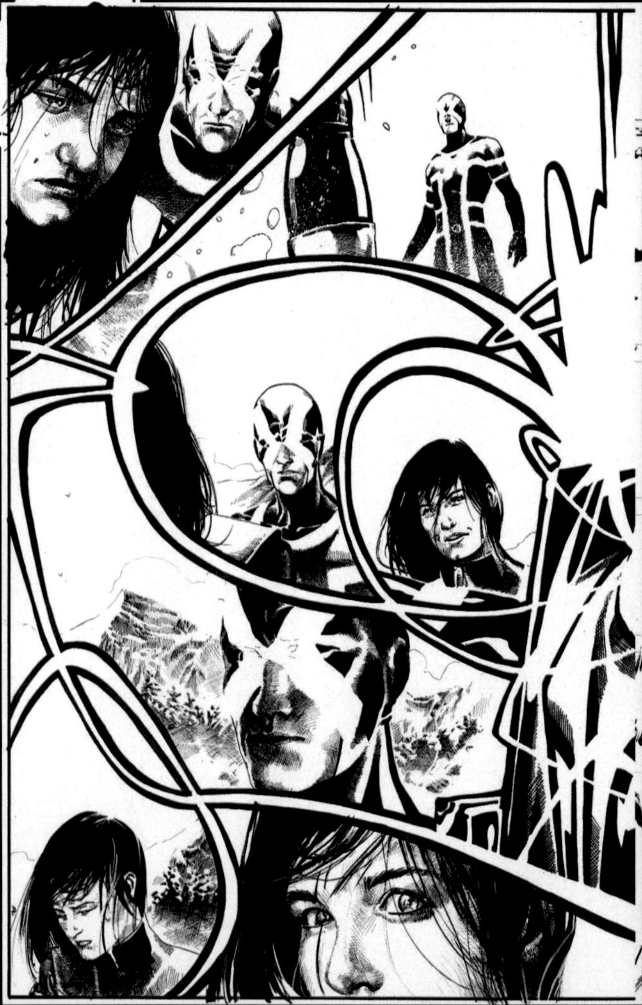

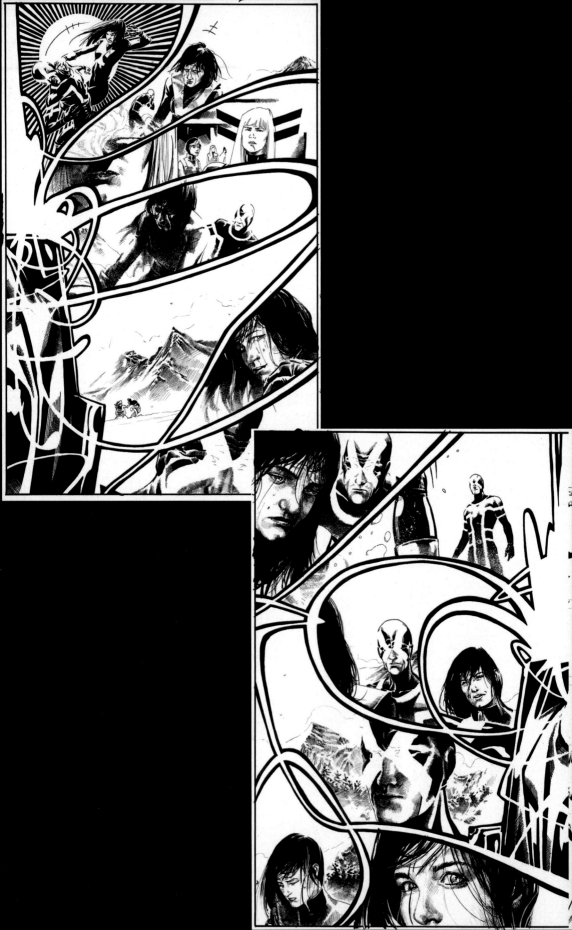

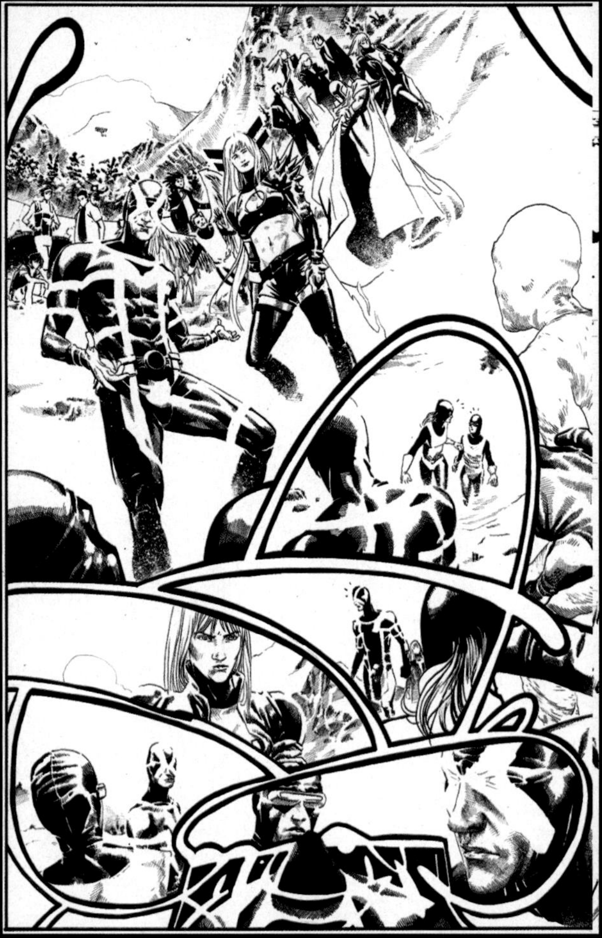

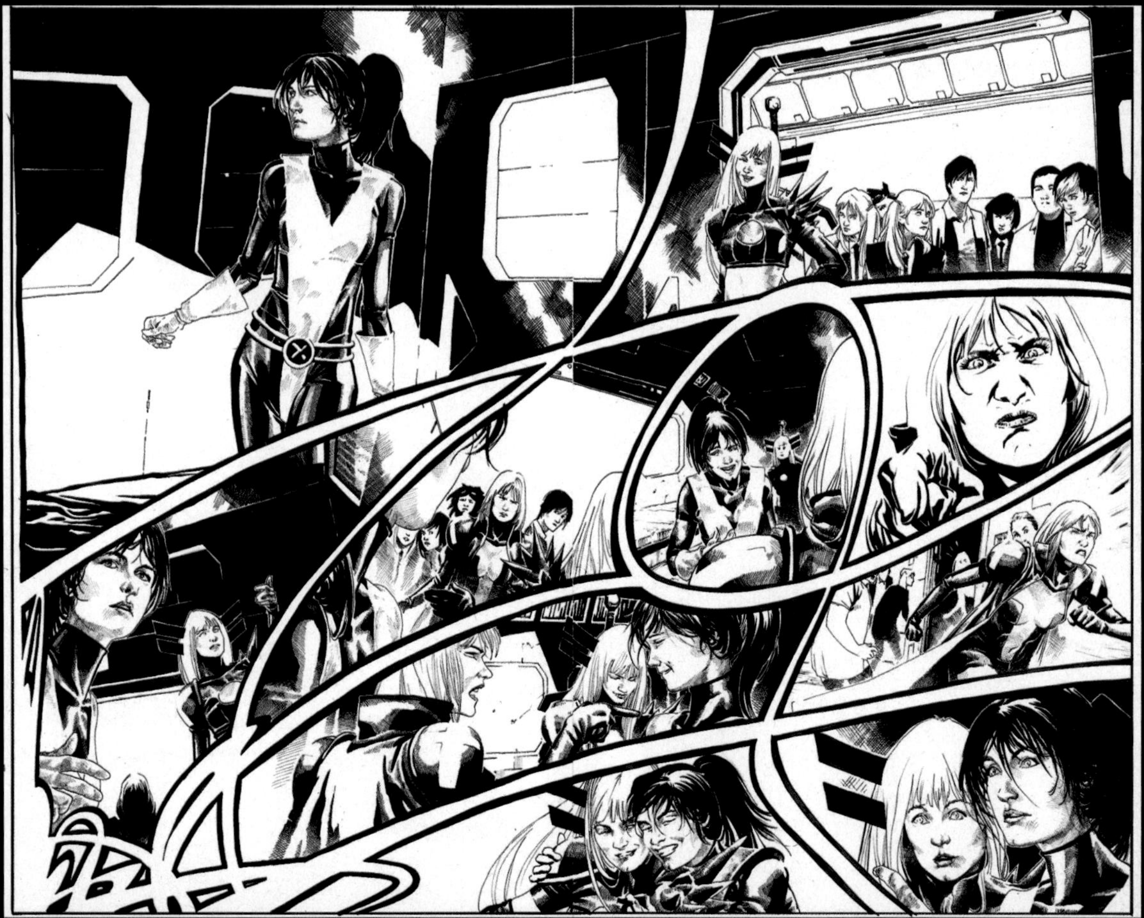

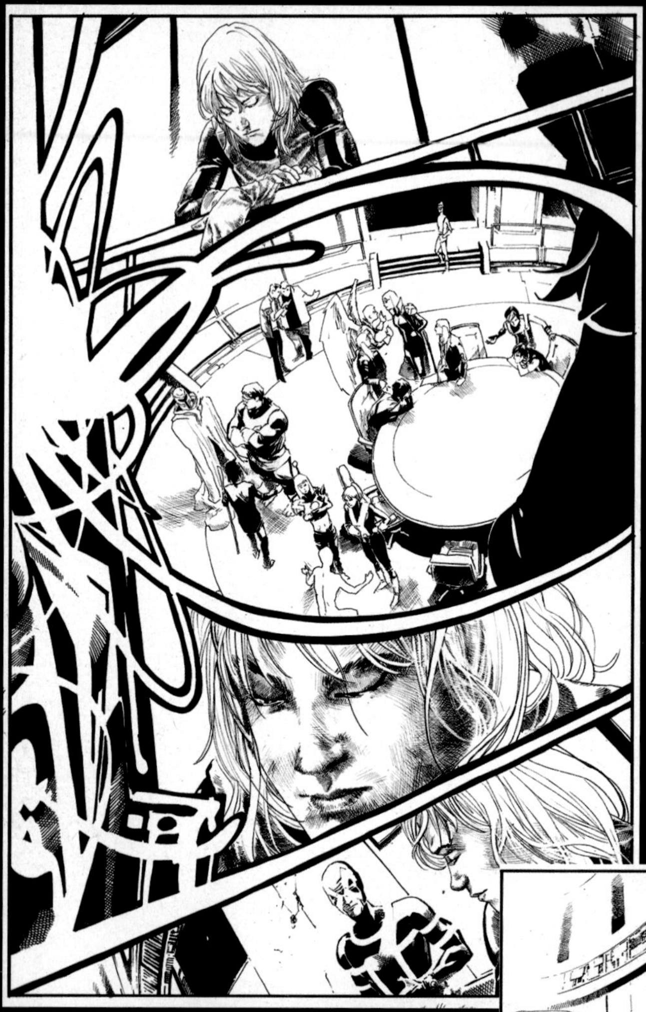

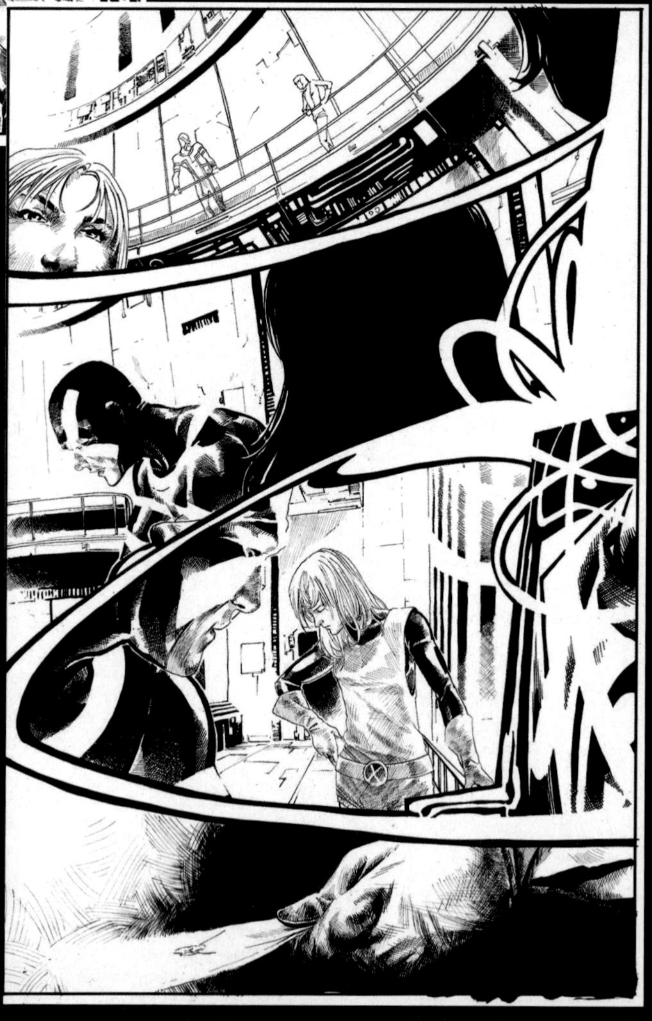

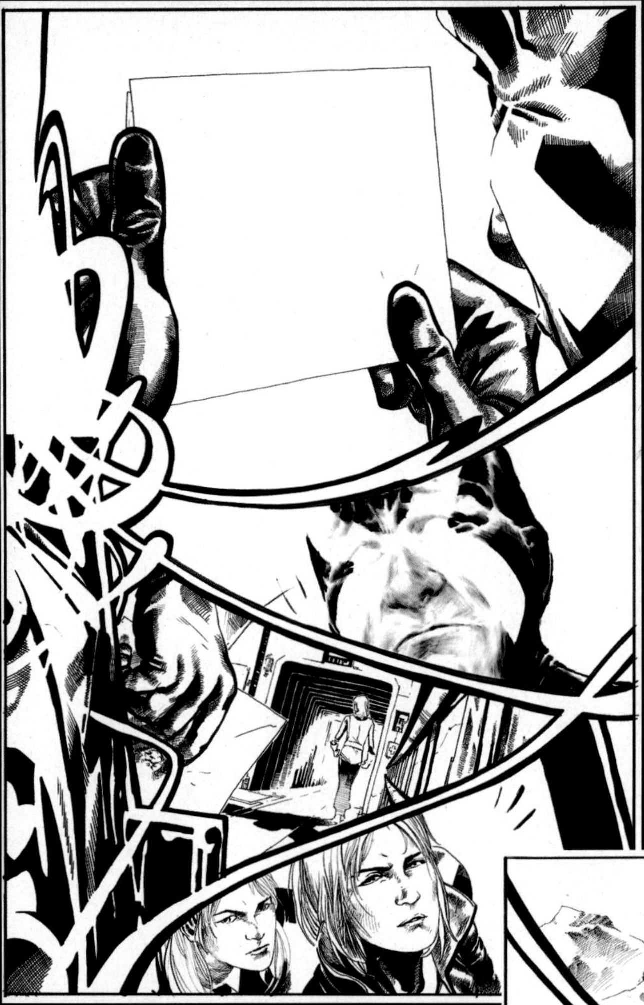

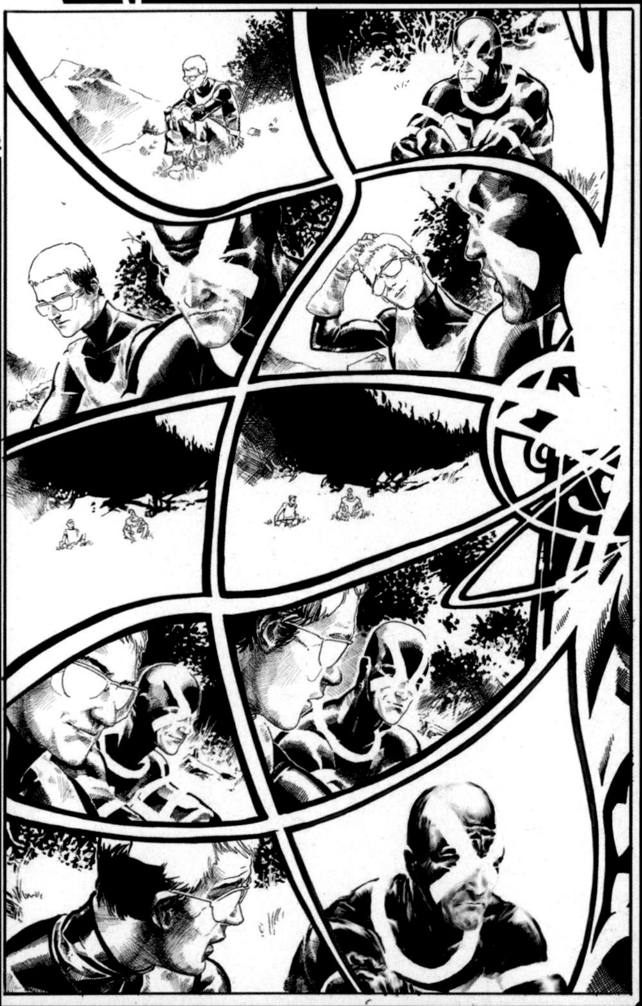

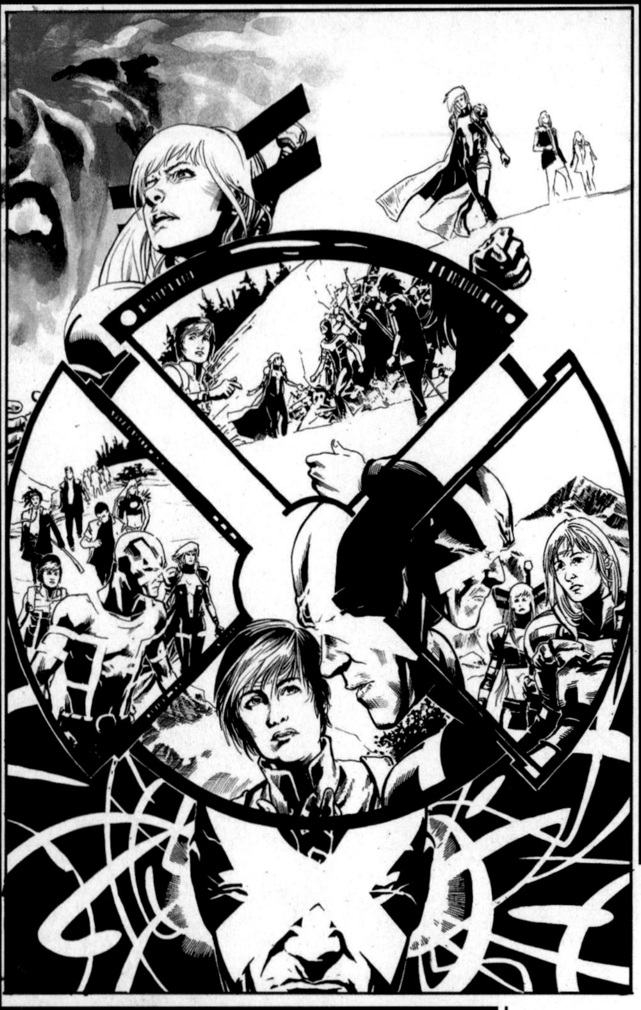

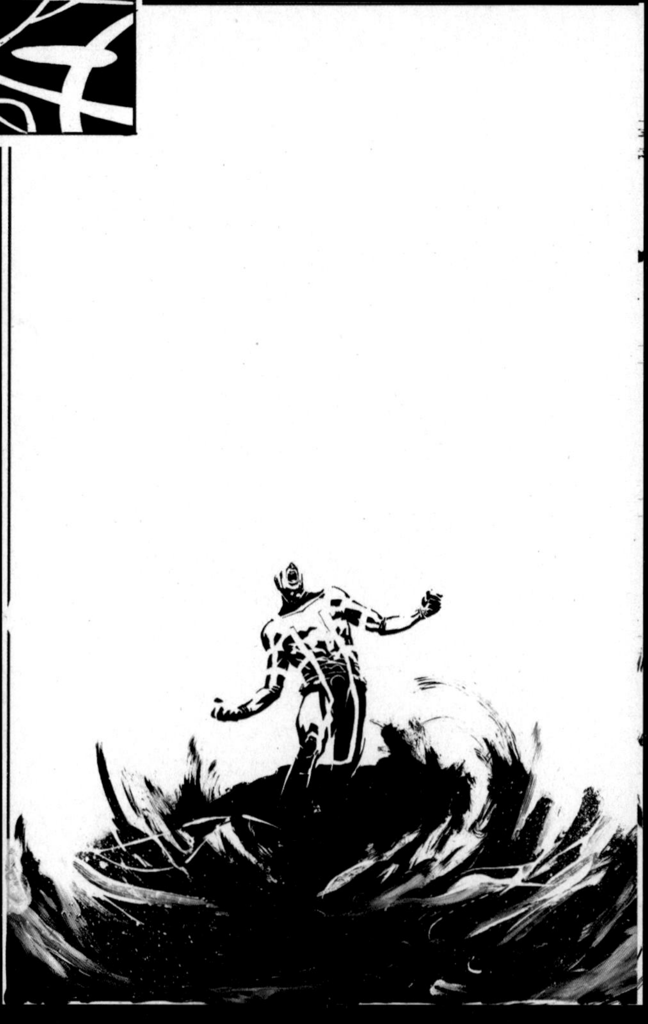

UNCANNY AVENGERS VOL. 1: THE RED SHADOW
WRITTEN BY RICK REMENDER • ART BY JOHN CASSADAY
978-0-7851-6603-0 • DEC130776

© 2013 MARVEL

MARVEL AR AUGMENTED REALITY

MARVEL AUGMENTED REALITY (AR) ENHANCES AND CHANGES THE WAY YOU EXPERIENCE COMICS!

TO ACCESS THE FREE MARVEL AR CONTENT IN THIS BOOK*:

1. **Locate the AR logo within the comic.**
2. **Go to Marvel.com/AR in your web browser.**
3. **Search by series title to find the corresponding AR.**
4. **Enjoy Marvel AR!**

*All AR content that appears in this book has been archived and will be available only at Marvel.com/AR – no longer in the Marvel AR App. Content subject to change and availability.

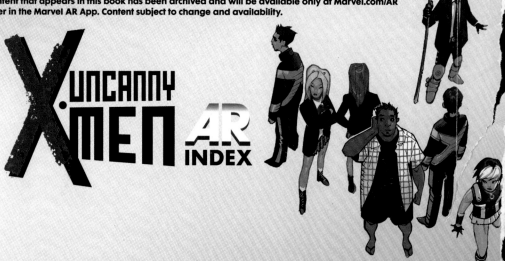

UNCANNY X-MEN AR INDEX

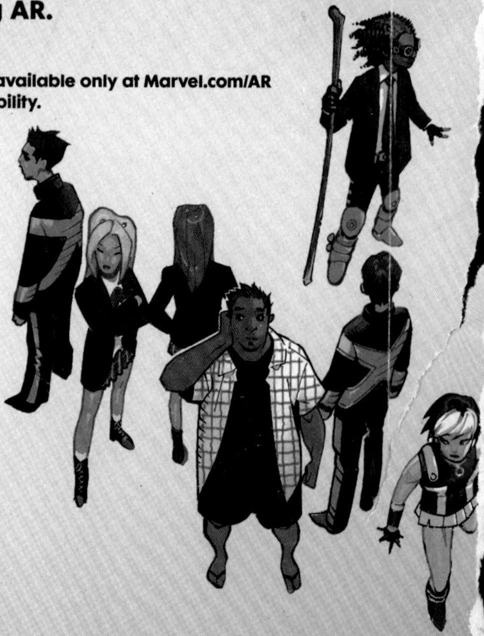